Alan LeMay

ALAN LEMAY

A Biography of the
Author of *The Searchers*

Dan LeMay

McFarland & Company, Inc., Publishers
Jefferson, North Carolina, and London

Frontispiece: Alan LeMay, 1916.

LIBRARY OF CONGRESS CATALOGUING-IN-PUBLICATION DATA

LeMay, Dan, 1929–
    Alan LeMay : a biography of the author of The searchers /
Dan LeMay.
        p.   cm.
    Includes bibliographical references and index.

    ISBN 978-0-7864-6690-0
    softcover : acid free paper ∞

    1. Le May, Alan, 1899–1964. 2. Authors, American —
20th century — Biography. 3. Screenwriters — United
States — Biography. I. Title.
    PS3523.E513Z75 2012
    813'.52 — dc23
    [B]   2012014087

BRITISH LIBRARY CATALOGUING DATA ARE AVAILABLE

Front cover image: John Wayne and Jeffrey Hunter in
The Searchers, 1956 (Warner Bros./Photofest)

Manufactured in the United States of America

McFarland & Company, Inc., Publishers
  Box 611, Jefferson, North Carolina 28640
  www.mcfarlandpub.com

Contents

Acknowledgments   vii

Preface   1

1. Washout   3
2. Origins   6
3. Heading West   22
4. Rancho Una Vaca   31
5. Recovery   41
6. Hello, Hollywood   44
7. *Reap the Wild Wind*   50
8. Life in the Film Colony   56
9. World War II   69
10. The Foto-Electric Games   76
11. *Mark Twain*   81
12. *The Story of Dr. Wassell*   90
13. *The Rurales*   96
14. *Useless Cowboy*   102
15. A Year at Warner's   108
16. *The Walking Hills*   116
17. The Business of Filmmaking   122
18. Independence   130
19. Working with the Military   144
20. Television   153

21. Racing 156
22. Legacy 163

Appendix: Story List 183
Notes 193
Annotated Bibliography 197
Index 203

Acknowledgments

Much of the information in this book comes from the greatly-appreciated efforts of others. Mary Ann LeMay (my wife) did virtually all of the genealogy work and convinced me the biography should be written. Joan Skinner LeMay Newlove (my sister "Jody") provided memories and insights, particularly from the late 1920s through the 1930s. Jon Tuska of the Golden West Literary Agency is an expert on Western literature; he added many elusive titles to the list of Alan's published works and offered editorial suggestions. Glenn Frankel, Pulitzer Prize–winning retired columnist of the *Washington Post*, is writing a book on *The Searchers*, and our sharing of research materials was most helpful. To all of these people I give my heartfelt thanks.

The history of Alan's early life and that of his immediate ancestors is sparsely documented, and some gaps are difficult to fill in. Marilyn Johnston of the Cloud County Genealogical Society (Kansas), Suzanne Hahn of the Indianapolis Historical Society, and Gail Greib of the Stetson University, DuPont-Ball Library Archives, were especially helpful.

I also owe a debt of gratitude to those of our ancestors who were thoughtful enough to write autobiographies, or otherwise save family history documents. I have noted the brief autobiographies written by Daniel Leander Brown, Karen Sophia Jensen LeMay, and John LeMay, who also saved Alan's correspondence. And special thanks to Alan LeMay who, by virtue of these saved letters, wrote much of this book.

The three-picture sequence in Chapter 21 of Alan crashing his race car is reproduced with permission from the photographer, David Iwerks. Alan's father, John LeMay, was an avid photographer and provided a wealth of candid shots, four of which appear in Chapter 18, "Independence."

All other photos are from the LeMay Family Collection (see annotated Bibliography) unless otherwise noted. Photographers are given credit in all cases where they can be identified. My thanks to all of the people who have enriched this biography with their art.

Preface

This is the story of the man who wrote *The Searchers*, a novel about an epic quest that features a complex hero-villain described by some reviewers as a hero and by others as an obsessive bigot.

John Ford and John Wayne turned the novel into a film that has grown in stature over the years to become a cult favorite. Its lasting popularity is frequently attributed to Ford's spectacular filming in Monument Valley, and Wayne's towering performance. But more important to its durability is the controversy over its troubling theme of racism.

Reviewers have analyzed every aspect of the film, attributing to it deep meanings about the clash of cultures, and the thin line between heroic determination and evil obsession. The racism theme dominated the news in the civil rights atmosphere of the 1950s when the novel was written and the film was produced. It still festers today.

Much has been written about John Ford, his character, and his prejudices. But very little has been written about Alan LeMay, the original author of the novel. This biography is intended to fill that gap.

Alan started writing while still in school, made a living at writing his entire life, and never held a significant job other than writing. But he claimed that it did not come easily for him, and he habitually saddled himself with crushing schedules to make his work meet his own grudging acceptance.

Despite long hours of writing, he still found the time to write letters to his parents. His father saved these, and we are fortunate to have them as a valuable insight into his life, his opinions of the way Hollywood works, and his insider's view of the fascinating business of filmmaking. The excerpts used here are unedited; I have not changed a word of the quoted material.

Most of his letters were addressed to his parents, and he always referred to his father as "Dad." That is also what I always called Alan, so in this book I call my dad "Alan" to avoid confusion.

1

Alan's life was dominated by writing, but he did not become one-dimensional. He did many things most of his contemporaries would never consider doing, and did them all with great enthusiasm and an obsessive zeal to excel. He participated in amateur boxing, light plane flying (long before it became either routine or safe), played polo with some of the best in the world, started and ran a cattle ranch, played tennis ferociously, and began racing sports cars long after his hair had turned gray.

Through the window of daily correspondence a picture emerges of a highly competitive man, sometimes moody, seldom pleased with his own work, and highly critical of other writers whom he considered generally (with notable exceptions) to be incompetent. Alan did, after all, earn a good living for his family over the course of his entire adult life solely by freelance writing, an accomplishment which qualified him as an expert, and earned him the right to judge his rivals. He was good, and he knew it. In everything he did, whether playing tennis, polo, or chess, racing or writing, only the best was acceptable. Life to him was a contest, a zero-sum game, and he loved to win.

As his second wife, Arlene, said, "Alan could be tough to live with, but he was never dull."

—1—

Washout

Rain had fallen nearly every day for three months. The pasture was a sea of mud, and 20 pregnant whiteface heifers had turned it into a quagmire. The smell would have been suffocating if it weren't for the biting wind out of the north. Two exhausted cowboys, slathered in mud, were trying to save the calves that the cows refused to drop. A heifer in labor lay in the mud with Alan LeMay's writing hand deep inside her trying to circle the unborn calf's head and forefeet with a lasso before his arm became too numb to function. When he finally got the noose in place he pulled his arm out and motioned the cowboy on horseback to haul away. Skillfully, Gil Strick backed his horse until the rope was tight. As the whiteface gave a violent heave, Gil backed the horse and a newborn calf was delivered from his warm cramped quarters into open air and icy muck. Welcome to Rancho Una Vaca!

Gil had introduced Alan to the technique, called calf pulling. Gil was an experienced cowpoke and rodeo bronc rider whom Alan had hired as a mentor and assistant rancher to teach him the cattle business. The birthing technique worked; they lost only one out of the 20 newborns. Calving season shouldn't be this hard, but Southern California's record-breaking rains in the winter of 1936–37 had taken their toll on man and beast alike.

Rancho Una Vaca (the name means One Cow Ranch) was the home of the LeMay's Lazy Lightning brand, and the smallest commercial beef herd west of Chicago. It was on the north side of the San Diego River, across from Santee. The usually dry river, raging from the record rains, had washed out the Lakeside bridge and the "dry" crossing at Santee. This left the Old Town bridge, sixteen miles of mud track down river, as the only way out. Rancho Una Vaca was cut off from civilization.

The isolation added to the gloom. A year ago this place was on the rise. While the world had been in the throes of a depression, the LeMay

3

family had been riding high on the returns from Alan's prolific writing. Rancho Una Vaca had been his Shangri-La, a refuge for writing and a showplace for Sunday afternoon polo parties. Alan had played on a number of teams throughout Southern California, and at Una Vaca he could, for the first time, stable his string of polo ponies right there on his own ranch, and practice on his own polo field just outside of his office. He had commissioned the noted architect Starling Watson to design a grandiose expansion of the adobe ranch house, and the first phase had been completed, adding a three-car garage and servants' quarters. The dream ranch was taking shape.

But the Great Depression was finally catching up with *Collier's* and the other "slick" magazines that were Alan's main source of income. The big corporate advertisers were cutting their budgets, so the magazines no longer could afford to buy as much high-priced material. They still bought a few of Alan's stories, but they began rejecting all but the best. He re-titled the rest and sold them when he could at salvage prices to the pulp magazines under the *nom de plume* Alan M. Emley.

The costly remodel of the LeMays' adobe ranch house ground to a halt for lack of funds. The house itself dragged down Alan's mood as the rain soaked the mud walls and the house reeked of mildew. Little "Sun Bowl" electric heaters in every room couldn't dispel the clammy atmosphere.

Writing is mentally exhausting, and Alan was, in the best of times, seldom happy with his. His successful stories took long hours of concentration, and multiple rewrites to refine them to the point where he could grudgingly accept the result. The entire product had to come out of Alan's brain, and that was now preoccupied by fears of failure. His wife, Esther, had been a helpful collaborator in his early career, acting as much more than secretary, offering advice, and even doing some of the writing. But now her suggestions went unaccepted.

Rancho Una Vaca, the writer's refuge, had become in reality the writer's ruin, distracting him from writing and drying up his income stream while the extravagant ranch improvements and lavish lifestyle drained his reserves. With the rejection slips and money problems came discouragement, recriminations, and the gnawing worry that if the next effort didn't sell, the family would be in dire financial straits. The worry split the concentration that was his only source of income. It was a creativity death spiral.

In the depressing atmosphere of the gloomy spring, Alan's mood turned black. He had worked his way up from obscurity to fame in his field, but now, suddenly, he couldn't write. He couldn't pay the ranch bills.

He couldn't even provide for his family. He started drinking too much. He blamed the weather. He blamed the editors. He blamed Esther, and she started drinking just to cope. Inevitably, their marriage collapsed, and Esther filed for divorce. Freelance writing has no parachute, no severance pay, and no unemployment dole. Beaten and broke, Alan left Rancho Una Vaca and returned home to his parents in Illinois.

His own words were the disbelieving words of defeat: "Me ... who have done what I've done ... been where I've been ... seen what I've seen..."

— 2 —

Origins

In his depressed condition, Alan had no faith that he could come back as a writer. His failure seemed to hit him harder because everything had been going so well ... until everything went wrong at once. Higher highs and lower lows, that was his style. But he came from sturdy pioneer stock, a heritage of men and women who were self-reliant survivors. The family had a history of taking care of each other in times of need, and for Alan LeMay this was one of those times. Returning home to his parents at the age of 38 could have been a further embarrassment, but with this family it was the natural thing to do.

Alan was very close to his parents, John and Maude Brown LeMay, and was strongly influenced by two of his grandparents, Karen Sophia Jensen Lamay, "Sophie," and Daniel Leander Brown, "Papa Brown." Alan's grandmother, Sophie, came to America from Denmark as a 19-year-old immigrant, following her friend and minister, the Rev. Nels Nelson, to Kansas.[1] The Reverend Nelson had done much toward attracting the attention of Danes to the opportunities to be found in the American West. The greater part of the Danish settlements in Cloud County, Kansas, came through his influence.

Sophie's new life could not have been a more extreme change for the young woman from Denmark, but she quickly developed into the archetypical pioneer woman. The frontier in Kansas was far from settled in 1870. The Reverend Nelson had his new homestead destroyed in a raid by 60 Indians. They killed three settlers, stole what they could carry, and burned the rest.[2] Sophie must have heard of this attack shortly before she left Denmark, but she came anyway.

Within a year after her arrival in Kansas Sophie met and married Oliver Lamay [Jr.][3] an expert hunter and harness maker, but an inexperienced farmer. The newlyweds lived for a short time with Oliver's parents on their homestead, two miles south of Jamestown, Kansas, twelve miles west of Concordia.

House built by Oliver LeMay (Sr.) in 1870, near Jamestown, Kansas. Birthplace of Alan's father John LeMay, April 25, 1873 (photograph by John LeMay in January 1942).

They lived in a wooden house that Oliver's father built in 1870. Oliver [Sr.] was a Boston man, and did not want his family living in a dugout. Wooden houses were rare. River banks grew enough poles for the roofs of the dugout homes, called "soddys," but there were few big trees to mill into conventional lumber. Oliver's father had hauled the lumber himself, 70 miles over the nearly trackless prairie from Junction City. Alan's father, John, was born in that house on April 25, 1872.

That same month, Kansas had a history-making three-day blizzard. But in defiance of the weather and the sporadic Indian raids, the young family decided to start their own homestead 70 miles farther west. Oliver dug them a sod house, and began to learn about farming. This house was described later by Alan's father, John:

> The dwelling was a one room dug-out, made by digging into the side of a hill or stream bank, with a fireplace in the back and walls of prairie sod (buffalo grass). Roof of sod as well, supported by poles cut from the growth along the stream. A haven for snakes in cold weather.
> My father [Oliver] wasn't much of a farmer (he was a city man from Boston and at this time only twenty years old) but he was a mighty hunter which was an avocation which he loved. I was told later by men

who knew him that he was the best rifle shot in Kansas. My mother told me that buffalo herds passed by in sight of the home frequently and she reported that on one occasion a herd came by, my father grabbed a gun and ran out, shot a buffalo and brought it down almost in the dooryard. He approached the fallen animal to bleed it when the buffalo rose and charged. My father saw a little gulley and threw himself into it. The buffalo ran right over him without injuring him and a few paces farther along fell dead.

Alan's description of the soddy in his novel *The Unforgiven* is essentially the same as his father's description of that first prairie home. Oliver planted some crops, but the next summer the area was hit by the Great Grasshopper Invasion of 1874 that wiped out all crops. Conditions were harsh.

The Lamay family stuck it out on their homestead for a few years, but Oliver decided that he was not a farmer and the family moved back to Concordia where Oliver opened a harness manufacturing business. His father had been a harness maker in Lowell, Massachusetts, so it was a trade he understood, and in which he excelled. He very quickly became known for his fine leather work, and the business grew rapidly until he employed as many as ten harness makers. He owned the building that housed his shop, and also a tiny residence on 7th street, just outside the business district. But he never outgrew his love of hunting.

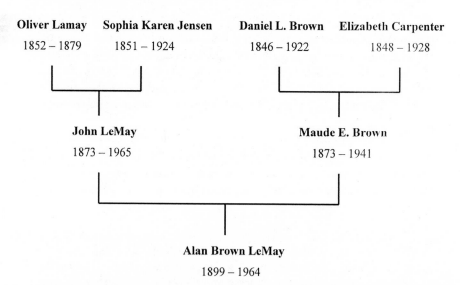

| Oliver Lamay | Sophia Karen Jensen | | Daniel L. Brown | Elizabeth Carpenter |
| 1852 – 1879 | 1851 – 1924 | | 1846 – 1922 | 1848 – 1928 |

John LeMay
1873 – 1965

Maude E. Brown
1873 – 1941

Alan Brown LeMay
1899 – 1964

Ancestry chart of Alan LeMay. There were three Oliver Lamays or LeMays: Alan's great grandfather, his grandfather, and his uncle, but none of them used the distinguishing Sr., Jr., or the 3rd.

It was on one of these hunting trips that he was caught in a blizzard and was severely chilled. Pneumonia developed and on January 8, 1879, he died at the age of 26.

Three months before Oliver's ill-fated hunting trip, there had been massive Indian raids in that same area. A band of Northern Cheyenne, led

Harry, John, and Oliver Lamay with their mother, Sophia Karen Jensen Lamay, ca. 1886.

by Chief Dull Knife, had fled from their reservation in Oklahoma to return to their homeland in the Black Hills.[4] But on their trip through Kansas they laid waste to as many farms as possible, killing the settlers and taking scalps. The death toll in Kansas alone was variously reported as 75–100 settlers. This campaign has entered the history books as The Last Raid in Kansas, and served as the historical basis for Alan's first novel, *Painted Ponies*.

When Oliver [Jr.] died, his oldest son John was nearly six, son Oliver was four, and little Harry was born the month after his father died. Their only daughter, Mary, had died four months before at 17 months. Since making her brave decision to seek a better life in an unknown land, young widow Sophie Karen Jensen Lamay had adapted to frontier life, learned a new language, married and had four children, lost one, and lost her husband. And she had been away from her home in Denmark for less than eight years.

In his dedication of *The Searchers*, Alan wrote: "To my Grandfather, Oliver LeMay, who died on the prairie; and to my Grandmother, Karen Jensen LeMay, to whom he left three sons under seven." Sophie (Karen) lacked formal schooling in the English language, but saw to it that her boys were well educated. She put them all through school and even college, and lived until 1924 when she died a week before her 74th birthday. It was her spirit, unremarkable in those challenging times, that inspired Alan to write about the pioneer families in *The Searchers*: "These people had a kind of courage that may be the finest gift of man: the courage of those who simply keep on, and on, doing the next thing, far beyond all reasonable endurance, seldom thinking of themselves as martyred, and never thinking of themselves as brave."

After Oliver's death, his brother Thomas took over the harness business for the family, and did well. Thomas Lamay later became County Clerk of Cloud County. In this capacity he worked closely with Daniel Brown, the mayor of Concordia, bringing the Lamay and Brown families together in this small town.

* * *

The Brown's side of Alan's ancestry had been living in Indiana. Daniel Leander Brown, Alan's maternal grandfather, was born in 1846 in Plymouth, Indiana, about 100 miles north of Indianapolis. He lied about his age to volunteer for the Union in the Civil War, and came home early after being wounded on June 20, 1864, in the battle of Kennesaw Mountain, Georgia.

After the war in 1867, Daniel married Elizabeth Carpenter in Union Mills, Indiana. He was elected sheriff of LaPorte County in 1872. Their daughter Maude was born in LaPorte, Indiana, in 1873, the same year that John LeMay was born in Kansas.

In 1879 Daniel Brown moved his family to Concordia, Cloud County, Kansas. He opened a law office there, became the probate judge from 1883 to 1888, and was elected the mayor of Concordia from 1889 through 1891. During this period he bought and sold a number of farms and plots of land in the area, and became quite prosperous.

The youngsters, John LeMay and Maude Brown, attended the Concordia school together, starting when they were six or seven. John later said that the school was a one-room, all grades affair. He recalled reading aloud, as the students had to do while learning, and coming to the word "giraffe," which he had never heard of. He read on, nevertheless pronouncing it "griffy." Everyone except Maude laughed and made fun of him. He was so touched by her kindness that they became best friends, and soon started a love affair that never waned.

They both graduated from Concordia High School in 1890, and John went off to the University of Chicago. In 1892, the Brown family also left Concordia, moving to Indianapolis because their son, Dan Jr., was very unhappy with his living conditions at school there. Young Maude went with the family to Indianapolis, but John and Maude stayed in contact as best they could.

While at the University of Chicago, John played football for the famous coach Amos Alonzo Stagg, and traveled with the team to games in California where they played the best West Coast teams. This was the forerunner of the Rose Bowl championship series. Chicago brought a minimal team, and sometimes Coach Stagg had to play to get 11 men on the field.

Besides the college grind and football, John was a member of the prestigious University of Chicago Pi Club. Their flag showed a pi symbol (π) superimposed on a club (♣). The members contributed their spare change to a club fund, and when the fund had grown big enough to buy each member a pie, they went out for a feast. Each member got a whole pie, because one rule of the club was that a pie should never be cut.

With the determined help of his mother, Sophie, John completed his studies at the University of Chicago, graduating with a Bachelor of Science degree in 1896. He became a Professor of Physics at Lake High School in Chicago,[5] beginning his teaching there while he was still a student at the university. This kept him too far from Indianapolis, home of the Brown family and their beautiful daughter Maude. The commuting problem was solved when John was able to land a job teaching physics at Indianapolis High School, where he also taught a laboratory course in physical measurements, and wrote the textbook for the course.

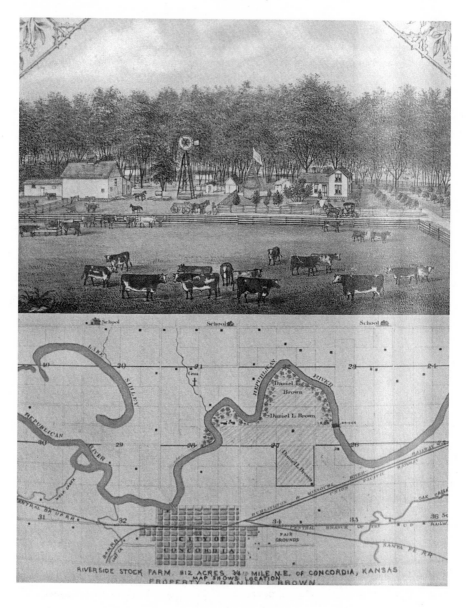

The Daniel L. Brown farm near Concordia, Kansas. A flood in the 1930s moved the Republican River to the south of the farm (print made from 1885 Cloud County, Kansas, Atlas).

John and Maude were married in Indianapolis on December 28, 1897, and after a two-week honeymoon moved into their first house at 433 N. Delaware Street, Indianapolis. Maude's father, Daniel Brown, had opened a law practice in Indianapolis, and in January 1898 bought a large house at 3239 N. Illinois St. Before long, the newlywed LeMays, having trouble making ends meet, moved in with the Brown family in their new home on North Illinois Street. That may have been the plan when the Browns bought the big house just a few days after the wedding. A year and a half later, Alan LeMay was born, and the three generations stayed in the same house.

During the first ten years of Alan's life, the LeMay family was quite poor, and remained in the home of Alan's grandfather, Daniel. This is when Dan decided he did not like being called "Grandpa," and became known to the family as Papa Brown. Alan's father, John, worked hard at several jobs, and the young LeMay family saved in every way they could to earn a place of their own. Alan remembered rather bitterly that he had to wear his mother's old shoes to school, and was chased home by taunting schoolmates when they noticed.

It wasn't until 1910, when Alan turned 11, that the LeMays were able to move out of the Browns' house into the one next door. By this time Alan's sister, Betty, had been born, and Papa Brown, who had done well in Kansas real estate and in his law practice, may have been inspired to help the LeMays so that everyone could have more breathing room.

* * *

Late in 1911, a Presbyterian minister, the Rev. A. C. V. Skinner, was transferred by the church to Indianapolis. He, his wife, and three pretty daughters moved into the house across the street from the LeMays. Their middle daughter, Esther, was a year younger than Alan, and the two became good friends. The friendship grew stronger over the three and a half years they both lived on North Illinois Street, and remained so after they were separated by a family move.

Alan's father, John, and his two brothers, Oliver and Harry, formed the LeMay Brothers Company, Grocers, and John became the manager. In 1909 they had three stores, and this grew to four the next year. Then two of those closed, and after 1912 they disappeared altogether from the City Directory. John decided that groceries were not to be his life's work, and so he sold out and went to work for the Payne Die Casting Co., a job more suited to his science and engineering education. This was the first stop on the road to a lifelong career in metallurgy. He worked his way up to manager by 1913, and the next year moved to the Aurora Metal Com-

John LeMay, 1896.

Maude Brown, 1896.

John LeMay, 1939.

Maude Brown LeMay, 1939.

pany, in Aurora, Illinois, as their chief metallurgist. John spent his entire career at the Aurora Metal Co., pioneering the die casting of aluminum bronze, and eventually retiring as Vice President. He had come a long way from the soddy on the Kansas prairie.

John spent the winter of 1914–1915 settling in at his new job in Aurora, while the family remained in Indianapolis to finish the school year. Then in the summer of 1915, the LeMays moved from Indianapolis to 24 N. Locust Street in Aurora. Alan LeMay and Esther Skinner began a long-distance relationship that went on for the next seven years.

During his first winter in Aurora, Alan was a senior at West High, played on their football team, joined the Literary Society, played in two class plays, and was the associate editor of EOS, the school annual. Under his graduation picture it says, "A diamond with a flaw is better than a pebble without one." It could also have mentioned that he was clearly not gathering any moss.

For Christmas that year, Alan gave his mother a hand-made calendar with a sketch and short poem on each monthly page. All of the subjects focused on nature and the outdoors, but with a melancholy tone. In contrast with his later treatment of Indians in *The Searchers*, Alan showed a sadness for their plight. For example, the June calendar had a sketch of a dour Indian, with this poem:

> When the forest shall mislead me,
> When the night and morning lie,
> When sea and land refuse to feed me,
> 'Twill be time enough to die.

* * *

In the summer of 1916, Alan's grandfather, Papa Brown, retired from his law practice in Indianapolis, and moved to Aurora to be closer to his daughter Maude and her family. Papa Brown, with his commanding presence, his evident leadership mentality, and his successful career as a soldier, constable, sheriff, attorney, and mayor, was the alpha male of the clan. With World War I raging in Europe, the potential involvement of the United States was a hot topic of conversation and Papa Brown was outspoken in his expression of patriotism and national pride. It influenced the entire family.

When the United States entered the war in April 1917, John LeMay became a 4-Minute Man. This was a group of trained volunteer speakers formed under Woodrow Wilson's Committee on Public Information who gave talks lasting exactly four minutes to garner support for the war effort and help sell bonds. The 4-Minute Men spoke anywhere they could get an audience — at movie theaters, churches, union meetings, lodges and granges. This took considerable effort and initiative, and illustrated his commitment to patriotic duty.

In this atmosphere, Alan was inspired to volunteer for the Illinois National Guard. He learned, however, that his high school education was not enough to earn him a commission, so he was eager to get a year of college behind him. His mother, Maude, always a strong influence, began investigating colleges for Alan. She wrote the following letter to the president of Stetson University in Deland, Florida[6]:

> We have been very favorably impressed with the catalogue of your University and are seriously considering sending our son to you for the coming year. He has spent three years in the Manual Training High School of Indianapolis, Indiana, whose reputation you probably know, and this last year in West High School of Aurora, Illinois, receiving his diploma yesterday.
>
> The Registrar of the University of Chicago assures us that his preparation is more than adequate for entrance there and we take it for granted that it will be satisfactory to you. However, before sending the boy so far, we wish assurance that such is the case...
>
> Our son wishes to prepare for journalism and plans to spend at least the last two years of his course at Leland Stanford. The requirements there are sufficiently elastic to allow him to spend his freshman year on the following subjects, — English, Biology, History, and Language. The

Daniel Leander Brown, as a soldier in the Grand Army of the Republic, and as an attorney and Sheriff Emeritus. The desk, an original Wooten, is still in the family.

language requirement in the English department at Stanford calls for four years work in one language, besides some work in a second. Our son chooses to put the bulk of the requirement on Spanish, considering it desirable for South American opportunity.

Maude had several more rounds of correspondence with the president of Stetson, checking on everything from living conditions to student attitudes, before she finally approved Alan's enrollment for the fall semester of 1916. He studied hard, and said later that the long hours in class put him to sleep, and that he took up smoking so he would stay awake by getting his fingers burned. It started an addiction that he could never break. But his grades were all good, and he was elected to membership in Phi Beta Psi.

With a year of college behind him, Alan got his Army commission as a "Shavetail" (a newly-appointed Second Lieutenant) and soon advanced to First Lieutenant, horse and reconnaissance, 124th Field Artillery of the Illinois National Guard. This was his first real experience with horses, and it began a lifelong love affair.

The same month that Alan finished his year at Stetson, his sweetheart, Esther Skinner, graduated with honors from Shortridge High in Indianapolis. Her yearbook had the comment: "Esther Skinner, Therapon. Honor Roll. Esther is an incurable tease, but in spite of it, she has a host of friends.... One of the prettiest girls we know." In the fall she entered Western College in Oxford, Ohio. But Alan and Esther were still keeping in touch.

After Stetson, Alan took a year off to earn some money before entering the University of Chicago, his father's alma mater. During that year, and while he was in school, he held a staggering variety of jobs. As he later described it in a brief autobiographical note that appeared in *Adventure Magazine*, September 1, 1927:

> I have acted as horse wrangler in Colorado, swamper in Wisconsin, fisherman off Florida, super-cargo on a schooner in the Caribbean, geologist in the Colombian Coast jungles, and sparring partner for a welterweight in Chicago. I've also tried several other things, none of them for very long, but each, I was told, for long enough.

At the same time he began writing fiction. He sold his first published story, "Circles in the Sky," to *Detective Story* magazine in 1919, while just a sophomore. He followed that with "Out of the Swamp," which also was published by *Detective Story* a few months later. These short stories did not pay much, but he enjoyed writing and seeing his work in print, and it was something he could do at night while he worked and went to college. And

Esther Skinner at Western College, Oxford, Ohio. Alan on "the Schooner" off Colombia. Spring 1921.

played football. He played on the University of Chicago varsity team as had his father before him.

He also wrote a play, *I Am Villion, a picaresque comedy in three acts.* It was done as a school project, but by this time he knew enough to copyright it in his own name. His analytical approach to his writing is revealed in a letter to his instructor:

Mr. R. D. Jameson,   March 3, 1922
University of Chicago,

Dear Mr. Jameson,

I enclose the stage directions for the color action to take place before the split drop.

I have not attempted to make the color action especially symbolic of the action of the play. However, anyone thoughtful enough to look for symbolism can easily explain how the action I have written is symbolic.

The value of the action as I have written it I construe to lie first in the opportunity it gives for fifteenth century Parisian atmosphere in the street; and second, in the inconsequence, irrelevance, and utter commonplaceness of its composition. It is an attempt to give the production perspective. Most plays are hypnotic in their narrowness of focus. This has been felt and combated by numbers of playwrights; but I have never heard of the use of a device like this for the purpose. I have introduced material completely irrelevant, completely detached, and of little dramatic distinction, hoping by this to remind the audience that whatever goes on inside the Green Moon, life goes on outside just the same, and a vast variety of people remain absorbed each in his own particular life.

I doubt that the device would work, since the audience, never having seen it before, and looking at it casually, would expect to find in it something or other, more relevant, that is not there. But I think the idea is an interesting one. What do you think?

The "vast variety of people" I have represented by only six types, all told. But my feeling is that the repetition of some of them enforces the idea more effectively than single glimpses of a larger number.

The dog, appearing five times, unifies the scenes, and in addition represents a sure-fire human interest hit. I seriously consider taking the dog out of the split-drop scenes and putting him into the play. He would be attached to Jones. The entrances of Jones are supposed to be entertaining, and it seems to me the dog would heighten this. Also win the audience for Jones. I know it is possible for a dog to wreck good scenes by creating diversions — flea-hunts, and the like — but the scenes which Jones attends are mostly noisy ones. The proper actor — an elderly greyhound retired from the vaudeville stage — would sleep thru. I hate to abandon the picture of Jones putting the dog thru the window ahead of him in the first act.

Hoping to hear from you soon, I remain,

Cordially yours,
Alan LeMay,
191 Grand Ave.,
Aurora, Ill.

The play was performed by the Aurora Dramatic Club on June 9, 1922. Alan directed it, and his father played in it as the Innkeeper.

* * *

The year before, Esther Skinner graduated with honors and an AB degree from Western College, having gotten a year ahead of Alan while he was traveling and working. The Rev. A.C.V. Skinner was transferred again by the Presbyterian Church, this time to Monte Vista, Colorado, and Esther lived there after graduation.

The notation by Esther on the back of the picture of "the Schooner" is the closest we have to correspondence during this period. Alan graduated from the University of Chicago with a PhB degree in June 1922, and a few weeks later married Esther, August 9, 1922, in Monte Vista. Her father, the Reverend Skinner, officiated at the wedding.

The newlyweds moved back to Aurora and lived on Calumet Avenue on the western outskirts of town. Alan called the house "Thunderbird"; there was no particular reason, but he always named his houses and cars. Esther worked as a teacher to help make ends meet. Alan did some writing and sold a couple of short stories, but again found himself near poverty. He got a dreary factory job sewing for piecework wages, and found that he could go faster and earn more if he removed the safety devices. He did, and stitched his thumbnail to his thumb.

This was when Alan began his planned career as a journalist, writing for the *Aurora Beacon News*. He also wrote more pulp fiction and worked on a novel. He sold several stories each year, mostly to *Adventure Magazine*, where he was becoming a regular, often with a series of episodes using the same characters such as Bugeye, Whiskers Beck, and Old Man Coffee. At pulp fiction prices it took workaholic hours just to eke out a lean living.

In January 1926, Esther had their first child, Joan Skinner LeMay (Jody) and Alan finished his first novel, *Painted Ponies*. It was published both as a four-installment serial in *Adventure Magazine*, and as a novel by George H. Doran Company.

The story took place on the Kansas frontier at the time of the Last Indian Raid in Kansas, the year that Alan's grandfather, Oliver, had died so young. Most of the people's names and the town names in the book were fictitious, but the Indians were clearly identified as the Northern Cheyenne, and their leader, Chief Dull Knife, was identified by name as the actual leader of the Last Raid in Kansas campaign. The Republican River was named in the action, and that was where Papa Brown had built his farm. The actions of the Indians loosely followed the history of Chief Dull Knife's campaign, except that the novel omitted the Indians' atrocities. In that respect it contrasted sharply with Alan's later treatment of Indians in *The Searchers*. But the public sentiment at the time held that the Indians were justified in defending their territory any way they could, and Alan's primary motivation was not to report history, but to sell a novel.

* * *

Alan was intrigued by Mark Twain and the Mississippi, and decided to move to New Orleans to do the research for river stories. The three LeMays left Aurora and took an apartment at 520 Saint Peters St., opposite Jackson Square in the Vieux Carre. He did the research and wrote several novels. The first of these, *Old Father of Waters*, was serialized in *Adventure*

Magazine and published in hard cover by Doubleday, Doran, & Company, Inc. in 1927. It was also sold in paperback as *Rivermen Die Broke*.

The short stories kept the family going, but the novels were what finally began to bring him recognition. One salute was from *The Mid-West Review* in September 1927:

> After reading Lindbergh's "We," and after considering the romance of "Trader Horn," and knowing of the work of our young Mid-American author, Alan LeMay, we can't help but write a few words about the fascination and inspiration of the written word...
>
> For some time Alan LeMay's short stories have been a feature of the "Adventure" magazine.
>
> His book, "Painted Ponies," was a success in this country and has been published in England, and some of his short stories have been translated into French by the translator of O. Henry.
>
> Mr. LeMay's next novel, "Old Father of Waters," starts in the September issue of "Adventure" and will be published in book form by Doran.
>
> Mark Twain told what the Mississippi meant to a boy; perhaps Alan LeMay will tell what it means to a man.

Another Mississippi-based novel, *Pelican Coast*,[7] followed in 1928. But with his analytical mind Alan studied market trends in the fiction business, and became convinced that his best subject would be Westerns. To know the subject well enough to write about it, he had to go there and immerse himself in it as he had done for his Mississippi-based stories.

So the family moved again.

—3—

Heading West

Alan surveyed places where he could live and own horses, and decided on San Diego. The family's first stop in 1929 was a tiny house at Windansea in LaJolla that Alan named El Pueblo Ribera, which means Beach Town. I was born in nearby LaJolla, and was named Dan Brown LeMay in honor of Papa Brown. The beach house was really too small for the family of four, so they soon moved to a larger rental on Dove Court in the Mission Hills area of San Diego while they scouted for something more permanent.

They finally found the ideal place at 2166 Pine Street in Mission Hills. Alan named it Gopher Gulch. It overlooked Mission Valley, and had a separate building that Alan used as a study where he did his writing. The study was not exactly off limits to kids, but my sister and I were not very welcome there. If we were to ask Daddy why he spent so much time working in his study, we could expect a short answer such as, "You like to eat, don't you?" And our mother frequently had to tell us "maybe we can do that after Daddy sells a story." Many a childish request crashed on the rocks of "when Daddy sells a story." And many a celebration came with the mail that meant "Daddy sold a story!"

At the end of the day he would spend some quality time with us, although sometimes his working schedule went far into the night. When I was still a pre-kindergarten lad, I remember Daddy lulling me to sleep with a reading of some spooky poem about the Great Gray Green Greasy Limpopo River, or better yet a dramatic rendition of Vachel Lindsay's *The Congo*. I have a strong lingering impression of how it sounded as I lay in bed in the dark. It started rather slowly, built into a crescendo about cannibals and the boom of a blood-lust song, with a thighbone beating on a tin pan gong, and climaxing with a "Rattle-rattle, rattle-rattle, rattle-rattle, **BOOM**." There followed an eerie refrain of "Then I saw the Congo creeping through the black, cutting through the jungle with a golden

2166 Pine Street, San Diego, also known as "Gopher Gulch." The study where Alan did his writing was the wooden building down the hill on the left. It was still there in 2011. Photograph by Alan 1931.

track..." and so on in a deep, sonorous chant that tapered off into a finale of "Mumbo-Jumbo will hoo-doo you, Mumbo-Jumbo will hoo-doo you..." repeated over and over as I drifted off to sleep. It never occurred to me that this was a weird bedtime poem for a four-year old.

* * *

Alan's deliberate shift to Westerns was a watershed decision that determined the rest of his writing career. In a 1945 interview he described his thoughts to Lee Shippey, feature writer for the *San Diego Union*:

> My income was so low in those early years that my wife helped out by teaching.
>
> One night we had to go to a high school performance of Shakespeare. Despite its amateurishness, Shakespeare's genius reached across 300 years to make the audience laugh and cry. It shocked me to realize that Shakespeare hadn't even tried to please the art critics of his day. What he wrote was so broadly human it appealed to coachmen and hostlers in inn yards — and that made the exquisite lines stand out in contrast.
>
> I resolved to find out what America was reading. I was newspaperman enough to know how to get information and made a private survey which seemed to prove that nineteen in twenty readers preferred extrovert to introvert stories, and that the Western story was not only the most American but, as proved by "The Virginian" and "The Covered Wagon," was by far the most popular if written right. So, knowing nothing of the West, I moved to San Diego when I learned that then

there were more than 100,000 acres of open range in San Diego County.

I rented 90 of those acres within sight of my San Diego home, hired a wise ex-cowboy and rodeo rider [Gil Strick] and he and I went into the horse raising business. We often broke horses for dude ranch cowboys who couldn't gentle them. And just riding over the land inspired a lot of ideas of what might happen. I spent part of every day riding and learning, and tried to write what I learned into stories good enough for the best magazines.

I wrote every story five times. The first draft was three times as long as the fifth because I tried to put everything essential in it. Then my secretary listed every mention of every character. Next I weeded out all that did not keep the story on course to its climax and tried to make every step compelling and inevitable, even if often surprising.

He did well with the Westerns, breaking into the "slicks" when *Collier's* became his primary customer in early 1929. The first story they bought was originally called "There's a Million Cows in the Greasewood," but they put it in inventory for more than a year before it was finally published as "Cowboys Will Be Cowboys." Alan became a feature when the March 7, 1931, issue of *Collier's* proclaimed on its cover: "*Gunsight Trail,* A New Novel by Alan LeMay."

He was soon on a first-name basis with *Collier's* fiction editor, Kenneth Littauer, and their frequent correspondence had the tone of old friends. For example, responding to some publicity material Alan had sent (December 10, 1934), Littauer wrote:

Dear Alan:

Many thanks for responding with the autobiography and the photograph of the young first-nighter. Do you mind if we add a monocle?

Alan responded:

Dear Ken:

The wow effect in the photograph is not a first-nightie. It is a horse muffler suitable for drinking cocktails in after a polo game without changing the hoof-trampled shirt. I suggest that race blinkers will increase the art value more than a monocle.

As his name became recognized, the pay got better. The pulps had paid just a few cents a word, but with *Collier's* he averaged 18¢ per word in 1931, and 35¢ per word by 1936, despite the worsening Depression wages in the rest of the country.

Alan was beginning to hit his stride. He claimed that his income was inadequate, but he had hired a secretary and professional cowboy Gil Strick, and started a horse raising business. All this must have taken significant capital, or caused indebtedness. But horses had become his passion since the first "jughead" he had ridden in the Field Artillery, and it showed in his success as he settled into living and writing in the Western genre.

Family life centered around horses as well. There were polo matches held frequently around San Diego County, and Alan joined in with enthusiasm. Esther was a good sport and learned polo, playing on women's teams organized by the players' wives. The kids were relegated to "cooling out" the polo ponies by walking them around after the match while the adults discussed the game over martinis and a lavish buffet table.

An occasional Sunday morning entertainment was a "paper chase." This is another game de-

Alan LeMay, 1935.

signed to get the whole family out with the horses. A lead horseman would ride out through the unfenced brushland of Kearny Mesa, dropping an occasional scrap of paper. The game was to follow the paper trail and get to the end first, where there was some prize like a wristwatch. I was just five, but I got to go along one Sunday, riding a docile mare named Lady Bird. I had my own saddle, which I was very proud of despite its being old and worn. As everyone galloped off in different directions Lady Bird and I fell behind, so no one noticed when my old worn cinch broke, landing me and my saddle in the brush. I had been taught that a cowboy never leaves his saddle, so I started walking back toward the stable, dragging the saddle by one stirrup. It seemed like a long, long time before anyone noticed Lady Bird tagging along bareback, and came looking for me.

Cowboy Gil Strick heard from his local Indian friends that there were some excellent horses in a wild band that had been seen in the Carrizo Plains, the desert badlands between the Cuyamacas and the Salton Sea. So he and Alan took their horses there with visions of roping a magnificent stallion and bringing it home for breaking. They didn't find any such horse, but on their way back to the trailers they spotted a desert burro. They roped him, and gentled him by riding close on both sides of him while they teased him with little switches. By the time they loaded him into the trailer he was completely tame. We named him Carrizo after the Carrizo Badlands where he was found.

Gil had introduced Alan to the local Los Conejos Indian band, and Alan and Esther made a point of attending the tribe's occasional "peon" games. Two four-man teams would sit facing each other across a camp fire and try to guess which hand of a player held a black or white stick (peon) while all chanted "peon" songs. The games and chanting could go on for days without stopping. In those years, the local Indians depended on deer and other game for food, and the Forest Service's no-burn policy had allowed heavy brush to choke out the grazing lands. Gil helped the Indians by setting fires that would start spontaneously when no one was around, thus restoring the deer habitat while keeping the Indians out of trouble. This earned him year-round hunting privileges on the reservation, which later helped the LeMays with an occasional haunch of venison during World War II meat rationing.

During this period the LeMays were doing so well that they put both of their children into the prestigious and expensive Francis W. Parker School in Mission Hills. I went to kindergarten, pre-first, and first grade there, and had three years of French before the second grade. Parker had a "Pet Day" where kids could bring their pets for show, and one year I won first prize when I brought the burro Carrizo to school. But times were hard, and the economic downturn drove the school into near bankruptcy; Alan served on the rescue committee that saved it.

* * *

The decade of the thirties was known as the Great Depression. For the LeMay family this famous event was divided into two distinct parts: the "Great" part, and the "Depression" part. The "Great" part for the LeMay family was the period of 1930–1936. Alan's name became established so that he could sell almost anything he wrote. He averaged more than 20 publications a

Alan on Carrizo, 1936.

year, either short stories, short-shorts, or monthly episodes of a serialized novel. There was no television, and few movie theaters, so people read magazines for entertainment. Westerns were king, and Alan had learned to crank them out at a pace that kept the LeMay family in an enviable lifestyle. Here's a summary of his production during those great years:

1930 18 short stories, mostly for *Collier's*, plus the novel *Gunsight Trail*.

1931 12 short stories, 2 books (*Bug Eye* and *Winter Range*), and 9 episodes of the serialization of *Gunsight Trail* for *Collier's*, plus the start of the serial version of *Winter Range*. *Collier's* began to feature his name on the cover.

1932 14 short stories for *Collier's*, *The Saturday Evening Post*, and others, plus serialization of *Winter Range* in *Collier's*, and the book version of *Cattle Kingdom*.

1933 Eight short stories, serialization of *Cattle Kingdom* in *Collier's* as *Cold Trails*, the book version of *Thunder in the Dust*, and the start of its serialization in *Collier's*.

1934 Four short stories, including two relegated to the pulps under the pseudonym "Alan M. Emley," plus *The Smoky Years*, and the last half-dozen installments of *Thunder in the Dust*.

Alan joined the Padres Writer's Club, a San Diego group with such members as Stuart Lake (*Wyatt Earp: Frontier Marshall*), Vic Hurley (*The Swish of the Kris, Southeast of Zamboanga*), Max Miller (*I Cover the Waterfront*), Walt Coburn (*Stirrup High, Law Rides the Range*), and others. There were frequent articles in the local papers showing Alan playing polo, Alan and Esther with their collection of Great Danes, Alan and Esther returning from a trip, or hosting a party for the People That Mattered.

The LeMays became good friends with Eileen Jackson, the society columnist for a San Diego newspaper. Most of Eileen's articles were society page fluff, where the LeMays were frequently mentioned as party hosts or attendees, but sometimes a column had a human interest angle that gave insights into the subject's life. She quoted Alan in an interview:

Most of my stories virtually amount to collaboration and really should be published under both names. Mrs. Le May supplies many ideas and oversees the behavior of my female characters. She often gathers a good deal of the background material we use. Last summer she made a reconnaissance of fiction material in the Pacific. On the basis of the material she gathered a leading national magazine commissioned us to write a serial set in the Hawaiian islands. To try out island material we wrote a short story which appeared in *Collier's* ["Out of the Whirlpool," February 24, 1934].

First Mrs. Le May wrote all the description in this story. Personally I never had seen the locale. She also contributed the opening scene in the story, basing it on an old Hawaiian legend. The opening was considered

Padres Writer's Club, c. 1934. Back row: Murney Mintzer, three unidentified, Syl McDowell, Charlie Booth. Front row: Doc Quirk, Gil Strick, Jim O'Connor, unidentified, Eddie Orcutt. Seated: Alan LeMay.

brilliantly clever by the editors. They cited it as their reason for playing up the story as their lead in the issue.

When we're in a jam trying to make a deadline she often takes dictation all night. She says she thinks this is a lot of fun.

On the strength of Mrs. LeMay's recommendation concerning the Hawaiian Islands he will accompany her there next month to gather material for more stories.

When they arrived in Hawaii they were noticed by the *Honolulu Advertiser* of May 26, 1934, which published their picture wearing leis, with the following caption:

Alan LeMay, well known fiction writer for *Collier's* and *Cosmopolitan*, arrived Thursday with Mrs. LeMay for an indefinite stay at Waikiki. LeMay said that he will probably do some writing with Hawaii for a background while here, but indicated that his plans are more or less indefinite. It is his first visit to the Islands but Mrs. LeMay was here a year ago.

Author Vic Hurley and his wife moved into our Gopher Gulch house and took care of my sister and me for the "more or less indefinite" duration of the Hawaiian trip. Alan's stories based on the Hawaiian material included "Deep Water Island" and "Dark Tropic Sea," both serialized in *Collier's* in 1935 and 1936.

Alan and Esther also made numerous trips to Mexico. They became friends with a cattle rancher in Baja California, where Alan could ride unbroken horses, rope and brand cattle, and acquire firsthand all of the background necessary to write authentic Westerns for the most discerning readers. They visited sites throughout the West to absorb background details such as the color of the mud in the Pecos, and where a horse could cross it at the end of summer. Get it wrong, and the readers will write.

When Alan's fame as an author became established, amateur writers would send him manuscripts and brazenly ask him for suggestions on how to improve their technique. He was never responsive to these intrusions. He said that, in the first place, he expended all of his writing energy just

Alan on Lula H., 1936.

to make a living. In the second place, it made no sense to tutor his competition, and in the third place, he did not want later to be accused of plagiarizing the plot. He said plots were a dime a dozen anyway; it is how they are written that sells. He had his secretary open all of his mail, and she would send anything that looked like a manuscript back either unopened, or marked "Opened by mistake, not read."

Polo matches on weekends became a regular occurrence. They were mostly informal games between local teams, but the participants were necessarily the successful people who could afford a string of polo ponies. This earned them frequent mention in the society pages. For example, from the *San Diego Sun*, September 1934:

> POLO GAMES IN MISSION VALLEY ATTRACT FASHIONABLES
> Royal Naval Players Are Matched With San Diego Team in Two Fast Contests
> The polo matches between the Royal Naval players from HMS Norfolk, the British cruiser, and the San Diego team, hold the interest of society this weekend. The games are being played on the new turf field in Mission Valley, the first this afternoon at 3 o'clock and the second tomorrow....
> Mr. and Mrs. Le May are giving a jolly cocktail party in their Mission Hills home following the game today. The British players will be honored guests.

Life was good, and the next step up for Alan was to own his own ranch. He wanted a place where he could stable his ponies, have his own polo field, and maybe raise a few cattle. He found exactly what he wanted in Santee, just 16 miles east of San Diego.

—4—

Rancho Una Vaca

Alan's accumulated savings in 1935 were sufficient to buy a 20-acre ranch in the San Diego back country across the river from Santee. It had a peach orchard, an orange grove, a well and a reservoir for water, an old adobe ranch house, and a decaying barn. Alan named it Rancho Una Vaca (One-Cow Ranch.) The land was at the corner of two nameless dirt roads which Alan named Board Walk and Park Place.

Alan had wanted a ranch ever since he moved to San Diego, and now he devoted much of his time and energy to developing it into a showplace. He ripped out the peach and orange groves and put in a polo field. He had the inadequate water well re-dug, and patched up the swimming pool-size reservoir. It serviced not only the house, but the irrigation of the vast polo turf, and in the summer we swam in it.

The house was about two thousand square feet, authentic adobe, and built in Mexican style around a walled patio. It had a large living room, separate dining room, three bedrooms, and two baths. Alan hired the prestigious local architect, Starling Watson, to design an addition to the house, more than doubling its size and adding a three-car garage and servants' quarters. The remodel was to add a large master bedroom with two walk-in closets, a guest room, two more baths, and *two* studies. The larger study would have its own fireplace, and look out onto an added patio and down the length of a long, slender lap pool.

The decaying old barn was torn down and a new one built. The new barn was as elegant as anything housing thoroughbreds in Kentucky. It had a tack room with wall racks for saddles and bridles, small quarters for a groom, and four horse stalls down each side of a wide central aisle. Each stall had its own outdoor corral, an automatic waterer, and a feed chute that was loaded from the large loft above. Alan retrieved his pet mare, Lula H (the "H" was for Horse), from her boarding stable in Mission Valley, and bought several more horses to fill out his polo string. One was

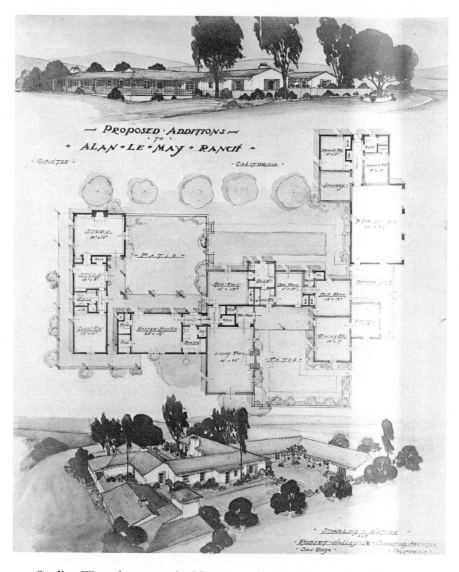

Starling Watson's proposed additions to the Una Vaca adobe. The original part is the square block in the southeast corner.

a spirited young gelding he broke himself and named Wildfire, setting up a piece of dialogue like: "Where's Alan?"

"He rode outa here on 'Fire."

To gain first-hand experience with cattle punching, he bought 20 whiteface heifers and a bull that he named Jim Farley. Jim Farley was

Franklin D. Roosevelt's Secretary of Agriculture, and bore a close resemblance to the whiteface bull. Alan worked the "L" for LeMay into a jagged cattle brand, and called his little herd the Lazy Lightning brand. The herd was scheduled to increase itself by 20 calves the following spring.

Alan made arrangements with a neighbor named Nichols to farm 40 acres of hay on the parcel southeast of the ranch. Twenty head was what he figured he could feed with that. He had consulted weather experts and almanacs, and all of the indicators were for a very wet winter. His local Indian friends said that even the squirrels were moving farther up the hillsides. The winter of 1936–1937 would surely be wet enough for a great hay crop. In the dry Southwest, the herd size must be planned according to the long-range weather forecast. The wetter it will be, the more the grass will grow, and the fewer the number of acres needed to feed each cow. Alan figured he needed just two acres per head.

* * *

By the fall of 1936, Bermuda grass was established on the new polo field. Crews went the entire length of the field cutting the wire-grass run-

Roundup of the Lazy Lightning brand, 1936.

ners with special knife-tined rakes so that each node became a new plant that could better withstand the pounding hooves of the Sunday afternoon polo matches. And with a beautiful polo field right outside his office, Alan took advantage of it for exercising his ponies while practicing hitting a ball up and down the field for hours. It was exactly what he had wanted, but it was a major distraction from writing.

Weekends became party time, with visiting polo teams from all over the world. Usually the matches were at Mission Valley, but more than once they were at Rancho Una Vaca. There was a touring team from Argentina, the British Naval team, and the Hollywood team came down from the Riviera Polo Club. Producer Darryl F. Zanuck, the founder of Twentieth Century–Fox, and producer Hal Roach played on that team. There were local teams from Coronado, Mission Valley, and La Jolla.

And there were other interesting people who stayed at Una Vaca, providing more distractions. An Argentinean professional boxer, Alberto Lovell, trained at the ranch for his bout in San Diego. Alan had done some amateur boxing, and worked out with Alberto as a sparring partner. We went to the championship match which Alberto won by a knockout, smashing his hand and ending his career in the process. Lew Walker, curator of birds at the San Diego Museum of Natural History, trained falcons at the ranch. He set up a pigeon cot and raised pigeons which he used to train his falcons.

Besides the pigeons, falcons, polo ponies, beef herd, and milk cows (actually there were now dos vacas at Rancho Una Vaca), we had dogs. We had a little white Sealyham named Shorty, and Alan's pet, a big black Great Dane named Jumbo. Alan thought that raising pure black Danes could be fun and profitable, so he bought Jumbo a girlfriend named Queenie. In what seemed like the natural scheme of things, the pack built up to a count of 13 at one time. Uno of the dos vacas was purchased just to provide milk for the Danes.

The press apparently found all of this entertaining, and Alan encouraged the publicity because it helped sell books, and because he enjoyed the trappings of fame. He cultivated the image of a successful Western writer, always wearing cowboy boots, and driving a flamboyant canary-yellow Buick roadster with red pinstripes on the sides. He wore high-heeled cowboy boots the rest of his life. He always said they were more comfortable for him, but the two inches they added to his height helped overcome his self-consciousness about his short stature.

Alan was at the top of his game. He seemed unbeatable. He even wrote his own Fight Song to the tune of the old Civil War song "Kingdom Coming"[1]:

I heard him say that he was mighty clever
And his luck was in today
But he was looking foolisher than ever
When the dust had cleared away.
He lost his shirt, Ha Ha!
His luck ran out today,
For he was big enough and old enough and shoulda known better
Than to bet against LeMay!

* * *

Collier's paid well and became Alan's mainstay, but he still needed more income. Since he retained his own copyrights he could resell his serials to others (book publishers, film producers, etc.) as long as it did not interfere with his primary customer. He asked his agent, Helen Everitt of Curtis Brown, Ltd., to test the waters with his *Collier's* fiction editor, Ken Littauer:

> [February 6, 1935] ... Also, I want to consult you on the question of selling the second serial rights, long after book publication, for use in these one-issue pulp magazines.
> LeMay is leaving the decision up to me, and I want your advice as to whether you think this damages his serial market in any way. All the best Western writers seem to go in for this, and it picks up some money on the side, but not enough to accept, if you think it's bad tactics.

Littauer replied:

> [February 8, 1935] ... About selling second serial rights in his stories after publication: certainly we have no objection to this. Publication of this sort is rarely noticed by people who read COLLIER'S. And even if it were noticed we can't see that it would do anybody in the least harm. You may as well pick up these crumbs and put them in the bank.

* * *

The "Emley" stories in 1936 were the first signs of trouble. They were published in pulps under the Alan M. Emley pseudonym because they were rejected by the slicks, and Alan didn't want them to detract from his established reputation for the higher-priced market. Their sudden appearance here was due in part to the Depression, which finally caught up with the advertising income of the slicks. But equal blame could be given to the distractions that interfered with Alan's concentration and undercut the quality of his writing. As the rejections piled up, Littauer almost pleaded with Alan to produce something they could use. In one letter he wrote:

[April 5, 1937] ... Can't you think of something else in the way of short fiction that might be up our street? Believe it or not, we miss you badly.

The rejections meant that Alan was spending much of his time in wasted effort. So when a story sold, the paycheck seemed meager because he still was slowly sliding into debt. He pushed his agent to try to get him a raise, and Edith Haggard wrote to Littauer:

[May 26, 1937] ... I am delighted that you are buying NIGHT BY A WAGON TRAIL by Alan LeMay and I assume that the price is $500 for first American and Canadian serial rights.

I am still brooding over the idea that he should have a raise on short shorts. Don't you think something might be done?

Littauer promptly replied:

[May 27, 1937] ... I still don't see why we should raise LeMay's short short story price. Five hundred dollars is one hundred dollars more than we pay most people. Do you know anybody who would do better by you? If you do, that's different.

And the rejections kept coming. Alan's efforts continued to get discouraging responses to his agent from Littauer such as:

[July 29, 1937] ... Here is ODD THING AT CLAMNECK by Alan LeMay.... It is a very old gag and I don't think we ought to use it again. In fact I don't think anybody ought to use it again, not even Alan LeMay.

And just a week later:

[August 5, 1937] ... This one by Alan LeMay called THE VANISHING WINDOW offers nothing but some very odd monkeyshines. This is not enough to make a good short short.

The big distraction was the ranch. The climate forecasts were more than correct. It rained. The new hay came up as scheduled, but the rain didn't stop. It set records. It washed out every river crossing all the way down to Old Town San Diego, and I missed most of the second grade because we couldn't get across the river to the Santee school. The new oat field soon was drowned in mud, and hay had to be imported from the Imperial Valley to keep the herd fed. All the cattlemen had the same problem, so feed costs skyrocketed.

Thus began the "Depression" part of The Great Depression. The constant rain created a gloomy mood that was hard to shake in the dank adobe ranch house. Mildew began to grow, and small, smelly black beetles called "tule-bugs" were everywhere. When the lights went out at night they scurried up the rough walls, and sometimes would drop from the ceiling onto the bed. The atmosphere reeked of mildew and tule-bugs. Alan's grand-parents had endured worse conditions in their Kansas prairie "soddy," but there it was expected.

As things grew worse, Alan tried to convince himself that he was worrying needlessly. The day after his birthday he wrote the following back-handed essay on worry in a letter to his parents:

> Friday, June fourth 1937
>
> Dearest Mother and Dad:
>
> I am now 38 years old. In review, it seems to me that I have spent most of the thirty-eight years worrying. Looking at this as the one big specialty to which I have devoted myself, I feel that I have done very well as to amount, intensity, and continuity of worry, but my accuracy has been deplorable. I have at all times had on hand a good well-timed stock of impending disasters, and if one per cent of them had ever come through with the goods I would indeed be in pitiable shape today. Yet after thirty-eight years in the shadow of imminent calamity I am amazed to note that I am still here. I am not only here, but I am just as well off as I ever was in my life; in fact in every way I can think of I am probably better off. This does not check very well with the consistent opinion I have had in the past as to the difficult situation I was always facing. I am afraid that I can only conclude that as a worrier I have laid an egg....
>
> I have so long been afraid, for example, that I would go broke that a good bankruptcy would have been a relief. And what did I get for all my trouble? Just one long series of narrow escapes. Year after year I have come as close to bankruptcy as I have come to getting in the movies, and that's about the best you can say for it.
>
> From falling hands we throw the torch. Let somebody else pick up the white man's burden. All my really original ideas for anxiety are threadbare, and as far as worry is concerned I have shot my bolt. I don't give a damn whether I go broke or not, and to hell with it. Thirty-eight years of fruitless anxiety! That would take the tuck out of any-body.
>
> Love, Alan

But his money worries were quite real, and so were his anxieties about the rejections from *Collier's*. The burden of these perceived failures left him vulnerable to the gnawing belief that his bad luck had become a pat-tern. So he was not prepared for what happened next.

My sister Joan was to spend the summer with Alan's parents in Illinois, making her first trip by air. Her flight was diverted due to weather, had to refuel at a small air strip at Laramie instead of its scheduled stop at Cheyenne, and the result was that Joan appeared to be missing for several hours. The plane was not actually missing, but the airline failed to communicate what was going on. In his dark mood, Alan thought he had sent his daughter to her death.

His fears were not without reason. He had flown many times, and enjoyed the speed and convenience, but he was wary of the safety. He had lost more than a half dozen manuscripts to airmail crashes. Alan was a big fan of Will Rogers, who died in a much-publicized plane crash with Wiley Post in 1935, and that accident was fresh in his mind. This was a time of barnstorming pilots, wing-walking daredevils, air races, and frequent new records for speed and non-stop distances. Airplanes were working their way into the mainstream for mail and travel, but they crashed a lot. Navigation was rudimentary, radio communication was unreliable, and such problems as water in the fuel and ice on the wings were just beginning to be solved.

Much earlier, before Christmas, Alan had written his parents a soothing letter about what to expect on an airline flight. They were coming out from Illinois for Christmas, and they had decided to try the newfangled air travel experience. Alan's letter didn't get there. The Western Air Express mail plane crashed near Salt Lake City, and the letter spent the winter in the wreckage on a cold Wasatch Mountain peak. It was found when the snows melted in May, and was finally delivered with an understated rubber stamp on the envelope that said "DELAY DUE TO AIR MAIL INTERRUPTION NEAR SALT LAKE CITY, UTAH, DEC.15, 1936." Its arrival, just two weeks before Joan set off on her flight to Chicago, renewed Alan's worst fears. Joan arrived safely a few hours late, but Alan was shattered. He wrote the following letter to his parents. It is unusually frank, and illustrates the depth of his mood:

> Monday, June 28, 1937
>
> Dearest Mother and Dad:
>
> Well, that's over with, and I never want any more of it. I guess with advancing years I have simply lost my ability to take it. I have nothing to say against air travel, and would be willing to use it myself, but the nature of my profession makes me over-imaginative and nervous. Ernest Haycox, in a letter to the editors of *Collier's* which they published, suggested that writers, through many years of trying to write better than they are able or know how, develop an enlarged imagination, as athletes develop an enlarged heart; he says that enlarged imagination is a writer's occupational disease.
>
> I believe this to be a good statement. I estimate that I have traveled more than 35,000 miles as an air passenger, and that I traveled more than 20,000 before I began to feel fear. Whether or not I remember this correctly, it nevertheless is true that I have developed a morbid, unreasoning fear of the air; I lighted at Honolulu from Kauai so green-faced

that everyone commented on it, after a trip so uneventful that both pilots were reading a newspaper....

I have lost air mail stuff no less than seven or eight times. One BUG EYE story written in LaJolla was down in the flames not only once, but the same story a second time, before it finally reached its destination.... I cannot forget that if we had used the planes as casually and frequently as we use the air mail, the entire family would have been lost by this time, one by one.

Naturally, to the best of my ability, and I believe successfully, I have concealed this reaction from Joan (you can tell better than I can whether or not I was successful).

Joan set off most gallantly. It was possible to see that internally she was full of doubts and flusters; she turned red and white by turns and kept asking little worried questions about details, such as her baggage and the plane changes. But she maintained a gay, happy, and fairly calm exterior....

We drove back to San Diego the same night. And after a hideous and sleepless night, morning brought word that her plane was missing.

To me, in my unreasoning terror of the air, the night had been an age-long horror, and the morning news closed in with the slow, crushing grip of an implacable doom. Worse than the sheer lack of news was the evasive manner of the airways people whom we continuously haunted by phones. You would have thought, to talk to them, that none of them had ever heard of the flight, the plane, the route, or the schedule. In contrast with their usual swift accuracy, I took this evasion to mean that they knew much more than they were yet willing to tell.

Finally we wormed out of them that during the night the plane had fueled not at Cheyenne, but at Laramie, and the reason was given that Wyoming was under a ceiling-zero fog. This incredible report bewildered us. It is my business to know something about the climate of the west, and to the best of my knowledge and belief Cheyenne has not seen a cloud the size of the hand, this time of year, since 1872. It isn't even in the dust bowl. What it does have is mountain range upon mountain range, close set and precipitous. Until you finally reported Joan in at Chicago, after nearly five hours' suspense, all we could find out was that section one had been in for hours but that Joan's section was unreported since it refueled — mysteriously far off its course — at Laramie.

All this was terribly hard on Esther; yet she is one who views air travel with confidence and liking. With my pathological fear of the air, the experience was shattering.

The relief of knowing that she is safe does not seem adequate to undo the damage of that terrible night. Of course none of this must be communicated, by any unguarded inference, to Joan. It would be a sorry thing if she should obtain from me, by contagion, any part of this shameful cowardice, but I think that her return by air had better on some pretext be abandoned. Will you therefore please cash in her return ticket at the air office there, with a view to sending her home by streamline train? I am trying now to finish and sell my serial in time to be able to come east to meet her.

Since learning of her safe arrival I have been able to think of nothing except how little I have been able to do for her, how little of myself I have given her. Yet I do not see how I can do more. I don't feel as if I have much of anything of value to give her, or anyone. I feel empty, and all shot up.

Love, Alan

He did not snap back from this experience, which was more than an isolated panic. Bills had piled up from the ranch remodel, the cattle feed, the parties, and the full-time help. Rejection slips from the slicks were depressing, and the meager checks from the pulps for the re-titled Alan M. Emley stories didn't cover the red ink. The weather had been nothing but record-breaking rains for months, and the ranch was a swamp. The saddles mildewed in the barn. The precious polo field was a sea of mud. Everywhere Alan looked he saw his dreams in decay. His mood was black, and he couldn't write.

His marriage suffered badly during these emotional times, and finally fell apart in the summer of 1937. Joan was still in Aurora visiting Alan's parents, so on July 20 he left the ranch for the last time, as he and I took the train to Illinois. Esther filed for divorce, and the chapter on *Rancho Una Vaca* closed.

— 5 —

Recovery

It was my understanding that the visit to my grandparents was to be a summer vacation, but after all three of us were in Aurora, Dad took my sister and me up to the privacy of the attic and explained that we were not going back. Joan and I survived a very homesick year at Mary A. Todd school in Aurora, but we sure didn't like it. Our grandparents were as nice as they could be, but we still hated it.

From my viewpoint as a young child, the Rancho Una Vaca years were the good times. Going back through the correspondence of the time, I can see that I was sheltered from much that was going on, at least in Alan's mind. His problems with the magazines were not entirely of his own doing. The other side of the story was that the Depression had cut corporate advertising budgets, so the magazines themselves were in trouble. To make matters worse, there was a plethora of excellent writers competing for the shrinking market. *Collier's* had a huge stockpile of fiction ready to publish, and little cash to buy more.

Alan's writing had been our only source of income, and the good times had required a high production rate, which he had met by selling an average of two stories per month during the early thirties. It was little consolation that other good writers preceded him when he was cracked loose from his grip in those last sad days at Rancho Una Vaca.

Back home in Aurora, away from the distractions and frustrations of the ranch, Alan quickly regained his competitive drive, but he still wrote very little that sold in the tough Depression market. His production of published stories dropped from more than 20 in 1936 to eight in 1937, just five in 1938, and five in 1939. The market was thin, but it existed for quality material. Ken Littauer, the fiction editor of *Collier's*, wanted more of the old LeMay. In a letter to Alan's agent, Edith Haggard, Ken wrote,

41

[November 50, 1937] We would like to have a serial by Alan LeMay and will undertake to render a decision on four installments of the story together with a synopsis of the balance.

The opportunity was there, but Alan's concentration still lacked something, and the rejections continued:

[February 21, 1938] ... We are returning Alan LeMay's story LADY IN SEARCH OF SILENCE. I am sorry, but it is much too long for the weight of the plot and leaves the reader pretty well puzzled.

And another:

[February 23, 1938] ... We have decided finally against SPRING PRAIRIE by Alan LeMay. The tension in this story is never sustained. It is full of good bits, but they are only bits. It isn't LeMay at his best or anything like his best.

I am terribly distressed about the situation, but I can think of nothing to do to improve it. Please tell Alan when you write him that I am concerned and sympathetic.

Under these conditions the cash flow from his fiction writing was doing little to pay off the ranch debts, so Alan cast about in other directions. He tried to get *Collier's* to send him to the war zone in China as a

Alan as a student pilot in a Tailorcraft, 1938.

foreign correspondent, while also gathering fiction material. The idea fell through because *Collier's* already had a news correspondent there. So Alan did some reporting and writing for the *Aurora Beacon News*, and worked for the little Aurora radio station as the "engineer." It is there that he met and began dating Arlene Hoffman, who was the station manager, and was soon to be his second wife.

The memory of Joan being "lost" on an airline flight still rankled in Alan's mind. It bothered him most that he had been defeated by his fear of flying. So in typical LeMay fashion he attacked his fears head on by learning to fly. He took lessons at Fox Valley Flying Service, soloed, and earned a pilot's license. He even started to buy a Cessna single-engine plane in partnership with a Dr. MacElroy, but the partner defaulted on his share, ending the idea rather acrimoniously.

In a move to profit from his experience, he wrote several flying stories. He described "Forced Down a Little" as "a complete dog — I can't do anything with it." But he thought three others were promising: "Bat Out of Heaven," "Flying Horseshoe," and "Rainbow Round My Ship." None of those working titles showed up in print, but three others did: "Uncertain Wings" (*Collier's*, 26 November 1938), "West of Nowhere" (*Collier's*, 29 July 1939), and "Interrupted Takeoff" (*Collier's*, 4 November 1939).

In June 1939, events conspired to end his flying, when he was called to Hollywood to be an "advisor" to Cecil B. DeMille at Paramount Pictures.[1] Then World War II stopped recreational flying for the duration. But he still thought about it, not as a phobia but as a hobby to return to when possible.

He never did renew his pilot's license after the war, but that was because of other interests and inadequate spare time, not because of any residual paranoia. He had faced that and beat it. If he had had any further doubts about who won that fight he would have heard the bell and come out for another round.

— 6 —

Hello, Hollywood

Cecil B. DeMille sent a telegram to Alan in June 1939, inviting him to come to Hollywood as a story consultant. The job looked uncertain, but the money was good, so he left Aurora immediately. My sister and I stayed behind with our grandparents.

His first assignment when he arrived at Paramount Pictures was *North West Mounted Police*. The tentative "Story Consultant" title was DeMille's version of probation; he was hedging because Alan had never written a screenplay. As soon as DeMille saw Alan's work his title was changed to "Screenwriter." The circumstances of his being recruited for this film are recounted by Jesse Lasky, Jr., in his *Whatever Happened to Hollywood.*[1]

> DeMille, seeking a more primal tint of virility on his palette, had decided on a new combination of writers. Alan LeMay was lured from short-story writing for *Collier's* and *The Saturday Evening Post*. Lacking any screenwriting experience, he was assigned to collaborate with me. Having survived two DeMille pictures I was now considered almost seasoned. This meant, among other things, an acquired ability to roll with the insults. And, as the Boss put it, I was supposed to keep Alan from "going too far wrong." Tried and true script carpenter C. Gardner Sullivan was assigned to clean up the mistakes behind us.

A month after arriving in Hollywood, Alan felt sufficiently settled to send for Arlene. They rendezvoused in Las Vegas where they married on July 22, 1939. His new friend from Paramount, Jesse Lasky, Jr. and Jesse's wife, Donna, went along for the celebration. The newlyweds went back to California to their first home, a spectacular rental house on Lookout Mountain above Hollywood, at 8946 Appian Way. It had a view extending from Los Angeles to Santa Monica, with Catalina Island in the distance. It had previously been rented by Errol Flynn. Lew Ayres and Ann Sheridan had the only houses above it on the mountain. Alan had barely cashed his first paycheck from Paramount before his standard of living was raised to match it. Because of the ping-pong schedule of joint custody, my sister Joan and I moved in just two weeks after their marriage, which Joan remembers did not thrill Arlene.

Alan's early efforts at Paramount were well received, but it took a considerable adjustment to get used to the differences of screenwriting. After a few weeks' exposure to the Hollywood version of writing he gave this brief analysis of his own style in an August 1, 1939 letter to his parents:

> Dear Mother and Dad:
>
> I have not set the world on fire in pictures; I can see now that I have always been a literary writer rather than a dramatic writer — I have written so well and so easily that I have told stories that are no good unless I write them, and here they have to have naturals dished up such as anybody can tell. So I will have to make a special study, and change my attack. This needs a lot of explaining, but for the present, just take my word for it; I would never have found it out if I hadn't come here.
>
> Love, Alan

Alan was used to having complete artistic control over his work. But at Paramount there were meetings daily, or oftener, to criticize each scene. DeMille's comments were typically vitriolic, not constructive, and quite intimidating to a rookie screenwriter. Writing for DeMille, Alan said, was like learning how to feed a Siamese cat: by selective vomiting. What the cat will finally keep down is not usually something you would have chosen.

Alan and Arlene, 1940. Photograph by John LeMay.

Nor had his years of solo writing prepared Alan for the culture shock of team writing. Alan's attitude about a collaborator's contribution was frequently "if I had wanted it that way, I would have written it that way." Indeed, his early experience at Paramount was showing him that the team concept seldom went smoothly. In a December 11, 1939, letter to his parents, Alan describes how it went on *North West Mounted Police*:

> Things here go very well indeed, and somewhat better than to be expected. The usual parade of writers that always goes on and off a DeMille opus, have been with us; one by one they have flopped and got the gate. A haunting dread of failure is not allayed when one sees high-priced crack screen writers falling down to one's right and left all the time. First off the picture was Jeannie MacPherson, who wrote "King of Kings." Next the great Spig Wead (Ceiling Zero) came and went leaving in the picture a single line which must have cost $15,000. (Three words at $5000 each.) Next Gardner Sullivan lost himself in the amazing intricacies of the plot, and came out of the woods to find he was also outside the gate. (Not long ago Sullivan was absolute tops around here — about $8000 a week.) Next came and went Clements Ripley, Cosmo writer, author of a great new picture about Paul Jones. He lasted one sequence. Finally came Bart Cormack, known to me in the U of C, [University of Chicago] a screen writer for fifteen years. He lasted three weeks. One more writer may yet be called in "to bring a fresh mind to the cutting." But Jesse Lasky and I finish alone.
>
> This gets me the record as the only outside writer ever to stick it through a DeMille picture, first to last. It also is supposed to get me a few modest offers, including one from Paramount to stay on with a raise. I think I ought to get another screen credit or two quickly, if I can. No other picture takes so long as a DeMille.

Alan was fortunate to have Jesse Lasky, Jr., as his mentor and main collaborator on his first Hollywood script. Jesse had experience working for DeMille, and could reassure Alan that the insults and expletive-laced critiques of his work were entirely normal. Jesse was patient and friendly, and had a more benign view of team writing than did Alan. In *Whatever Happened to Hollywood*, Jesse said[2]:

> I am frequently asked how two people can actually write together. Obvious methods of collaboration differ with the personal preferences of the collaborators. Sometimes one talks and the other types. Sometimes they type in separate rooms, then exchange drafts for polishing. The perfect collaboration, like a perfect marriage, requires diplomatic genius and extrasensory perception. The combined writers are supposed to augment and stretch each other's capabilities without inhibiting creativity or ever offending each other. Since producers were frequently the common enemies, strong alliances were pretty essential to artistic survival. Though not quite Damon and Pythias, Alan and I got along well.

DeMille's staff generally gave each other moral support (except in the competition for screen credits), which helped to weather the Boss's frequent tirades. One of them anonymously wrote "The DeMille Fight Song," sung to the tune of the USC Trojans fight song:

> Fight on for old C. B.,
> For William Pine, and Dorothy.
> Your salary's down to three,
> Or maybe two,
> Or maybe one,
> Or maybe none, fight on!
> It's all in fun, fight on!

But the long days and unending pressure took their toll on Alan, and he blamed his own ambition for keeping him on the treadmill from which he was constantly planning his escape. In answer to his father's question he wrote:

> [September 24, 1941] You asked me if I still think the hard drive of ambition is a bad thing, and the only way I can answer is to say I don't know. I probably am forced to conclude that it's a bad thing for oneself, but good for one's family. Civilization is now so stepped up and all the family services so concentrated on those who bring in the money, that I do not see how anyone with family responsibilities can keep out from under the wheels without going full out.
>
> I would feel better about the whole thing if I had not been imprisoned all day in a cubicle where we had to burn the electricity through one of California's most brilliant, sunny effects. Personally, I would much rather round up cattle or go fishing. But there is not much use in questioning these things until the children are raised; after which I mean to retire happily upon the Government.

* * *

As filming began on *North West Mounted Police*, Alan and Jesse were assigned to another DeMille project with the working title of *The Rurales*. But they still had to cope with last minute script adjustments, which made for very long days. Alan was returning to his habits as a workaholic, and Arlene was becoming a movie widow. Alan was also learning how to survive among the carnivores of Hollywood, where screen credits were essential to success. He wrote of this in a letter to his parents:

> [April 8, 1940] ... Our present work is a good deal complicated by repeated and almost incessant calls to the sets where "North West Mounted" is shooting to add or alter lines. This is a very good thing for it gives me an opportunity to keep in contact with the actual shooting. But it is not what we are paid for (Jesse and I) since we are charged against the "Rurales" picture and feel that we must turn in a full day's

Standing: C. Gardner Sullivan, Jesse Lasky, Jr., William Pine. Seated: Alan LeMay, Cecil B. DeMille. On the back of the photograph is written: "In DeMille's office — a conference on the *North West Mounted Police* screenplay. Note the photographs of Mounted Police and Canadian scenes pinned on the wall and lying on the desk. Pine is DeMille's associate producer, Sullivan and Lasky were assisting Alan with the script. On the desk in the foreground is a replica (mounted) of the Golden Spike used in 'Union Pacific.'"

work on the "Rurales" in addition to the trouble-shooting on the "North West Mounted."

[Gary] Cooper is doing the best job of his life and Madeleine Carroll is amazing everyone with a moving, emotional performance — besides looking like a perfect angel in color. The picture is shooting about four days ahead of schedule and several have said that the script is the best prepared they have ever seen, which is not a thing we can take credit for, but avoids a discredit which would fall on us if the opposite were true.

Gardner Sullivan will get third credit on the screen with an admitted one per cent of the screen play on a political gyp; his protection being in DeMille's declaration that he wrote under the name of DeMille. You can't get around a thing like that and there is nothing we can do about it. There may be some political capital in the principle of the shenanigan knowing perfectly well that we got a good trimming; but I doubt it.

In short, everything except the Sullivan credit looks as good as it possibly could in what will always be a very uncertain business, at best.

North West Mounted Police finished shooting on May 13, 1940. During filming Alan had become frustrated by the extensive rewrites and by DeMille's directing style. By the time the final product was released he had lost his enthusiasm completely. Even when he worked alone and had full artistic control he was seldom satisfied with the results, but here he also disagreed with the directing and editing. Mercifully, he did not go to the first sneak preview in Westwood Village, which was a disaster not of its own making. As Jesse Lasky, Jr., reported in *Whatever Happened to Hollywood,*[3]

> it was scurrilously alleged that Paulette Goddard had participated in an unrehearsed love scene with a famous director at Ciro's. Hardly believable to anyone who knew Paulette, who, aside from being a lady of taste, would under no circumstances have fed her reputation to the Hollywood locusts.

Nevertheless, the rumor inspired raucous hoots, and shouted references to Ciro's, during Paulette's on-screen love scenes. Jesse was mortified, but C. B. was unfazed. He adjusted the order of some shots, made a few trims, and after the unsubstantiated rumors had faded they previewed again in Santa Barbara. This was the version that Alan saw as his first viewing of the final product, out in public, where he could see his name on the screen, and strangers could judge the final result of his efforts.

This second preview was an unqualified success, and so was the film when it went into roadshow[4] release. Despite the acclaim Alan was not happy at all. He wrote to his parents:

> [October 31, 1940] "North West Mounted Police" is such a hashed-over product, every line hammered down into plastic pulp and cast into some synthetic shape, that I recognize very little of it as my own. I do not care for the picture very much. I think it is choked, overcrowded, melodramatic and mainly out of reality or character. However, it does seem to be a box office smash, which I suppose is the main thing. At present it is running 192% of "Union Pacific."
>
> After a year and a half in pictures I do not care for this branch of writing very much. This is definitely a directors and producers business. I do not think you would have gathered from the premiere that such a thing as a script had any part in the picture. The producer, director and actors take all the bows, and the writers play the part of the meanly inefficient cogs who hold everything up. This is strictly not good enough.

—7—

Reap the Wild Wind

For the first of many times, *The Rurales* was set aside while Alan tackled a new DeMille project: *Reap the Wild Wind*. This story by Thelma Strabel originally ran in *The Saturday Evening Post* in three installments.[1] Paramount bought the film rights, and DeMille started Alan, Jesse Lasky, Jr., and Charles Bennett on the screenplay soon after the last installment was published.

DeMille liked to kick off new projects with occasional working sessions at his ranch or on his yacht, and this was one of those times. A previous time was when they started *North West Mounted Police*. That trip came shortly after Alan married Arlene, and caused her to say that they spent their honeymoon on DeMille's yacht, except that she didn't get to go.

The days on the yacht were much the same as those at the studio, possibly with a more creative atmosphere and fewer outside interruptions. But at sunset the ambiance was transformed, as the somewhat starry-eyed boy from Aurora reported to his parents:

> [August 13, 1940] The main feature of the yacht, like the DeMille ranch, is the extraordinary food. One of the dinners, for example, went like this: The famous DeMille rum cocktail, mixed with the greatest ceremony by DeMille himself, of priceless ingredients; undoubtedly the finest drink of any kind I ever tasted. DeMille drinks nothing during the day nor after dinner, but always has a cocktail before dinner. With the cocktails were hors d'oeuvres which featured Hungarian goose liver, definitely different from pate de foie gras, and a rare delicacy, difficult to obtain. We then had thick oxtail soup, made with the only genuine oxtails ever used around here. The main feature was birch partridge — a white meat partridge which has to be captured wild when young in Canada, and raised with greatest care in captivity. There were only twelve of these west of the Mississippi River; now there are only six. With the birch partridge we had Piper Heidsick, 1927. We finished with a peach blanc mango in a rare old Kirsch.

In social moments, as at dinner, DeMille becomes a host of the superlative old southern gentleman type, in violent contrast to his angry tornadoing at all other times.

While out on the yacht I practiced staying under water with a glass face mask. We are going to use some underwater stuff in "Reap the Wild Wind," and the special effects department is planning a terrific budget. It is in my mind to bid upon making the underwater transparencies, if the set-up seems favorable. What they call transparency plates are the film which they project upon a screen for purposes of re-photographing with actors in the foreground. Such shots as the water-tower wreck in "Union Pacific," the snow-slide wreck, and so forth, are all made by this method, first making a transparency plate of miniatures, then playing actors in front of a magnifying projection. The plates I am thinking of would be Kodachrome underwater backgrounds to be projected against the back of a plate-glass studio tank.

There is the possibility that they will expect to spend $50,000 or more upon the few simple transparency plates required. Their cost would run this high because of the number of people they would use in the crew and the unwieldy apparatus they would feel to be necessary. All I would need is a tripod ten feet under the sea, and a water-proof camera box. I would have to go to Key West to make the shots, and they would have to be made upon speculation.

Someone apparently threw a wrench in that plan; it was not mentioned again. But it shows a little of what was constantly churning in Alan's active mind.

As work on the screenplay progressed, Alan kept up a running insider's commentary in his frequent letters to his parents:

[October 31, 1940] We are toiling away at the usual fast, steady grind on "Reap the Wild Wind" which no longer bears any resemblance to the original *Post* serial. DeMille has been in New York. We were supposed to mail him the treatment Wednesday night, so Tuesday night he calls up and wants to know where the hell the script is. We were happy to be able to say it was in New York. With a flash of unaccustomed intuition, we had mailed it Monday.

The working atmosphere at Paramount is revealed in a letter written on New Year's Day while being bothered by the constant studio office interruptions:

[January 1, 1941] It looks now as if the Wild Wind script will be done in the middle of February, and that I will end work on it possibly the first of March. The old man is getting very jittery again, and Charles Bennett's hypnotic power over him seems to be slipping a little. He is still my diplomatic corps, however. It is a great satisfaction to sit back dreamily as DeMille begins ... telephone....

As DeMille begins loading and firing, and to know that I don't have
to say a damn word — Charles will put up the verbal counter-barrage....
The telephone interruptions are no worse than usual. It always goes like
this. Ring, ring, ring, I don't know how they think of all the things to
phone about.
   Yesterday I was photographed with DeMille and Bill Pine receiving a
blue ribbon ... my secretary wants something....
   A blue ribbon plaque for ... phone....
   For our parts in the best box-office picture to premier in November.
Pay-off: The plaque is cardboard. Mounted Police will not be in any of
the selection listings because it is a 1941 release. Present showings are
advance pre-release showings at advance prices.... I'll have to give this
up now....

With these conditions being typical at the studio, the charm of
working at DeMille's ranch or on his yacht can be appreciated. The script
was finished in early April 1941, and was highly praised by everyone
who read it. Alan was enthusiastic and cautiously optimistic. He said that
it will be a terrific melodrama and will probably beat the box-office
record of *North West Mounted Police*, providing they don't gum it up in
some way.

By August the filming was well along, and Alan went to see what the
product looked like. The special effects were breaking new ground and the
sets were elaborate. Alan felt justifiably proud to have authored this production, and it showed in his report:

[August 7, 1941] I went down to Paramount to visit the "Reap the Wild
Wind" set. The scene was the deck of a schooner afloat in the big
indoor tank, with a big transparency behind it showing sea breaking
upon coral reefs and other vessels in the background. About a hundred
and fifty people were engaged in making the shots.
   I was told by [Bill] Pine and others that the results so far (about two-
thirds through) are superb, both in technical and dramatic effect. The
miniatures, showing schooners racing at sea and such like shots, especially are considered to be most astounding, perhaps the best that have
ever been seen on the screen. The picture is already six days ahead of
shooting schedule, but $150,000 over the budget. It will cost
$1,800,000 as against the $1,650,000 budgeted. Nobody has dared tell
the old man this yet. But the front office execs are delirious with delight
at the picture and have no fear that the box office will be satisfactory at
any price.
   As I mingled with the crowd at the edge of the tank, DeMille caught
sight of me from the quarterdeck and called me up to the camera
through the public address system. He was very cordial. But he looks
extremely tired and has become so savage that Cliff Clay, his script
man, walked out in the middle of the picture, ending all employment

in pictures forever; and the next day Frank Calvin, erstwhile son-in-law, quit as research man, two things that nobody ever thought would happen.

A couple of days later, he took Arlene and me to see the underwater location at Malibu. Situated above the Pacific Coast Highway, it was a giant aquarium made just for this film. Few movie sets, if any, were so expensive, and Alan was clearly impressed.

[August 9, 1941] Arlene and I [and Dan] went out to Malibu to see the tank stage where they are shooting the underwater sequences of "Reap the Wild DeMille." The assistant director, Arthur Rosson (brother of the famous camera man, Hal Rosson) is shooting all the submerged stuff. Art Rosson is a bedeviled but swaggering little man with a nose like Cyrano de Bergerac.

The tank set is amazing, resembling the giant Aquaria at Marineland, Florida. It carries about twenty feet of salt water in an oval tank about 125 feet by 160 feet, and has a secondary circular tank about 60 feet in diameter. Windows of high pressure glass are set everywhere for the use of the big lights.

Using the tank, they pump it dry, put up a complete set, then flood it and add various fish. The marine life they are using includes some lobsters as big as a kitchen chair; an 18 foot leopard shark; and an 8 foot eel.

The big shark only survived a day or two but they obtained some wonderful shots of it, circling the divers, I am told. The eel was a failure, mostly running under the camera, which is submerged and hooded, and trucks around like a dry camera. A lot of brilliant little Hawaiian reef fishes were used by caging them between seven glass plates and shooting through this at the action.

The cameramen and grips work in oxygen-fitted diving helmets, complete with telephone. $42,000 was spent upon color experiments alone, so that the underwater color will be the most clear and bright ever taken underwater. A special varnish which saves light underwater was the principle trick they discovered for obtaining this result.

But the most amazing thing of all is the giant squid with his 25 foot mechanical tentacles. He works hydraulically from an amazingly intricate control board. He can pick up a diver by the helmet and write his name.

If this won't get them through the wicket, I am at a loss to know what to astound them with.

The filming was complete three months later. Reports from the insiders at Paramount continued to be enthusiastic about the picture, and Alan began to see it as a further boost to his skyrocketing career. His excitement shows in this note to his mother:

[November 18, 1941] ... I have every chance of rating number one in screenplay again next year. This is bragging, but I don't know how you would ever hear of it unless I told you. (Original story next year will go to Thelma Strabel).

In January 1942, Alan and Arlene saw the final cut of *Reap the Wild Wind* in a private showing at Paramount, and Alan was not pleased. His taste, even in action drama, was more subtle, and he was embarrassed by DeMille's gaudy flamboyance. The world premiere was to be held in the El Capitan theater in Hollywood, and Alan had this to say about that:

[January 16, 1942] Paramount has bought a small legit theatre in Hollywood called El Capitan and will make it into a little picture show house. This means that for the first time in the history of the industry a limited number of Hollywood people will see Paramount films.

Motion picture people have often heard about Paramount films, through Paramount publicity, but none of them have ever seen one before, due to you have to go all the way downtown for it. Going downtown in Los Angeles is no project to be taken lightly and nobody has ever felt willing to take a chance on a Paramount film to that extent.

Paramount is going to open El Capitan with the one thing they have got which certainly nobody has ever seen before in the history of either pictures or biological science. They are going to lead off with "Reap the Pink Squid." Here the Hollywood audience — virgin as far as Paramount is concerned — will see all the pictures they have never seen before, because they are all here, tangled up in this single job of foul play. But neither this audience nor anyone else has ever seen a sixty-foot pink monster with the ten arms and the movable glass eyes.

This opus (not to be confused with octopus) is to be road showed, which means that it is to be shown for its first year or less at clammy high prices with reserved seats. The road show idea in itself does not make much money, but usually results in a very heavy take in the regular run, if the picture is one that can stand it at all.

The film premiered in March 1942, and Alan wrote his own version of the event to his father:

[March 18, 1942] Tonight we are going to see "Reap the Wild Wind" at its premiere. I paid $5.50 a seat for this, though we have seen it already, because I thought Arlene would be regaled by the pomp and circumstance. I guess there will be pomp and circumstance — there always has been at this price.

And the next day he wrote:

Well, we went to the premiere. The new theatre is very nice. The manner in which the curtain is raised got applause.

Judy Canova arrived in a buggy with two white horses, driven by a Sergeant from the ack-ack. Huge pictures of DeMille were hung over the street every hundred feet for two blocks; but failed in their purpose, if, as I assume, it was to keep the street clear. The curbs and part of the street were packed for a block and a half to watch us celebrities arrive. I never felt sillier, and thanked God for my blessed obscurity. I will never again criticize the producers for suppressing the identity of the authors.

The picture did not look quite as bad on second showing as it did the first time—I guess I am getting used to it. It is definitely not as bad as "North West Mounted." It has no line in it that can compete with the world famous stinker about "fouling the lodge of a great chief with the blood of a dog"; but then we can hardly expect more than one gem like that in a generation.

After some pretty good opening views the picture gets off to a very bad, silly start. It becomes rather amusing in the second quarter, in spots; and the rest would be a pretty good story if it were not for the bald, artificial, melodramatic statements of plot, out of which DeMille's direction is able to wring the very worst possible effect.

The giant squid runs an entire reel. It would be pretty good if they would let me take a pair of shears and cut it to about a third of its present length, but as it stands it contains many shots justifying the appellation: "world's most bewildered inner tube." The fight with the squid contains a great deal of standing about while the control men practice waving the arms about, apparently unaware that they are broken in three or four places.

The ends of the tentacles look exactly like window-washing mittens, and what mystifies you is why the thing does not go flat in a cloud of bubbles when it is stuck.

However, the audience sat and took it very well and the whole thing is probably a great popular success, and at worst is DeMille's best picture.

At the close of the performance there was a hideous embroilment of automobiles in the parking lot and in the streets, and nobody ever got out of there, so far as I know, except Bob Hope and me, who slid out one, two, leaving a horrible mess behind us. This was due to the superior intelligence of us comedians.

It was not unusual for Alan to be dissatisfied with his final product. It may have been defensive, a preemptive strike against criticism. But as the results came in on *Reap the Wild Wind*, DeMille could not have been more pleased. It was Paramount's leading money earner, both for the year and for all time. Alan reported to his father:

[March 23, 1942] Hanagan, Dozier's assistant at Paramount, told Henri Verstappen that DeMille swears by LeMay—says the sun rises and sets in LeMay—there aren't any other writers. So from this we learn that no matter how cheesy a bum you are when they got you, you shina lak gold when they can't get you.

Reap the Wild Wind is tearing the box office apart, and the critics are tearing RTWW apart.

— 8 —

Life in the Film Colony

1939 — 1948

Alan arrived in Hollywood in June 1939, an outsider in a foreign land. He knew no one. But despite the long hours at Paramount, Alan and Arlene made friends quickly and were soon immersed in a life-style that was completely new and exciting for both of them. For one thing, Alan was getting a regular paycheck and had more money than he had seen in several years, although he was still paying off ranch debts. For another, with his new status as a highly-paid Hollywood screenwriter, Alan felt obligated to raise the family's standard of living. Appearances were important. It was clear that they were not in Aurora anymore.

The first concern of the newlyweds was to get settled in their spectacular new home at 8946 Appian Way, on Lookout Mountain above Hollywood. Arlene's approach to this was to hire help. That was fine with Alan — Hollywood moguls did not mow their own lawns, and their wives did not cook dinner.

In compliance with the joint custody agreement, Joan and I spent the summer with them. For us it was interesting, but isolated. There were no children our age in the area. The view was terrific, and I enjoyed hiking the trails up the mountain, but at the end of summer Joan and I were glad to get back for our winter stay at our mother's house in San Diego, where our friends were.

By that time Alan and Arlene had also learned the disadvantages of ostentation. The house was isolated from Hollywood by a steep mountain road with 27 hairpin turns, and it had to be negotiated many times every day, to pick up the help down at the bus stop, to take them back, to shop, to go to a show, to do anything. The cost of rent and full-time help was staggering. Despite his high salary they were not accumulating any savings at all, and Alan became aware that his employment was week-to-week at the whim of an unpredictable tyrant. Reluctantly, he hired a business manager.

The manager's first recommendation was to move to a smaller place that they could maintain without so much help. Arlene was cheerful about the change, as she wrote to Alan's parents about their new apartment at 821–¼ Sweetzer in Hollywood:

> [October 22, 1939] ... It's exactly what I wanted. A really small apartment with large rooms. When I told the rental agent what I wanted they looked at me as if I were asking for the moon on toast, but we got it. We had become awfully discouraged, everything that looked at all nice was way up in the hundreds. And some of the little dumpy places, that were badly furnished, and poorly built want $115. So when we found this at a price much less than we dreamed of, we were very pleased.
>
> Alan is down to the studio today, something I don't like. I don't like working on Sunday so much, but I don't mind when he can work at home. But I just hate to have him go to the studio, because it seems that we see little enough of each other as is. But as Mrs. DeMille says I'm a film widow, right along with the rest of them.
>
> We're supposed to see the GATEWAY TO HOLLYWOOD SHOW this afternoon, to which Alan and I have a standing invite, thru Jesse Lasky. I hope that Alan can get thru to go by then. It's a very interesting show to see and follow. Much more so than the Lux Theatre, which we saw last Monday.

Joan and I spent Easter 1940 at this little apartment, and that was the only time we saw it. It was too small for Alan and Arlene, especially if Joan and I were to spend the summer with them according to the custody agreement. Alan had received a healthy raise at Paramount which the business manager grudgingly agreed could support a larger house, so they moved again.

This time it was a brick house at 507 N. Maple Drive, Beverly Hills, just a few blocks from the Beverly Hills Tennis Club. Alan complained that the $175 per month rent seemed like a lot by Midwest standards, but his raise and the six months at the smaller apartment with minimal domestic help had permitted a healthy level of savings. He was already formulating a plan of escape from screenwriting, as he wrote to his parents:

> [April 8, 1940] Our savings are accumulating very well and I hope to remain in pictures until I have a full year's expenses ahead; after which I would like to take a full year upon a book, something I have never done, but which I now feel is really necessary to bring my best work to the surface. At that time I hope to steal my present secretary from Paramount but don't know whether I shall get by with that. [His secretary for many years was Virginia Roddick, a petite little woman who liked to be called "Gus"].

The Maple Drive house had enough room for Alan to have an office to himself at home. He always had several projects going at once and so needed a place to work away from his frequently changing studio office. The adaptation of a couple of spare rooms into a small office complex was a major remodel, which Alan described in the Round Robin. The Round Robin circulated between Alan, his father, his sister at Pinhook (her Massachusetts farm), his daughter Joan, and his son Dan.

> [July 16, 1945] This dump is now torn up to a degree which would pass for Pinhook by your accounts. The back end of the house is torn out, a crew of painters is in the dining room, they are sand-blasting the outside, and the gardener is nagging me to buy him a $450 tree to replace the one that blew down. We have changed the name of this place to Tobacco Path; it isn't in good enough shape for a road.
>
> Dan and I are going to get the hell out of here and do an escape in the desert. I have worn my brains to a frazzle trying to get something written in this maelstrom of interruptions, and I give up. If you never hear from me again, it is because Death Valley Al is almost impossible to take prisoner and drag back, once he makes it into the Funeral Range.

Dad and I had a great trip to the Mojave desert. We camped out and cooked hot dogs over a fire and slept on the ground in sleeping bags. I had made a couple of box traps to see what critters we could capture at night, and were rewarded with a kangaroo rat and several deer mice. Kangaroo rats are particularly docile and odor-free, making great pets. We named this one T-Square, because with his long tail he was sort of shaped like that.

Sleeping on the ground didn't seem to be the right thing for Dad's back, and we hadn't packed a lot of food, so the second night we had dinner in a Victorville restaurant and slept in a motel. Over a coffee shop breakfast Dad said he thought it might be time to be getting back, so that was it for the great escape. But I still remember it, 60 years later, as a special time with just Dad and me.

* * *

Alan always needed exercise to keep his spirits up and his weight down, and the Hollywood life was not suited to horses or polo. So he joined the nearby Beverly Hills Tennis Club which combined exercise with an opportunity to meet others in the movie industry. George Toley was the Club Pro, and the Toleys became two of the LeMay's best friends. Alan took the game very seriously, took numerous lessons from George and, according to Arlene, got mad at himself because he couldn't play like Tilden. Winning was important to him.

Alan and Arlene entertained a lot, and their guests seemed rather exotic to me. Alan sometimes described these events in his frequent letters to his parents:

> [August 6, 1941] Last night we had to dinner Elda Garvey, a friend of Arlene's, native of Aurora, formerly an actress in New York for a time; her husband, Lucius Cook, erstwhile New York director (I think erstwhile means ain't worked lately); Nicki and Toni Landi. Toni Landi, whose sister is Elissa Landi, is Austrian born, but a British citizen from a commission in the first world war after a scholarship at Oxford. He is a distinguished linguist, who has served I.C.I. (Imperial Chemical Industries) as an international expansion agent — a weird matter of secret diplomacy such as astounds me. He also is said to be related to Emperor Franz Joseph on the left side. He rates the title of Count, but does not use it. He sells insurance and shows jumping horses. His wife is a Belgian girl who plays a smashing game of tennis.
>
> They all sat around and talked until nearly one o'clock.

In turn, they were invited to many affairs at the homes of others in the movie industry. Celebrities in Hollywood did not maintain their status by subtleties and a low profile, and their homes and parties frequently left the Midwestern LeMays shaking their heads.

> [October 21, 1941] A short time ago we had Sunday afternoon tea at the home of Edward Everett Horton, over in The Valley. His house is a vast rambling provincial type, furnished mainly in English antiques, especially Queen Anne.
>
> The amazing thing about it is that all the rooms are about the size of Grand Central Station. The dining room has on the wall a canvas fifteen by twenty; it used to hang in the Palmer House in Chicago. It portrays a rooster nine feet high and an enormous wagon wheel. The dining room also has a musicians gallery with musicians on it.
>
> There were about thirty-five people present, and they were lost in this room.
>
> The other rooms are larger. The main living room, in which there was piano playing, is so large that you can just barely discern figures moving at the other end of it.
>
> Twinkle, twinkle little guy.

Alan was always thinking about ways to improve the movies he was working on or had planned. He once had Arlene take me to a riding stable with a raccoon skin and a rubber snake to see what worked best for spooking a horse (it was the floppy coonskin). His research even extended to music that might be used to enhance mood or authenticity. While working on the screenplay for *Quebec* he tried to find an authentic boatman's song to work into the script:

> [January 19, 1945] Last night we took some books of old French Canadian voyageur songs to the home of a friend — Gretchen Hastings —

who has a piano, and picked out the melodies. The songs are very disappointing, I am sorry to say. They harp monotonously on about three notes, and the girls were unable to catch the peculiar paddle-rhythm that is their chief distinction. But I got about six that I think can be fixed up. With crack arrangement, I hope they will be distinguishable from our usual modern.

Besides tennis and parties, there were other new things to do in what little free time Alan could find. An unexpected side effect of World War II was that motorcycle riding suddenly became the "in" sport. Wartime gas rationing was a serious problem for all who worked in the "non-essential" movie industry. Like many others, Alan could simply not drive to work five days a week on an "A card." The answer was a motorcycle, and the popular imports such as the Triumph Tiger and the Ariel Square Four were selling at quadruple their original price. Alan bought a Triumph Tiger from actor Dick Powell, and named it Honeychile in an effort to de-fang the Hell's Angels image. He tried to involve Arlene with a cute little Royal Enfield that he named Mrs. Cafferty, but she wouldn't touch it. Inevitably, with this fun-loving movie crowd, the motorcycles became much more than just transportation, as Alan wrote to his parents:

[September 27, 1943] Yesterday I went on a motorcycle ride with half a dozen fellows, among them directors Howard Hawks and Victor Fleming, stunt-rider Cary Loftin, and famous test pilot Vance Breeze. We first made a lovely scenic tour through Palos Verdes, a pretty community on the sea to the south, and along the cliff road. We then left the road, and I learned what amazing things a motorcycle can do in rough work. One event was a casual broad jump, made by running up what looked like a fifteen-foot sheer vertical side of a coulee. When actually tackled, of course, it was by no means vertical, and the motors went up it with amazing ease, sailing into the air very prettily at the top. Not everyone rode this, however. Results, Cary 11 feet, me 8 feet. I have a very good motor indeed. We also jumped and chased a jackrabbit, Cary gaining on it for a while, until stopped by a gulch.

Arlene looked down on all this as stupid little boys and their toys, and she would have no part of it. I was the beneficiary, inheriting Mrs. Cafferty and learning to ride at age 14. Dad said this would probably not meet with my mother's approval, and so would be our little secret. At the end of the war, rationing ended and Dad sold Mrs. Cafferty, and I inherited Honeychile. At that point I was 16 and got a license, so I rode the big Triumph Tiger home to San Diego. My mother didn't like it, but she put up with it. She was very patient.

The next summer, living with Dad and Arlene in Brentwood (at 12735 Hanover St.), I crashed Honeychile at the end of the long straight stretch of Sunset Boulevard by the Riviera Polo Club. I had just beaten a friend on a Harley in a drag race, went into the turn at the end of the straight too fast, and lost it. I rode back to the house on the back of the Harley and interrupted Dad at work in his home office. I told him I had been racing against the Harley and wrecked Honeychile. Blood was dripping from my skinned hands, knees, and elbows, but Dad's first words were "Did you beat him?" When we took the car back to pick up Honeychile, Dad proudly paced off how far I had skidded (115 feet).

Alan had a competitive nature that was more attuned to the Old West that he wrote about than it was to modern day Beverly Hills. His competitiveness extended into everything he did. He had taught me to shoot at an early age on Rancho Una Vaca, and he was not to be held back by conditions in the big city. One day we drove up Topanga Canyon with our .22 rifles and sighted them in, shooting tin cans in a box gulch. We didn't have time for a real contest, but Dad said we shot about a tie, which was high praise. The next day we shot a ten-round contest in the back yard and Dad won, with nine out of ten shots in the bull. He knew that firing in the back yard with sacks of dirt as backing was very illegal, but he said, "Civilization has always completely strangled grown men, and now it has closed in on boys. The hell with it — I am an outlaw."

* * *

Alan's best friend, going back to Mission Valley polo days, was a Navy surgeon and polo player named Bud Hering. During Alan's Hollywood years, he seemed always to be under the pressure of deadlines, and Bud was more than busy with World War II. So during the rare times that Bud was home on leave, they always planned a get together. Arlene wrote about one of those times:

> [October 27, 1942] Last weekend we went down to San Diego to see Bud and Irene Hering. We finally got Alan to face his former habitat. Going down there at 35 miles an hour [the universal wartime speed limit] I found fun. The sea is very lovely down thataway and we weren't in any particular hurry to get there — so we looked and talked. The Herings are such grand people to be with and we had much fun with them. Alan had a ride on a horse that he said was simply dreamy — thru these lovely hills and vales it must have been. Alan looked terrific in his riding (cowboy) boots, a black cowboy shirt, and beige whip-cord pants. I'd never seen him on a horse before, and he's a thing of beauty, believe me.
>
> We drove by Alan's old ranch, and it was lovely. I can well imagine how Alan hated to give that thing up. We really had a wonderful time.
>
> We had to drive back Sunday afternoon, because its "dim out" all the way down there, and that makes night driving tough.

The dim out was another wartime restriction. It permitted parking lights only, no headlights. The West Coast was considered to be a potential target area.

There was occasional correspondence from Bud while he was on duty in the South Pacific. Alan would always mention this in his letters to his parents:

> [April 16, 1944] I had a great letter from Bud Hering, my best friend, who is a Navy doctor, perhaps you remember. He is a full Commander, now, or Colonel of Marines, whichever; he has 80 doctors under him, and 1000 corpsmen, and is in charge of the medical for a divisional area including the present scope of attack in the South Pacific; he was at Tarawa, etc. His job rates a promotion, and his eagles may come through any time.
>
> He is finally coming home, for thirty days only. After 18 months of combat service he rated retirement to home duty, but "raised his hand at the wrong time," and volunteered to go back.

As the war neared its end, Bud occasionally came home and wanted to go camping on horseback. This was one of Alan's favorite pastimes, but Bud apparently caught Alan in a mood of frustration, preoccupied with his writing schedule:

> [August 12, 1945] Last week Bud Hering called up, freshly back from Okinawa. He didn't know when his leave was supposed to be, if any, so nothing would do but we must go down there immediately and go camping with him. This we did, and it shot the week. The peace overtures were going on most of the time, so it would have been an upset week anyway.

That was an interesting camping trip, and I got to go along. We rode the horses far into the wilds of Los Conejos Indian reservation and camped out several nights. While riding the horses back to where we had left the trailers, we got caught in a summer thunderstorm. As we crossed over a ridge on a dirt road bordered by a fenced field, lightning struck the fence beside us, no more than 30 feet away. I will never forget the blinding flash. It filled the entire sky overhead, giving no impression of being on one side or the other; the whole sky just lit up. Simultaneously there was a deafening explosion of sound, also directly above us. The horses panicked and took us at a hard gallop down through a draw and up onto the next ridge before we got them stopped.

When we looked back at where we had been, we saw that three of the fence posts were on fire, so we rode back to put them out. Kip Hering, Bud's seven-year-old son, held the nervous horses while the rest of us pulled off the saddles and beat the fires out with the saddle blankets.

I don't remember much else about the trip, but I will never forget that near miss bolt. I have talked to Kip about it recently, and he remembers it the same way. What surprises me now is that Alan didn't think it was interesting enough to give it a comment in one of his many letters. Oh well; a day or two before the trip the United States atom-bombed Hiroshima, which was also a memorable event, and he didn't comment on that either.

* * *

Alan's restless spirit easily tired of any place they lived, and house hunting became a perennial pastime. The family averaged about three years in any one house. Alan's opinion of each home followed the same pattern as it did for most of his films: initial enthusiasm, discovery of flaws, optimistic remodeling, disappointment with the results, and on to the next one. But finding the next perfect home was not easy, as Alan reported:

> [July 10, 1944] Saturday afternoon and yesterday we searched the San Fernando Valley for a larger house. The Valley is 95% poverty-stricken small citrus growers, 5% estates of wealthy picture people. Definitely not a buyers' market now; places of the size and type we want are few, and held for no loss. Only one we could use, $49,500, next door to an infantile paralysis sanitarium, and with five acres of citrus and other fruit, which I will have nothing to do with. Income property be damned. My best bet for income is to avoid harassment by nuisances in which I am not interested in the least. I have already owned citrus, and never saw it out of trouble for an hour.

Harassment by nuisances was an ongoing problem. At the studios there were constant phone calls and meetings, making his office at home a greatly-preferred refuge. But even there he could not avoid the distractions. Alan's frustration with not being left alone to write comes through in this letter:

> [November 24, 1944] The gardener wanted the front lawn fixed up, and brought a man to give an estimate. The man said two (2) loads of dirt would be required, and the bid would be $200!
> I said, "I don't want the lawn fixed, I like it the way it is." The man said, "Yes, but you need it bad, it looks like hell." I said, "So does yours look like hell, two can play this game. I will give you *one* load of dirt for *five* hundred dollars." He said, "But I haven't any lawn," and I said, "In that case it will cost you $600, where do you want it put, in your cellar?" He said quite piteously, "But I don't want any dirt," and I said, "Neither do I, as I told you to start with, we certainly see eye to eye on that question, brother, what the hell kind of an argument is this, anyway?"
> He went away, finally.

Although Alan frequently talked about getting out of Hollywood, it had become his home. In fact his long-term plan was to build his own house. It would have been impossible during the war; builders were unavailable, and materials were scarce or rationed. Alan was correct in his belief that this would be a good time to buy a lot, and the family spent many summer evenings after dinner looking at vacant lots in the Hollywood hills. I can remember looking at a lot with them just a few blocks above Sunset Boulevard in Hollywood. It was fading twilight, and a mountain lion walked across the next lot, not 300 feet away. He was heading down into town.

Most people look at lots with a vague notion of "I like it" or "I don't like it," but without any firm evaluation parameters. Alan, in his usual analytical way, had his specifications organized. That was probably why the idea never came to fruition. He described his thinking in a letter to his parents:

> [July 17, 1943] We have concluded that our present Hangout is very inefficient indeed, as a plant for handy living, and, what with inflation coming on, we think strongly of buying a lot for building on after the war. The lot we are looking for must be largely vertical, to avoid lawn; lie on a south slope; be protected on both sides by gulches; take no more than four and a half hair pin turns to get up or down; be east of Westwood and Bel-Air, but west of Hollywood, on the slope of the Santa Monica Mountains; get protection from the wind from a higher cup of hills behind; enter from the north or uphill side — that is lie on the south, downhill side of the street.

* * *

In Alan's single-minded working life, children did not play a big part. Even so, considering Alan's almost daily letters to his father, it is surprising that the LeMays' plans for an adoption were never mentioned. In October 1945, he mentioned it for the first time:

> Well, what do you think, you'd never guess in a thousand years —
> Arlene and I have adopted a little baby, only two weeks old! She came to us Thursday night on only twelve hours' notice, and you can imagine the dither we have been in.
> The baby is a little girl with brown hair and brown eyes, 7 pounds; her name is to be Mary Karen, and we mean to call her Molly.
> Aren't you astonished? I am.
> More later — but at the moment I am brutally swamped — eight pages behind the pace, to be exact....

Nearly a month later came his next report on their new arrival:

> [October 24, 1945] Molly has now been with us four weeks and has gained two and a half pounds. She seems a contented and healthy baby.

I am at home for the present, working on my novel. Though I seem set on two jobs, one at Warners and one at Goldwyn, the whole place is closed down on account of the strike.

* * *

Just after the above was written, there was a problem with the hot water heater, or a valve, or the thermostat, or something, which Alan tried to fix with the traditional good belt with a wrench. The result was a burst pipe that soaked him with scalding water. He was wearing a heavy sweat shirt which held the water like a sponge, and by the time he had it stripped off his burns were serious, and landed him in the hospital for a two-week stay. Back at home, he wrote:

> [November 7, 1945] Well, I got out of the hospital after being there two weeks to the day. I poop out very easily; I had not realized before that the toxins absorbed are the worst part of an extensive burn. The healing was at a virtually phenomenal rate, but the toxic effect kept me in a fever up to the last three or four days. But I am hardly the worse for it now, except slightly subdued in spirit.
>
> Molly looks much fatter and stronger and brighter than when I went to the hospital. She is now eight weeks old and has been with us three-quarters of her life.
>
> The strike ended after my first week in the hospital and Warners put me back on the payroll. My efforts in their behalf have been slightly lethargic, not to say enfeebled, but I hope to give them their money's worth in the long run.

A year after Molly arrived there was another adoption announcement, with no more advance notice than the first one:

> [October 13, 1946] Big news! Molly has a new baby sister! She was born last Monday, and came to us yesterday. Her name is Jane Bronwyn.

But then just two weeks later came other startling news:

> [October 29, 1946] I have been trying to get Arlene to write you, but in seven years I have never succeeded in getting any results this way except the answer: "I'll be glad to do it when I have time, but today it's impossible." So I don't expect much in this direction.
>
> Inasmuch as I have been up at six every day in order to be early on the set, and have worked my rewrite as we went along till about mid-night every night, I don't know whether I wrote you this before or not, but anyway, the new baby, whom I announced to you as Jane Bronwyn, was snatched back by her parents, so that we are as we were. Answering your question, as to what kind of name Bronwyn is, Bronwyn is a Welsh name, so cannot help being an old family name of ours through the line of Logan. Well, no matter now.

In most families the adoption of a baby is a huge event. It requires months, if not years, of planning, red tape, frustration, and emotional anticipation. But in this family Alan appeared, at least, to be aloof from all that. Molly arrived with no notice in the correspondence, as if left on the doorstep. Jane Bronwyn came and went rather unemotionally, considering how one might get invested in a new baby in two weeks. Mark's arrival six months later was also remarkably unheralded.

> [May 7, 1947] ... The spot news is that we have another baby here for adoption, a little boy one week old, and his name is Mark Logan LeMay.

A couple of weeks later, Alan's father and his sister's family got the following, more detailed report:

> [May 20, 1947] Here's the first picture of your new grandson and/or nephew and/or cousin. Doesn't show much, but gives an idea of the size.

With two growing babies, and additional help for Arlene, their house became crowded. They decided to move again, and found a house that Alan describes in far more detail than he ever devoted to the adoptions.

> [July 19, 1948] We are dumbfounded to find that we have bought a house. Virginia found an ad in the Reporter Friday morning, and Friday night Al Blum issued a check.
> This house is eighteen years old, with the style of architecture popular in California as of that period, and is located [at 1344 Monaco Drive] on the mesa opposite Riviera polo field.
> There are four bedrooms and three elaborate tile baths upstairs; two servants rooms and bath downstairs; a powder room-lavatory; a small breakfast room, or morning room; a large dining room; living room; a den we will call the family room and live in mostly; a butler's pantry; laundry; a chauffeur's room in a kind of a gate house; a four-car garage; over the garage a big so-called rumpus room lined with half logs with a fireplace, which I will turn into my study; a considerable work shop and tool house; a filled-in swimming pool, which we will leave filled in until the children are older. We paid $37,500 on a court sale to settle an estate.
> We were able to swing this by buying it with the tax money I owed the government, with the intention of selling this house to pay the taxes. Good joke on the government if I can't unload this one. For once we will have the room we need.

* * *

The primary effect on Alan of suddenly having two babies added to the family was the pressure of more responsibility, and the frustration of more interruptions. He loved them dearly, but his first priority was to pay the bills in the only way he knew how, and his self-imposed schedules left him with little spare time. Saddled with the long hours of a sedentary desk job, his health demanded that he exercise strenuously every day. When he did not take the time to exercise his weight ballooned and he resorted to extreme diets that sapped his strength and interfered with his ability to write. He mentioned his exercise frequently in his letters to his father:

> [September 14, 1944] Whatever else happens, I am scrupulously working out in the gym every noon — mostly hand ball. Yesterday beat the hell out of Dennis Morgan, young leading man — and pooped him to boot.
> [January 23, 1945] I play handball every day at noon, instead of lunch. My stamina is pretty good, and the more games we play the better my score gets, while the kids tire, but my speed and timing are both gone, forever, I should judge....
> [January 30, 1945] Picked up a chest cold, by playing badminton Sunday afternoon, and getting all hot and wet, then powering home on my shieldless motorcycle in the unfriendly chill of the dusk. A child would know better. Consequently spent most of yesterday wheezing and dozing on my office couch, useless to God or Warner Bros.

Alan was frequently exhausted when he finished a script, not only from the pressure of meeting a deadline, but also from the psychological letdown of breaking away from a project that had occupied his mind so intensely. Towards the end of some jobs it took a supreme effort to power through the fatigue of a too-long sprint without a break. And in rare cases a supreme effort was more than he could come up with, as he wrote to his father:

> [November, 1944, while working on *The Frontiersman*] Seemingly the function of putting words together, all day and every day, never any pause nor anything different, is something like a muscle, in that it gets tired and sore. I have had a very bad slow week, resulting in only one usable page of screenplay, believe it or not, and unless I get a fresh wind we are quite sunk on the very verge of great opportunity.
> I can still write scenes down, but am quite incapable of evaluating them, or indeed telling one of them from another.... So there isn't any great hope of an improved rate of letter writing at this time. The part of my brain that puts words on paper feels as if it were bleeding. Yes, I am sure it is bleeding.

In the world of freelance writing, there is never a good time to take a vacation. When Alan was working on a script there was always the pressure of a deadline, and when he was between jobs the sudden lack of a paycheck impelled him to work on his next novel, or whatever else he had going. Once in a while, Arlene would insist, and they would take a short vacation. For example:

> [August 21, 1948] Tuesday through Friday I took Arlene to Toyon Bay for a rest from getting the kids up in the morning. I mean, a rest from having the kids get her up in the morning.
>
> Toyon Bay is an isolated small resort on a cove on Catalina. The installation is a subsidiary of the Palm Springs Racket Club and can be reached only by water. The thing is small and few people there and no automobiles, so makes a good place to rest. It is also very expensive, but the trip was made possible by the fact that Arlene has taken to shopping all the groceries by hand, and making up menus out of frankfurter skins and herbs from the lawn, so we paid for the visit out of savings on the grocery budget — even though we cut the grocery budget in half six weeks ago.
>
> By way of resting, for the first day, I went aquaplaning, then I got on a surf board and went goggle fishing, then I played four sets of tennis and finished off with a good swim. On the second day I tapered off a little, but nevertheless finished my rest feeling as if I had been slugged in the head by a paving block on the end of a stick. I attribute this to the sun, because Arlene simply lay beside the pool and also came home very punchy in spite of getting to bed around nine o'clock every night. However, I feel all right today and I guess I have recovered.

Alan and Arlene always hosted a huge New Year's Eve party, and it was typically followed by a day listening to the Rose Bowl game while nursing a resolution-inspiring hangover. One year the last year's resolution was actually honored, as Alan reported to his father in a letter:

> [January 2, 1945] New Years came and went, and it witnessed a pretty flashy stunt on my part, in that I tended bar for a large party at our house and got through without ever taking a snort myself, and was the only guy in Hollywood without a hangover Jan 1. This achievement has caused a considerable West Coast sensation, and I have offers to sign testimonials for several products, including cathartic pills and a vegetarian diet.

And that, for the LeMay's, was life in the Film Colony.

— 9 —

World War II

Hollywood may have seemed to be somewhat aloof from the gathering war clouds; Alan seldom mentioned the war in his letters until after Pearl Harbor. But there was apprehension in the film colony. At first the concerns were mainly about what the war would do to the European film market. The studios expected foreign income to cease entirely, and they depended on that for their profit.

Even before the Pearl Harbor bombing, a Japanese attack on the West Coast was considered to be a very real possibility. In November 1941, Arlene volunteered for civilian duty in the Aircraft Warning Service (AWS). She went through some hasty training and became an Interceptor Spotter, Enemy. In this capacity, wearing head phones, she received the reports of thousands of observers, filtered through scores of special telephone operators (Tellers) and dozens of map workers (Filter Spotters). Standing before a vast map table, she plotted the information essential to air combat.

My mother, Esther, was doing a very similar job at the Filter Center in San Diego.

Despite the preparations, the sudden attack on Hawaii was a shock. Within the hour, Arlene was notified to report for duty at three A.M. Her schedule remained chaotic for weeks while the Filter Center scrambled onto a wartime footing.

The sneak attack generated a wave of patriotic fervor. Most visibly in Hollywood, famous stars volunteered for military service, and film crew workers at all levels volunteered or were drafted into the military. The lifestyles of those remaining behind were affected by rationing, surtaxes, shortages, and regulations. All sorts of unlikely people volunteered for civilian defense duties. Most found themselves doing excellent work at jobs which, for them, were totally out of character and beyond their expected capabilities. Everyone was affected; there were no bystanders.

Alan kept in touch with his New York contact, the fiction editor at

Collier's magazine, Ken Littauer, looking forward to the day when he could afford to get back to story writing. Whenever Ken was on the West Coast, they got together, as they did just two days after Pearl Harbor. At dinner, Ken told Alan that he was probably going to take an important Air Corps desk job in Washington, with the rank of Lieutenant Colonel.

Alan was amazed to learn that he could probably do the same thing, and the idea excited him. It would mean a huge loss of income, but his business manager said he could survive financially *if* he got a commission as Major or better. Having no current military experience, he would need to use the pull that *Collier's* had with contacts in Washington to get an adequate placement. (They had previously influenced the Secretary of State to give Alan a passport to China when all passports to China were shut down.) The prospect of having to use influence to gain a commission convinced him that he would not be filling a critical need. So the idea fizzled.

* * *

Alan's parents worried about the vulnerability of the West Coast to bomb attacks or invasion, because rumors were rampant. To allay their fears Alan frequently made light of the situation in his letters to them, such as this note a few weeks after Pearl Harbor:

> [January 17, 1942] I should judge there will be no search lights at the grand premiere of our pink monster [the giant squid in *Reap the Wild Wind*]. The search lights are practicing two or three times a week, spotting little silver planes sent up for the purpose.
>
> It is really a very pretty and fascinating sight to see the tiny silver speck, at a height from one mile up, trailing swiftly across the sky held locked in a convergence of beams as if it were being swung across the sky on a tripod of light.
>
> Actual raiding is done with black planes which are virtually invisible to search lights, unless there are clouds above on which their shadows may be thrown. We never practice with black planes. Since only black planes are used at night, the answer seems to be that the search lights are no good except in the daytime.

Hollywood recognized the sudden need for topical war films, and rushed into production. Alan saw what was happening, and gave this analysis:

> [December 16, 1941] Republic, the cheapest movie outfit in Hollywood, is coming right out with a picture featuring Honolulu, entitled "Remember Pearl Harbor." They start shooting Dec. 29, which will give them one week to write the script and four days to prepare the production.
>
> Paramount is coming out with a super-duper about the defense of

Wake Island, called "Remember Wake Island," we hope. Fred MacMurray is in this effort.

Fox is coming out with a lovely called "Prison Ship," showing romance in the hold of a Nazi prison vessel.

Columbia is coming out with something called "Salute to Tobruk," the idea lifted from a BBC program from London, and carrying an all-male cast.

Meantime the audiences are reported very restless at "International Squadron," which the army pilots say is the best air picture they have ever seen, (They did not like "I Wanted Wings").

That is enough for me. I positively will not touch any subject which even remotely conceives the possibility of any conflict later than 1865.

Many brilliant young (or fairly young) men are being pulled out of pictures into the service, such as John Huston, son of Walter Huston. John Huston was a writer who was elevated to writer-director, and who has been directing Bette Davis, "The Maltese Falcon" and other hot stuff.

There is going to have to be double-trouble and such hell hard luck as was never seen before to keep me from getting some good picture jobs if I want them. But if I get them and take them, I'll feel like a heel. Nobody can win in this kind of a shenanigan. I will either get stinking rich and hate myself or I will fail to do so and feel worse.

Alan had not foreseen the wartime version of the graduated income tax. He did not get stinking rich, and did not hate himself. He hated Roosevelt.

Alan's nearly daily letters to his parents had been an effort to take their minds off his mother's losing battle with cancer, and to make her last days more enjoyable. She died on New Year's Eve 1941. Alan went home to Aurora for the funeral. She was buried in the Brown plot at the Union Mills Cemetery.[1] None of Alan's saved letters touched on the sad events. The correspondence with his father resumed when he returned to Hollywood, and continued almost daily as before in a tone that belied his grief. He and his mother had been very close.

* * *

The sudden imposition of the wartime taxes effectively capped Alan's annual salary, killing the accumulation of savings that he needed either to join the service or to take a year off for a novel. Tax planning became a major concern, as Alan speculated on survival techniques:

[Letter, Alan to Dad, April 29, 1942] Roosevelt's idea for putting a ceiling of $25,000 on all personal incomes after taxation I suppose may be regarded as a national disaster and a big stride forward for communism. However, as it affects me personally it seems to promise to make my life very easy indeed. I can make that much money in half time, I think, and can spend the rest of the time figuring out how to be a better writer. It looks to me as if the movies are going to be in an awful hole. All their best talent will be without motivation for working more than a quarter or half the time, resulting in a fearful shortage of top-line stuff, I should think.

My draft number is 12,471— definitely out of this war. This new tax system may keep me from going into the service in any way, by preventing me from getting enough money ahead to free my obligations.

Franklin Delano Roosevelt used his wartime powers effectively to mobilize the country, but made many enemies in the process. Under his administration, the unions gained power over industry, and the Communist leader of the Longshoreman's Union, Harry Bridges, used that power to try to shut down shipping and cripple the war effort. Roosevelt's decrees under wartime powers kept changing, and kept everyone in Hollywood off balance.

[November 2, 1942] Well, we have had our hands full here, trying to find out what is the score. By direct order to the motion pictures companies, Roosevelt froze all salary checks of people who have earned a probable net of $25,000 this year. Nobody had a chance to claim exemptions or anything.

This did not affect me, but the next day an order came through that all checks over $200 were to be held up, temporarily, while they work the thing out. So when I get paid again is anybody's guess.

We spent yesterday in a conference with [Business Manager] Al Blum, who is holding down the Heinze Office while Wally is in Washington. Blum is a good accountant, but not much else, and was little help; except that he had a book of facts about the tax bill.

After our conference, Arlene and I spent the rest of the day hunting for a smaller house, suitable for her to do the housework in, and for me to do the gardening. We found nothing. The only probability was at an elevation of thousands of feet, very bad for the gas situation, and had inadequate heating. Outside of these faults it was beautifully built on a precipice with no garden at all. This little item I could have swung with a loss of only five or six thousand dollars. The hell with it.

We are going to fire the gardener anyway, provided I can get a lawnmower, which I think I can. Obviously we won't ever have time to play tennis again, so we are resigning from the tennis club.

In the picture business everything goes well. DeMille is a miracle of pleasant geniality, and everything we do is wonderful. I cannot account for this.

Under the present tax bill it looks as if I owe the government about $12,000 this year. The split return under the California community property act saved us from complete ruination. Fourteen states have the community property law and it was not done away with because it was estimated that these fourteen states could block the tax bill another 120 days. It probably will be done away with soon.

On the other hand, alimony is going to be exempt. This means that if Arlene and I should get a divorce (but continue living together) and I pay her alimony to the extent of half my net, we will save about $10,000 a year! Her parents aren't going to like this, I shouldn't judge.

Of course, Alan and Arlene did not get the divorce that was recommended by Roosevelt's policies. But the huge impact of the war is evident in Alan's confusion about what he should be writing next. He wavered between tried and true Westerns, escapist humor, and timely war stories. Just a week after Pearl Harbor he wrote:

[December 12, 1941] I have a very timely story about Honolulu which I could write in a couple of days, but find it has a missing link. I am now trying to think of this link and am being hindered by a cold. If I had only plugged that hole in the story before I came down with the cold I could probably go ahead and write it in a state of stupidity. So now I am trying to make Gus think of the missing link without much success; she just sits there and stalls.

This story is not going to stay timely much longer. If I do not think of the lacking element in a day or two I will say the hell with it.

As the war progressed, more and more things became expensive and scarce, and subsequently became rationed. Alan had no problem with gas and rubber rationing because of his motorcycle, but public transportation became nearly impossible. Troop movements and servicemen going home on leave kept buses, trains and planes overbooked most of the time. There was a priority system, and of course civilians were at the bottom of the list. Virtually all civilian travel was on a "space available" basis, and trip planning was futile. Arlene had usually gone home to Aurora to visit her parents twice a year, but wartime travel conditions put an end to that as well:

[November 9, 1943] Answering your question on Arlene's trip: She proved to have no reservation whatever, and sat up all the first night. During this she was persistently annoyed by a drunk, until rescued by a fighter pilot.

Knowing something about both drunks and fighter pilots, I would consider the drunk to be the lesser hazard.

The trainman explained that it is now habitual practice to sell more than one reservation to the same space, due to people trying to protect themselves by holding reservations they don't need, then no-show. I heard of a case in which a girl found that her compartment had also been sold to 8 marines.

This ends the semi-annual junkets for the duration. I appreciate the viewpoint of Arlene's parents. But from here on in — no soap. Little Bear has spoken.

As a freelance writer, Alan could expect periods of free time between contracts. But if he used that time for writing and selling magazine stories, the salary cap taxation would take nearly 100 percent of his earnings. The only way he could find to make his time productive was to write stories, and then not sell them until the tax situation was more reasonable. He explained this to his father:

> [November 11, 1942] I do have one long-view possibility for beating this thing. If I can establish a market for original screen stories, I can eventually build a back-log of stories. As yet the government has hit on no plan to prevent a man from carrying a reservoir of ideas in his head. The government does have a good chance to destroy the original-story market by putting a confiscatory tax on lump-sum payments, but this is not yet done, and we will have to continue to plan on the basis of such weapons as we have left.

President Roosevelt died on April 12, 1945, but more than a year later his pro-union legacy lived on, with crippling strikes as the inevitable result. Alan had always been a strong proponent of free enterprise and capitalism, but under the control of unions and monopolies the system was breaking down. Alan tried to sort out his thoughts in a letter to his father on May 24, 1946:

> Fine shape the country has got itself in this time. Civilized specialization, plus heavy industry, has developed to a perfectly logical upshot, in which a small group of men can paralyze the whole nation, and starve it. I may switch ground and declare in favor of public ownership of the "Paralysis Industries."

When Roosevelt died he was replaced by Vice President Harry Truman, a far-left small-time Democrat-Machine politician whose term was anticipated with dread. He surprised everyone by respecting the office and doing an unexpectedly good job. Alan was among those most surprised, as he wrote to his father:

> [May 25, 1946] Heard Truman's speech, and was dumbfounded to realize that he was actually fighting back, hard, too, and bravely, too. Well, I'll be damned.
> [May 27, 1946] ... What a lot of confused thinking is going on, relative to the labor situation! People say, "You can bayonet them into the mines, but you can't force them to produce." Beside the point. My present view is that government ownership of the paralysis industries could force a return to the supply and demand wages of the open shop,

as necessary for production. Provide arbitration to set the minimum wage — and then bid as necessary for such skilled labor as needed. If the price of skilled labor then gets high enough, more will become skilled, and the price will level off again. Present unionism is designed to maintain an arbitrary wage regardless of the labor supply, using organization to frustrate supply and demand. I think we should expect to pay through the nose when the market is short of genuinely skilled and genuinely necessary technicians. But possession of a paralysis industry can not be tolerated, whether by ownership or organization, now that the actual results of such possession have been demonstrated.

In the end, true to form, following the British traditional lead, we muddled through again. And in the meantime, Alan did what he could.

[July 12, 1946] Last night I went out to the paraplegic hospital with a group who go and play chess with the boys Thursday evenings. These are boys who were shot in the spine and are mostly permanent casualties. I was beaten two games.

–10–

The Foto-Electric Games

Alan always disclaimed his talents in engineering. He believed in the theory of alternating generations, and credited the family engineering aptitude to his father and his son. He lacked any formal engineering training, but he more than made up for that in inventiveness. The outstanding example of this was his creation of a series of games which were graphically animated by the "successive revelation of light," a concept sufficiently novel to earn him patent number 2,260,467.

The Foto-Electric Football version was produced commercially, and was the most successful. It was essentially a cardboard box with a light bulb in it, with a translucent top that illuminated the field of play from below. The player on offense had a number of opaque sheets with names like "end run" or "short pass," each with a hidden translucent track representing the path of the ball carrier. The player on defense had a selection of translucent sheets with names like "strong against end runs," having dots that represented players. The offense had dotted lines for passes and the defense had red dots for interceptions. There was a separate cardboard field with a sliding yard marker to keep track of field position. Every play in football was possible.

To run a play, the offense put in a sheet with the hidden track of the ball carrier, and the defense placed his translucent sheet over it. The defense sheet also showed the line of scrimmage and the yard lines. Then one player slowly pulled out a fishtail-shaped slide, revealing a trace of light going down the field. Where the light trace ran into a defense dot was a tackle, and the play ended there.

The most sophisticated feature of the game, and an important reason for its success, was the realistic outcome of the scoring. The result of countering an offense card with the best "strong against" defensive card achieved a different result each time because of variability in how the cards lined up when placed on the light box. So when knowledgeable football players played against each other the results came out with infinite variety, but with averages comparable to real games.

Sometime before 1940, Alan (in his spare time while still writing) developed the concept, went through the patent application struggles, and licensed the production rights to toymaker Cadaco-Ellis.

As the football game went into production he was already working on a baseball version, and upgrades for the football game. But as usual, the war was a major deterrent, as Alan wrote to his parents on December 30, 1941:

> I have thought of a great improvement for both the baseball and foot-ball games which involves the use of Polaroid. This doubles the number of spots possible in the baseball game, and in the football game permits showing of the movements of defense players without pre-revelation of the future of the ball carrier.
>
> There is no chance, however, of getting any Polaroid until after the war. It is amazing how often I find myself using the expression "after the war." After the war celluloid and Polaroid should be virtually free. And these little basic patents will enable us to do some very astounding things. [There was a second patent anticipated, but never issued.]
>
> Even if nothing further develops along these lines than is already in the bag, it looks to me as if these patents already assure a basic living security for my children, like insurance. It looks to me as if in full development it will run not less than five thousand a year.
>
> [January 6, 1942] ... Last night we had to dinner the Mazers of Cadaco-Ellis. Don Mazer is the dynamo type, very jolly, I should say about thirty-six years old.
>
> I spent the afternoon rigging up a partial model of my baseball game to show him and he was very enthusiastic, wishing to get hold of a complete model right away to begin production plans. This surprised even the very optimistic Jack Schurch [salesman for Cadaco-Ellis], who sees so many hundreds of games constantly rejected (including great numbers of ideas of his own).

Alan was overly modest about not only his engineering abilities, but also his mathematical prowess, another field in which he was largely self-trained. Getting the football games to play realistically, with reasonable average gains, pass completion percentages, and final scores, is not a simple process. It can be done the hard way, by trial and error, or the easy way with mathematics. Alan explained this in a letter to his father:

> [January 12, 1942] When Mazer was here he asked me to make him up a new set of plays, exchanging a very odd look with his wife as he did so. I now know what his odd look meant. I undertook to make up a new defense and a new attack; further volunteering to induct a system such that anybody could readily concoct any number of further plays against the same defense which would work out in whatever percentages desired.

The Foto-Electric football game.

To start with I made a drafting board analysis of the mathematics which Mazer had used in constructing his plays, and found that he didn't have any mathematics to it.

His whole set of plays was achieved by the most infinitely laborious process of cut and fit and try that you can possibly imagine! The poor fellow had to simply make a play, run it, and then change its course to alter its percentage and then find that his change had altered every play in the set. No wonder it took him five months to get a play system that would work.

When he exchanged that funny look with his wife, as he requested me to make him a set of plays, he evidently had nothing on earth in mind except to show me what a hell of a nearly impossible job it was.

I am happy to state that we have met the enemy and they are ours...

There follow three pages of words, some new to science, describing a graphical-statistical method of play design, and concluding with:

> ... A simple cross-fire check-up permits me with my system not only to cause any play to gain an average of 3½ yards, or any average that you want, but also governs the number of times out of 90 which it will make a touch-down and the number of times out of 90 that it will lose the ball.

I would not have gone to all this trouble just to prove to Mazer that I

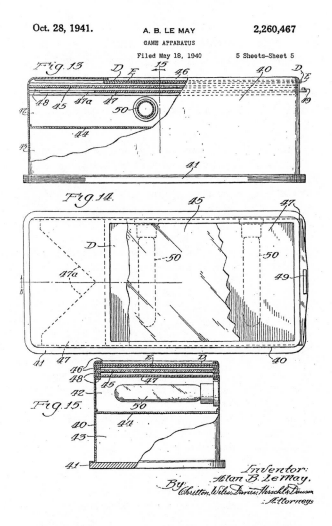

Oct. 28, 1941.   A. B. LE MAY   2,260,467

GAME APPARATUS

Filed May 18, 1940   5 Sheets—Sheet 5

Patent drawing showing the "Revolator" (item 47a).

could do it. The value of this effort is that it will permit them to go ahead with my idea for getting various coaches to sponsor envelopes of special plays. This plan was unfeasible, naturally, when it took a couple of guys five months to rig up each set of plays. With my basic sheets, anybody can take a set of tracing paper and build a set of plays in a couple of hours.

Of course, it was not that simple. What, for example, is "a simple cross-fire check-up?"

The football game paid some modest royalties, but production was limited by wartime materials allocations. The electric light and cord made the game exceed the allowable copper content. In 1944 its production was shut down for the duration, but Alan continued to work on the baseball game. Its development became my summer job in 1945. I got it to work, but it was a tedious job requiring a precision not easily achieved manually with India ink and an Exacto knife. But Alan seemed pleased, as he wrote to his father:

> [September 3, 1945] Dan successfully completed a model of the baseball game, on the basis of 80 plays, times 8 base situations, for 640 variations. The light box he built does not make use of glass. Dan's model works perfectly in actual play, with only some very minor faults such as pinched spots due to inaccurate tools and wrong materials. We have played a number of games and the scores and percentages in all ways conform to the Big League frequencies. I am very proud indeed of the kid on this one. His light box even seems to prevent undue warping from the heat of the light. Mazer is supposed to be here next week to look at it.

Alan, meanwhile, was arranging for the patent income to act as insurance for us kids. He explained this to his father:

> [May 7, 1947] Chritton, Schroeder, and the James boys have now completed the transfer papers whereby the football game patent and contract is put in trust, Jack Schurch getting 25% of the proceeds, Dan and Joan splitting the rest. I think I told you the game paid a little over $5,000 last year, to me. Dan will spend most of his summer perfecting the baseball game. The football game has eleven years to run and the baseball can be patented for seventeen more, so that I feel that these two of my kids will be fairly well protected for the present.

I had thought that my share of the patent earnings was mainly a bonus for my summer work on the baseball game. But more than that, Alan wanted me to have it because, as he said, in his life he had frequently been rich, but also frequently broke, and he did not want my education to hinge on his continued solvency. My share of the royalties did in fact pay my way through four years at Caltech, with some help from summer jobs and the full-time employment of my beautiful new wife in my senior year. The royalty income also gave me a fast education in budgeting, since the Cadaco-Ellis check arrived just once a year, around January, and the amount was always a surprise.

The original football game was a commercial success until the patent ran out, but the baseball game was never produced.

—11—

Mark Twain

When Alan first worked at Paramount he was somewhat in awe of his boss, Cecil B. DeMille. This was appropriate, since DeMille had a solid reputation for big films, and Alan had no screenwriting experience at all. He was, in fact, quite lucky to start his film career in such a prestigious position. *North West Mounted Police* was a great success, and Alan had outlasted the more experienced writers around him. DeMille liked Alan's work (though he seldom said so), and hired him back for the screenplay of *Reap the Wild Wind*. But by that time Alan had had about as much DeMille as he could take, and wanted to move on.

Being a freelance writer, Alan was not constrained by contract. He now had an agent to help line up new jobs, and he let it be known that he was available. At least he hoped that he was. DeMille was pushing assignments ahead of him that would be difficult for Alan to turn down without offending one of the most powerful men in Hollywood.

While he was still working on *Reap the Wild Wind,* an intriguing possibility was presented to him at a Christmas dinner in 1940. The host, Jesse Lasky Sr., told Alan in confidence that he had tied up the rights to a film on the life of Mark Twain, and if Alan were available when the project started, he would get the script job. Spencer Tracy was planned for the title role. Alan could not have been more enthusiastic!

But he had the *Reap the Wild Wind* script to complete, and evenings he had started working on *Useless Cowboy* as a serial for *Collier's*. The effort was wearing him thin. He had not had a vacation since he came to Hollywood, and felt that he was getting saddle sores, as he said in a letter to Mother and Dad,

> [January 9, 1941] ... One thing I could not put off was the reading of some material about Mark Twain which Lasky Sr. gave me to look at. If I do not have to work on *The Borderman* [later renamed *The Rurales*] at the end of this picture, I mean to take a month on the desert, probably

at Victorville, during which I will begin the preparation of the picture *Life of Mark Twain,* and combat my bronchitis.

This was the first time Alan had mentioned his "chronic bronchitis" in a letter to his parents. The real problem was probably his two-pack-a-day cigarette habit. His doctor got him to smoke Parliaments because they had a little wad of cotton in the mouthpiece and were supposedly safer to smoke, but Alan said they were like sucking on a steam kettle, and smoked more of them to compensate.

For a while he tried a cigarette holder that used a regular cigarette as a filter. The idea was to put the first cigarette from the pack into the filter compartment, and when that pack was used up to throw away the icky brown tar-sodden cigarette that had been doing the filtering. But sometimes Alan couldn't resist, and smoked the yucky one as a special treat.

* * *

When *Reap the Wild Wind* was completed, Alan was able to leave Paramount and take his secretary with him. They immediately started work on the *Mark Twain* project.

> [June 2, 1941] ... I have worked the past month on the Mark Twain treatment for Jesse Lasky, Sr. Virginia Roddick [Gus] and I worked together on this. She is the girl who was my secretary at Paramount, and whom I lifted from Paramount, as I think I told you. She has been with me on this as "Junior writer," paid by Lasky. We worked extremely hard, much of the time night and day, and produced what we think is a hell of a great treatment. It looks now as though we had wasted our time, however. All this time we have repeatedly explained to Lasky exactly what we were doing and I do not believe he has understood a cussed word. The treatment ran 107 pages, we read it to him bit by bit as we went along, up through the first 80 pages, and received nothing but hearty cheers. We then turned in the whole thing, and now find him in a state of complete bewilderment and incomprehension. From this we learn not to write speculative copy on privately owned subjects.

Thus the *Mark Twain* job was abruptly terminated. Alan was in good shape financially because of the long stint at Paramount, and had said he would take a month off and then write a serial. He did actually take a week off, and then started on *Useless Cowboy* while playing a lot of tennis. In the meantime a number of film offers came in, none of which were suitable for one reason or another. As was usual for Hollywood, the situation suddenly changed again.

> [August 27, 1941] The long lapse in correspondence is due to an extraordinary burst of activity which has wound up with me at Warner Bros, writing Mark Twain, after all.

With me on the picture is Harold Sherman who wrote a play which in obscure ways gives him an equity in the material, which is otherwise owned by the Mark Twain estate. So far his ideas have been useful and in support of my ideas, so that we have already established a complete story line, accepted by Lasky. We are now engaged upon the treatment. I got only a hundred dollar up in price on this job.

In less than two weeks they had a treatment that was well received, as Alan reported:

[September 3, 1941] Mr. Lasky returned yesterday and read our first two sequences in full treatment, and I have never heard such enthusiasm in my life. Everything about the job was praised as a whole and point by point, without one single criticism or suggestion, constructive or otherwise. I have never seen anything like it in my life, and sat with my chin on my knees.

The present correct figure is $850 as you thought. [More than $11,000 per week in 2005 dollars.]

Working with collaborators was never one of Alan's strengths, and the honeymoon with Harold Sherman was over in another week. Coincidentally, Mark Twain became the subject of an unexpected newspaper editorial. This came just seven weeks before Pearl Harbor. The news centered upon the war in Europe, and debate raged in the press about whether or not the United States should get involved or remain isolationist. The editorial was written to place the ever-popular Mark Twain in the camp of the isolationists, as Alan commented in a letter to his father:

[October 18, 1941] Since you do not read the Hearst papers, you probably did not see the front page editorial column, "In the News" last Monday. It was devoted entirely to Mark Twain and referred to the Jesse L. Lasky production.

This is one hundred per cent to the good for us, but the only reason it got in there was that the boys had dug up a thing of Mark Twain's called "The War-Monger's Prayer," a bitter sarcasm suitable for advocating the Isolationist cause. I do not feel that the fragment is likely to do any real harm in the direction of isolationism. When Mark Twain says "cause our enemies to wander upon bleeding feet," everyone is likely to recall that the bleeding feet of the enemy are about six hundred miles into other people's territory.

Lasky was delirious with joy and immediately saw ways to get more free publicity by starting a controversy. He called up Clara Gabrilovitch, Mark's daughter, and urged her to write a fiery denunciation, demanding that another fragment of Mark Twain's, pleading England's cause, be printed.

Clara, who has a battling temperament, was only too happy to undertake this until she talked to my collaborator, Harold Sherman. He persuaded her against it and authorized her to tell Lasky that he was the

one who talked her out of it. This Harold considers a masterful stroke
of diplomacy, designed to show Lasky how influential he is with Clara.
Personally I immediately bet Harold five dollars that Lasky would step
down hard on the next thing we wrote. This he did. But I have not got
the five dollars yet.

A week later they finished the master-scene script and were laid off,
but that was normal scheduling, not pique at Sherman's meddling. A contract writer was to do the final script, but Alan was not optimistic about
that process:

> [October 24, 1941] Harold Sherman and I completed our master-scene
> script of Mark Twain, all but the camera shots, and a Warners contract
> writer, name of Howard Koch, is now going to script it, and we are laid
> off.
>
> The theory is that we will get credit on the screenplay with Howard
> Koch, the script being already completed in all essentials.
>
> In actual practice Koch will immediately think of seven thousand
> things from the life of Mark Twain and from other pictures which can
> go in instead of what we have in; will immediately tear the structure
> down, and instantly find himself in such a hopeless tangle that he can-
> not even get it back the way it was before. When he has floundered
> about with it for three or four months, and increased the length of the
> script by seven or eight reels, none of them usable, six or seven more
> writers will be thrown at it; and this will go on for about a year or a
> year and a half, at the end of which the idea will be shelved due to no
> story line.
>
> At the present moment however everybody is delighted and have
> nothing but praise for the magnificent job we have done.

The slow destruction of the script by Howard Koch and others pro-
ceeded exactly as Alan had predicted, until finally, six months later, Alan
was invited back to fix it:

> [March 5, 1942] To the best of my knowledge and belief, although you
> can never tell in pictures, I am the only one working on this screenplay
> now. Howard Koch, Ann Froelich, Harry Chandlee, James Henry For-
> man, Bernard de Voto, Julian Street, all having been kicked off. None
> of them left behind them any semblance of structure, or any scenes,
> dialogue, nor bits that are anything but a source of confusion. It looks
> for the moment as if I have this thing licked, but that is exactly like
> picking which horse on the merry-go-round is ahead.
>
> Howard Koch's exit was rather interesting. When I left the script,
> and he followed me on to it, he naturally assumed that he had heard the
> last of me, and scrupulously obliterated every single word that I had
> written. My return found him slightly embarrassed—about like a small
> boy who is cutting the seat out of the old man's underwear on the
> wash-line when the old man shows up. Pulling himself together, Koch

read the first copy I turned in, about half the play, and turned to his employer with an ultimatum. He said he had never seen such bad copy in his life, that he was convinced that they must be kidding him, and that either he or LeMay must go.

The answer was, "Goodbye."

Harold Sherman is coming back on the picture when he gets back from the East next week. I encouraged this because he is relatively harmless, and the execs on a big picture are very unhappy unless a sufficiently large flow of money is going out, like the United States government. He has got to sleep on his own couch this time, though. I don't mind being kibitzed, but I hate to be heckled every two words.

The basic story line of the script continued to be troublesome. Alan said the problem was the subject itself: it was too even and undisturbed a climb to success over a long life. He thought he had a solution for it, but there was a lot of work to do and he worried about what was happening to the budget as the rewrites dragged on.

[March 14, 1942] ... At the price I am getting, and with the expenditure of a million dollars waving around in abeyance, there can be no mercy on the horses. I have just had to call off a dinner date because we are going to confer tonight (Saturday). This is all right with me; but the schedule I have undertaken to meet is a corker; so far I am on the beam.

Lasky alternates now between a great strengthening of confidence and a fever of worry amounting to unholy terror. The increased confidence is due to the fact that "Sergeant York" has greatly exceeded the take of the record-breaking "North West Mounted," and everything else except "Gone With The Wind." It is now freely estimated that it will gross ten million. Lasky's cut comes to a million and a half in this case. The gross on "Gone With The Wind" was twelve million, on "North West Mounted" about four and a half million.

Paramount was checking up again to see when they could get me on "Rurales." Warner Bros. was checking up to see when they could get me on "Captain Hornblower." I was checking up to see when I could finish "Useless Cowboy" and do my baseball game.

I don't know where all the time goes.

The script was completed in April 1942, and Irving Rapper was assigned as the director. He was to be introduced to the script by a reading, presumably to convey mood, tempo, and emphasis. Alan was picked to do the reading:

[March 20, 1942] To my embarrassed surprise I am nominated to read the script to the director. My answer to this, which may or may not be a fat-headed one, is to make arrangements with Lucius Cooke to coach me on reading.

While I was writing for print, it did not matter whether I could talk

or not — nobody listened to me anyway — but in this business oral
exposition and dramatic reading are a professional bottle-neck.

The reading went well; Lasky was "deliriously happy" and Alan was
moderately pleased with the outcome. The script went to the front office,
and Alan went to Paramount to work on *The Rurales* for DeMille.

As the *Mark Twain* cast was assigned, Alan was called back to Warners
repeatedly for further script adjustments. These visits gave him the opportunity to follow the preparations for production. The film had a million-
dollar budget, which was lavish in that day, and Alan was awed by the
elaborate props and sets. He described this to his father:

> [June 23, 1942] The Warners Bros. art department is doing more work
> on "Mark Twain" than even DeMille has done on his pictures. Every
> single camera set-up has its own drawing. They even design a drawing
> for a steamboat whistle blowing, or a close shot of the steamboat's
> name, as well as composing the figure arrangements in every action
> shot. They have already made drawings all through the Mississippi
> River and Western sequences, and they look simply gorgeous.
>
> The famous type-setter upon which Mark blew $200,000, and for
> which I made sketches, has been constructed in miniature preparatory
> to building it. They followed my sketches and I think the result is a
> very funny gadget indeed. Five large mechanical storks slowly revolve,
> picking up wads of type in their beaks.
>
> The make-up department under Perc Westmore has made a complete
> set of portraits based upon March's face, showing the gradations of
> make-up [as Mark Twain ages]. March is going to look marvelous.
>
> You never saw a project get such loving care from so many highly
> able people. And the atmosphere is completely different from that
> which surrounds DeMille's tigerish opuses. Everyone is happy, enthusi-
> astic and beaming, and the speed at which they are covering the ground
> is amazing.
>
> [June 24, 1942] ... The steamboat model which I mentioned the
> other day, is really one of the masterpieces of all time; you never saw
> anything like it. The reasons that they are making it in miniature
> instead of sending a camera to photograph some boat on the Mississippi
> are that there is no longer any such magnificent boat afloat anywhere,
> and anyway the effects can be more flexibly controlled in tank miniature.

The sixty-day shooting schedule took place in the summer of 1942.
In July, Alan was back on *The Rurales* for DeMille, and in August he was
pulled off for a more urgent DeMille job on a war picture, the biography
of Dr. Wassell. But Alan took time from his work at Paramount to participate as he could at Warners on an informal basis. This was an opportunity to learn more about producing and directing, and was the type of
experience he would need to produce his own films.

[June 25, 1942] I have been given a pass admitting me to all sets during the entire shooting, and have been invited, even urged, to camp at the directors elbow. One reason that they are so nice about this is that I will be quite useful in this position. It is impossible to write a script such that all the lines are satisfactory when actually read; for one thing, different actors can read different types of lines, but are not necessarily interchangeable in their readings, and you wouldn't know what kind of emphasis to give the line until you see what the actor's natural way of playing it is. This is of course unpredictable, so many lines have to be rewritten on the set.

Another thing is that nobody ever has enough ad lib on hand for the background voices in crowds and so forth.

Still another thing is the invention of business when everything, such as props, is directly under your hands. Once DeMille was held up for a solid hour trying to find out why Madeleine Carroll was still hanging around for her scene with Gary Cooper — the fire-side one where he made her the coffee. Nobody had ever noticed that poor Madeleine just had to sit there counting her teeth in order to be on hand. I was the hero in this case — if I hadn't been I would have picked another where I was — and had her putting her medical kit back together, rolling bandages and so on; and the shooting, costing hundreds of dollars a minute, was able to proceed again. It was a good thing, the old man had already bitten himself in three places. He didn't thank me. He gave one horrible glare and turned purple in the face, then wheeled about and did what I said.

When the shooting was finished, Alan, Arlene, and Virginia Roddick (Gus) were invited to see the results in rough cut form at a private showing at Warner Brothers. Alan was not sure what he thought of it, but he gave this analysis to his father:

[September 29, 1942] Saturday night we saw the first rough cut of "The Adventures of Mark Twain," without montages, inserts, dissolves, musical scoring, sound effects, or special effects such as double exposure. Gus and Arlene saw it with me.

I will say at once that the result is mystifying and equivocal. Arlene thinks that it is a smash hit on the popular side, "a gold mine in the cans," unpredictable with the critics. Gus seems to think that it has a pretty fair chance all around, good chances with the critics, and the public unpredictable.

I lean slightly toward Gus's view, but with greater mystification than either one, but feel that it is certainly no disgrace, and at worst is a good balance credit for the DeMille box office melodramas.

The production as such is magnificent, the river sequences particularly being completely out of the world. Under present conditions it may very well stand out as the last of the great multi-million productions. But the photography, unfortunately, is largely without sparkle.

March's performance is on the whole excellent, and in many places the make-up is superb. But in other places, especially in the later middle, the make-up is not so good and in two or three scenes is shockingly bad, something like Cyrano de Bergerac.

Alexis Smith is really wonderful as Livy, and will rate as a great dramatic discovery. She is able to make me cry at will. This is a great surprise in a girl who has never acted in anything except penthouse clothes models before. But her name has no pull, and neither, for that matter, does that of Frederic March.

The old-style Mark Twain gag lines, with which we are so familiar, and which we so feared would be flat, come out as amazingly funny as played. The picture is riddled with them, and they seem to maintain a quite lively and happy mood. At least one of the comedy scenes is as funny as I have ever seen. But in many other places the director, who does not understand comedy, and seems to feel it is cheap, has completely smothered the comedy routines, leaving them valueless.

There is nothing in this that is hammy or in bad taste. But the director has confused under-acting with under playing, which are two different things — the former desirable, the other bad — with the effect that nonchalantly bad timing robs the key scenes of any dramatic effect.

As a biography, I think it is outstanding, with a more intensified combination of laughter and tears than any other biography I can think of on the screen. But the fact remains that it is still a biography and my violent and long-continued effort to change it from a biography to a story has almost completely miscarried. This is about half due to the difficulty of the problem exceeding my ability to cope with it and half due to the fear of the producers that I had gone overboard in certain things, with the result that my main dramatic point is quite lost. Where I had intended to show frustration reversed at the end, the picture shows simply the logical reward of a well-rounded life of effort.

The minor characters are cast way over and above what their parts had a right to suggest. John Carradine, Donald Crisp, Walter Hampden, appear in parts so small that no one should have had the guts to ask them to read them.

My credit on this is for absolutely solo original screenplay, based on nothing. This credit will be challenged, but will hold good.

Papa Brown used to say, "The longer a man lives the more he finds by Jesus Christ out." This has not worked out in my case. If I continue to know less and less I will soon have to be fed with a spoon.

I am going to try to get them to dub in a few lines which make reference to the story which I had planned, but probably won't get anywhere.

When it comes to credits, Hollywood shows its fangs. A writer's future assignments, and the price he can negotiate, depend on his list of credits. And solo credit is ranked well above any shared credits. To counter the expected favoritism, nepotism, and studio politics, the producer's decisions on credit could be challenged. In the case of writers, the challenge was arbitrated by the Screenwriter's Guild. Alan explained this to his father:

[October 7, 1942] Warners, as I guess I said, awarded me absolutely solo screenplay credit, based on nothing. But now the incredible Harold Sherman is challenging, and the credits are being arbitrated by the Screenwriters Guild. A committee of three reads the evidence submitted, without hearing, and the decision is final without appeal. Sherman hasn't a leg to stand on, but he submitted nearly a half ton of treatments, covering every possible event in the life of Mark Twain, and the Committee may possibly be bewildered by it. I replied with a four page statement, and a handful of cross-indexed evidence in support.

We will hear from this in a matter of days.

The arbitration went in Alan's favor, mostly:

[October 20, 1942] The credits on "Mark Twain" will read: Screenplay by Alan LeMay; Adaptation by Alan LeMay and Harold Sherman; Additional Dialogue by Harry Chandlee. I get a card on the screen all by myself.

The film opened at road show prices and did moderately well. In the end it was profitable, but was not the raving success that had been anticipated. A major reason was probably the lack of a star; neither Frederic March nor the completely unknown Alexis Smith had drawing power at the box office.

When he had had time to reflect on it, Alan was disappointed in the film. His storytelling talents had been held in check by the facts of the biography. He had taken on the job with the enthusiasm warranted by the subject, but could not get his ideas to the screen. He thought again of how much better he could do if he had artistic control.

Two years after shooting had started, Alan wrote to his father:

[July 28, 1944] I'm glad that you liked "Mark Twain." I still remain very disappointed in it, and I am very much afraid that its shortcomings are going to show in the box office. The week of road show, at outrageously advanced prices — $1.20 General Admission! — was very spotty indeed. It set records locally, but in some places died on its feet. It is now in general release at regular prices since the 22nd. It held a second week here, then folded — not too good, except for its heavy take here as a road show. The reports from the rest of the country should begin to show in a day or two. Well, maybe some day I will have a chance to give the answers on these things myself. I'm working on that now.

Love, Alan

—12—

The Story of Dr. Wassell

As soon as the *Mark Twain* script was done, Alan was back at Paramount working (again) on *The Rurales* for DeMille. He had barely picked up the pieces of that when DeMille reversed course again and had Alan and Charles Bennett start on a biographical war story about Dr. Wassell. The story was based on real characters and actual events, and thus was more constraining than, say, adapting a novel to the screen. Gary Cooper was to play the title role, and his schedule made it imperative that shooting start within three months. Alan explained the situation in a letter to his father:

> [August 8, 1942] We were taken off of the Rurales picture last Tuesday, and put onto the Dr. Wassell job.
>
> This is a strictly rush performance, because Cooper is supposed to play it, and if he does we will have to begin shooting in November. This calls for a twelve-week job on the screenplay, a relative cinch if I were working by myself, and quite possible working in collaboration, but what with DeMille changing his mind every day, calls for miracles.
>
> Dr. Wassell's achievement was the evacuation of ten seriously wounded and burned men out of Java; they had been left there as impossible to move, under the circumstances, and were the last out. A hair-raising series of hazards and torments were met by Dr. Wassell with ingenuity and a singularly dogged pluck.
>
> The survivors have all been interviewed by everybody on the picture except Charles and me, who are only the writers who must characterize them. However, one of them is coming in to see me this afternoon, and two of them are to report to us Monday. And Dr. Wassell (Lieut. Commander, really) is assigned to the picture by the Navy. Part of the gross receipts go to the Navy Relief, is the angle.
>
> The most interesting part is the character of Commander Wassell, who is strictly Arkansas — a drawling, slow-moving sweet character with a background of fourteen years in China as a medical missionary without impairing his Arkansas dialect, and an interesting double love story.

90

The idea is to flash back to his background during the tense moments of the escape climaxes.

We have a chance to get a superb script — if not prevented. But you know C.B.

The screenplay got off to a fast start, with DeMille in a good mood. But even in a benign mood DeMille was hard to please, and accepted little of the material without extensive conferences and revisions. The main point of contention was that DeMille wanted more melodramatic action, but would not let them diverge sufficiently from the facts, even though the facts did not contain what he wanted.

It is not clear who came up with the idea, but an organizational change in the writing staff relieved Alan of the daily conferences so that he could write alone as he wanted to.

[October 7, 1942] Here at Paramount, DeMille has split Charles Bennett and me. I am writing ahead alone, and Charles is writing behind me under the close direction of DeMille. This is wonderful. As things were before, I was doing one hundred per cent of the writing, anyway, since Charles admittedly cannot write American dialog. But I had to get in early enough to do all my writing before he got here, because he liked to spend all the time in talk. Nothing could go forward until he had literally memorized every line I meant to put down. Sometimes this took days, so that we were at about twenty per cent efficiency from a stand-point of speed.

Bennett's rewrites were often harmless, but they were a continuing annoyance to Alan, who gave an example:

He would take my copy, say, "If I just straighten this up a bit," and bitch through it with his pencil, creating a few sillinesses, putting "But" at the beginning of each sentence, and putting in participles where they didn't belong. His best angle was amplification, like this:

(LeMay original) Smith: (Angrily) What?

(Bennett rewrite) But Smith's eyes flash, walking across the room. He reaches the door, standing still. He speaks directly to Jones, as follows:

Smith: (speaking directly to Jones, angrily)—What?

He falls silent, stopping.

So I am very happy to be rid of this nuisance collaboration. My new, much faster copy is getting by with DeMille much better, and it is relatively no effort. What they do behind me I don't much care; DeMille always bitches up the whole thing anyway, and there is no use feeling badly about it.

All of the inefficiencies of the endless rewrites added up to a schedule crisis that kept Alan working overtime under tremendous pressure. As Christmas approached, he wrote to his father:

[November 11, 1942] There isn't any possible chance that I can get away for a few days, or at all. We have to shoot January 2, and the script is about half in shape. Every day's delay decreases the possibility of making the picture at all. For one thing, Cooper will make only one picture next year, since one is all the government allows him to be paid for, and he wants to make it at once. For another thing, if the picture were delayed as long as March, it would become impossible from the standpoint of the procurement of materials. For another thing, the extensive government cooperation which we are getting will swiftly cool off from here on, and most of the production effect of the picture is based upon what the Army and Navy are doing for us, such as all the air work. For another thing, the public is going to cool off rapidly on war pictures and many think we are already very late with this picture; I am one of those who think so.

The rush on the picture is so great that production preparations have gone forward on sequences which are not even written; so that I repeatedly find myself fitting the scenes to sets which are already being built. As when the other day I found that all the shots had already been designed in an air field sequence I was trying to write, and another day when I found that the production department was planning to blow up three bridges instead of one. Art Rosson, the second unit director, is on the south border of Mexico shooting backgrounds.

The urgent completion dates kept skidding. When this job started in August it was absolutely essential that shooting start in November. Now it was the following March, and the schedule, if anything, seemed to be more relaxed. As Alan has said before, "Nothing takes so long as a DeMille opus." To his father, he wrote:

[March 2, 1943] The way things go now, we get down to the office fairly early, in order to do our rewrite, which is elaborate and extensive, before quarter of two. At quarter of two we are called to lunch, and go to the commissary, where we wait half an hour for DeMille to show up. We then spend an hour over what left-overs the commissary feels able to supply, and go into conference. Seventeen interruptions postpone the opening of the conference, which really gets going about quarter of five. Interruptions thereafter fall to a frequency of about every two minutes, but we manage to accumulate about ten pages of rewrite instructions by half past seven, in time for DeMille to get home for an eight o'clock dinner.

I then tool home on my motorcycle in the bitter-cold dark. You have no idea what a cold wind there is on a motorcycle. A relatively mild evening feels like the winter wind off Lake Michigan.

After a late snatch at dinner I work until eleven or so; at present I am still rewriting Useless Cowboy.

HW

SEQUENCE "A"

FADE IN:

A-1   FOLLOWING THE MAIN AND CREDIT TITLES, the Voice of the
       Commentator is heard over beautiful STOCK SHOTS, personify-
       ing the East Indies, and ranging from a towering Hindu tem-
       ple to a rich rubber plantation. We see heavily laden
       elephants moving majestically; tropic trees beside white
       beaches; terraced rice fields and great buffalo-drawn carts;
       a spreading tea plantation, etc., etc. (Picturesque shots
       as procurable.) Through these:

       COMMENTATOR: Many centuries ago Marco Polo brought
                     word of fabulous lands, rich with spices,
                     jewels and gold... the mysterious Far
                     East! His unbelievable tales proved
                     true. For seven hundred years the Indies
                     were the goal of high adventure, until at
                     last their riches became a part of our
                     lives... vital source of rubber, sugar
                     and tin. Then, down from the north swept
                     a dwarfish horde of island men.

       The SHOTS FADE, giving place to a SIMPLIFIED MAP OF THE FAR
       EAST. A blood-red arrow crawls southwestward from Japan,
       driving down the China coast, through Thailand and the Malay
       States, aiming at the gates of Singapore.

       COMMENTATOR: One by one fell strongholds which had
                     stood for decades. Hongkong! Bangkok!

       A second crimson arrow crawls southeast from Japan, down
       through the Philippines, Borneo and the Celebes, the two
       arrows closing upon Java like ice-tongs.

       COMMENTATOR: ...Manila! The Celebes! Only Singapore
                     remained -f as the great Japanese pincers
                     closed on Java... ~~jammed~~ heart of the Dutch
                     Indies.   vital

       The CAMERA IS MOVING IN TO CONCENTRATE ON JAVA and the Java
       Sea.

       COMMENTATOR: Caught in the terrible trap of the Java
                     Sea, a little handful of Dutch and
                     American fighting ships made their hope-
                     less stand against the navies of Japan.

       DISSOLVE TO:

A-2   TWO SWIFT CUTS OF NAVAL BATTLE ACTION

       a. A battle-strewn deck, as great guns thunder above.

       b. An arresting FLASH of a broadside firing.

       DISSOLVE TO:

5-19-43

Alan's original opening sequence.

By March the script was completed except for the neverending final
adjustments. And then the weather in Java created what was, to Alan, a
major disaster.

> [March 26, 1943] Yesterday our research department finally proved con-
> clusively that there is no fog in Java. This is a very major disaster
> indeed, and completely destroys the everlastingly troublesome and
> largely meaningless "F" Sequence, which is in there where the climax

ought to be. At long last we had finally managed to fight our way to at least a semblance of menace and suspense, to keep the audience in their seats, but without the fog we have nothing at all—no "F" Sequence, and no picture. What luck!

We have always tried to throw "F" out altogether, but no hope.

The "F" sequence was saved by substituting heavy rain for fog, and was left in. This attention to detail, keeping locales true to life, is not common in Hollywood but was always important to Alan. The script was wrapped up around the first of April, and Alan was immediately put back on *The Rurales*.

Since he was still at Paramount, Alan frequently looked in on the shooting of *Dr. Wassell*. His main objective was to learn more about producing and directing. But he did not always agree with what he saw.

[July 13, 1943] One thing that I don't see any sense to, is DeMille's practice of rehearsing the stand-ins hour in and hour out, without the principals even being on the set. Every detail of gesture is worked out this way; then after great cost of time, the principals are brought on, and they have to learn the whole routine. It looks to me as if DeMille ought to be able to work that stuff out in his head, if he had any great ability of visualization.

I don't think I believe in such detailed direction anyway—"Raise your hand an inch—not so much"—and all that. I appreciate the conscientious and meticulous attention to detail, but in this extreme I think it leads to a mechanical effect, in which the players cannot do their best emotionally.

It was a year later, April 1944, before *Dr. Wassell* was finally released. This was late in the war and, as feared, the public was growing weary of war pictures. Nevertheless, it was well received, as Alan reported to his father:

[April 17, 1944] "The Story of Dr. Wassell" previewed in Washington before most of the heads of Govt., and the acclaim was terrific. It will premiere in Little Rock April 26, and release at will thereafter. Both Wassell and Twain look like very great smashes.

Few Americans in 1944 understood much about the cultures of the South Pacific, or what had been going on there in the early stages of World War II. Alan wrote an opening sequence that summarized the situation beautifully. In less than two minutes of graphics and narration it tutored the audience on how the story got to this point and what was at stake. It would have captured the viewer's interest, educated them on important recent history, and made the rest of the film more enjoyable and understandable.

But when the film was released, the opening sequence had changed. DeMille had substituted his own narration about country doctors and motherhood, against a still-shot background of a bronze statue of a horse and buggy. It is a nice horse and buggy, but it does nothing to orient the viewer for the confusion of battle that immediately follows. Alan's original opening sequence, reproduced on page 93, explains his frustration with not having artistic control.

—13—

The Rurales

It was not apparent until much later, but DeMille may have used *The Rurales* just as a fill-in to keep staff writers busy. Alan was not a staff writer, but DeMille did not want him to get away. He first started on this screenplay with Jesse Lasky, Jr., in the spring of 1940, just after finishing the script of *North West Mounted Police*. At first he was very enthusiastic, and saw great possibilities for it as he wrote to his parents:

> [April 8, 1940] Our "Rurales" picture has developed extremely well under the working title of "The Borderman." [Bill] Pine seems as pleased as he dares to be; he has told DeMille that if DeMille does not want to produce it he will produce it himself or they can turn the story over to Paramount to produce as a big non–DeMille Paramount. I think myself that it has stuff in it better than anything I have ever seen in an outdoor action type of picture.

They didn't get very far before DeMille shifted gears and had them start instead on *Reap the Wild Wind*. As was usual with DeMille, the *RTWW* script dragged on and on but always with *The Rurales* scheduled to be next. Alan was tiring of DeMille's rants, however, and did not like the prospect of starting another film with him, as he explained to his parents:

> [September 15, 1941] By way of the grape-vine we hear that DeMille still imagines that I am going to script "The Rurales" as soon as he is finished with "Reap the Wild Wind." This may prove very embarrassing and difficult to get out of, but I don't want to work for him again if it can possibly be avoided. The easiest thing would be to give him a price which he would not pay and which I could not refuse; but I would have to give other people the same price, which would simply mean I would be through writing pictures. That might be preferable at that.

Alan's agent lined up several potential assignments, but the timing was a little off and Paramount jumped in:

[July 12, 1942] ... They simply asked what price we were quoting, and paid it, and since I could show no other commitment there was nothing to do but take it. I am getting $1,250 [per week] plus $35 for Gus. It is supposed to be a two-picture assignment, the Rurales and Dr. Wassell, both of which DeMille is making. Charles Bennett is with me on both.

"Reap the Wild Wind" has broken the Paramount box office records for all time, superseding "North West Mounted Police" and this may be partly why DeMille is extremely genial just now, I really wouldn't know him.

As Alan got back into *The Rurales* he became aware that the story line had developed serious problems, and his collaborator was not helping. Worse, the story was not typical DeMille at all. Alan expected that it was only a question of time before DeMille woke up to the fact and blew his top.

But after several months of effort the script began to shape up in a form that was acceptable to DeMille, and mostly tolerable to Alan. But one scene stuck in his throat.

[July 27, 1942] Everything is going pretty well here, except for one scene in the picture. This scene appears to have been concocted by DeMille, and is unfortunately the key point of the plot, without which the rest of the picture cannot be played. Everybody is very happy with the thing except Gus and me; we think the audiences will howl and fall in the aisles.

The substance of the scene is that Gary Cooper marries Rita Hayworth. Why do you think he does a thing like that? Because he likes her? No. Because he thinks she's pretty? No, he hasn't noticed her. Because she wants him to? No. She doesn't like him, either. You guessed it. He marries her to save her from a fate worse than death.

In contrast with his views on *The Rurales*, Alan was enthralled by *Mrs. Miniver*, starring Greer Garson. The two films could not have been more different, but they elicited comparison anyway.

[July 28, 1942] The other night we saw "Mrs. Miniver." We found it very real and moving; and for me it packs the hardest punch I ever saw in a picture. This is partly because of the excellent performances, and partly because of the fine direction; but it is also because they had the guts to use five or six reels in establishing acquaintance with the characters, and an affection for them, before anything dramatic is asked to happen.

Seeing this fine job made us feel even worse about my present assignment, in which animal-like peons run ravening through haciendas, for no reason that we are let in on. In the name of reality DeMille insists that all hacendados be shown as of unwavering grace and charm, making the whole nightmare even more incomprehensible. When asked why the peons are so hostile to charm, he replies with impatience that any-body understands revolutions, and he is amazed that I don't know that.

This brings us to the touching and delicately balanced scene in which the daughter of the hacienda is bound and thrown on a pile of loot to be gambled for.

DeMille now tells us that this scene, above all, must be written exactly like "Mrs. Miniver."

After all this time he can still astound me.

Alan's frustration in being stuck with this material shows in a letter he wrote to his best friend, Bud Hering, the polo-playing navy surgeon, on August 18, 1942. He described the basic plot of *The Rurales*:

In the first reel there is this Mexican tomato Rita Hayworth, and she is a rich bitch, and she is going to marry a Mexican citizen named Ray Miland. Just before they get married the tomato's old man makes Ray Miland a present for free of a hacienda that reaches for miles and miles and is planted in nothing but mile upon mile of peso bushes. So Miland spits right in the old man's eye and ditches the tomato and goes off and joins a revolution. I ask them (the producers) why this Mexican citizen does this, and they tell me don't ask foolish questions, he's sore.

So next Ray Miland joins a rebel army and immediately gets to be boss, and he sends a cookie named Wallace Beery to get some groceries, and the cookie burns down the tomato's hacienda. I ask them why the cookie does this thing and they tell me don't try to understand what he does, he's nuts.

So next this cookie and his gorillas put all the boodle from the hacienda in a big pile, and they tie the tomato's hands behind her back, and throw her on top of the pile for good measure, so now all the Mexican citizens have a gambling game to see who gets first pick of the boodle, and this is the damnedest gambling game you ever see. They all load their guns and cock them and stand around the table, and all throw their guns in the air, and when the guns come down they all go off killing many a citizen. The theory is that when there is only one of them left he will have first pick if he is able. I ask them does every citizen in Mexico have to have this one tomato, and they say oh no, only a few citizens want the tomato, the rest want first pick of the bridge lamps.

So next in comes Gary Cooper and he says to the tomato what cooks, toots, and the tomato says these monkeys have cut me in on a fate worse than death. I should have said that Gary Cooper is a Texas train robber, and has virtually sabotized the whole revolution by holding up all the trains and stealing all their damn weapons, and are they baffled. So Cooper says to the tomato, this is indeed an uncouth thing, boys, I will marry the tomato and save her from a fate worse than death. The tomato says she guesses this is the best deal she can make; I will marry you, she says, and be your wife in name only, because I hate you, you ugly chump you. I ask them why the tomato speaks so to Gary Cooper, who is only running out his neck, and they tell me none of your business, all you have to do is make this sound real like Mrs. Miniver.

I say what a cinch and they say naturally.

There followed an eight-month recess from *The Rurales*, while Alan was pulled off by DeMille for the expected assignment on *The Story of Dr. Wassell*. As that was wrapping up, he switched back to *The Rurales* script, and wrote to his father:

> [March 23, 1943] ... That Rurales story, which they cooked in its entirety while I was out of Paramount, cannot possibly ever be shot; neither Mexico nor our own State Department can possibly accede to it. So I will probably get credit for a flopped script, whatever I do about it. But I think maybe I can stand that, now.

DeMille was still shooting *Dr. Wassell*, and Alan was anticipating that the script he was working on would be scrapped when DeMille returned. The daily struggles with Charles Bennett were wearing him down, and without any approvals from DeMille it all seemed futile. His efficiency dropped, and he needed a rest.

> [May 6, 1943] I am thinking seriously of taking a week's vacation. First of all, this may be the back-handed way of getting speed on this. If I do, I will use it to go on a pack trip in the mountains with Bud Hering, who thinks he can get leave.

He suggested the idea to Bud, and found the overworked Navy surgeon more than eager to get some time off also. Bud wrote back to Alan:

> Dear Alan: May 10, 1943
>
> Have been building castles and trails in the sky since I have heard definitely that you are coming. Let's see now, am having Ghost shod this morning, have been graining heavily for past two days, have fixed up a pack saddle, got the sleeping bags, must get some K rations, carbines, ammunition, cooking gear, have the tent and cots for the gals; now here is the plan to date:
>
> We shove off early Thursday morning from the ranch, going over in back of El Capitan Lake and cutting up Eagle Pass to Pine Hills and winding up we hope in the evening at Cuyamaca. We will ride Scooter and Ghost and take Old Folks along as a pack horse and spare in case of a lame bronc or such. The girls go by car to Cuyamaca, taking one or two of my men along to set up a tent and make camp.
>
> We spend the night there and start off the next morning for the desert, possibly going down into the Oraflume and coming out somewhere south of Banner, making camp that night on the desert if we can make contact with the gals. The next day we might ride up to the San Felipe ranch and go up that canyon as far as Warners or can ride the

other way and go over the pass into Pine Valley. This may be a two-day jump and in that case we would have to truck the horses back from Pine Valley which same can be arranged very easily.

As far as equipment goes all you need to bring is your own tough body, hardened by DeMille cynicism no doubt, your good wife, with some riding and roughing togs, and any little conveniences that you might think of. Ammunition for the new thirty carbine is almost non-existent to date so if you can get ahold of a carbine of some sort and ammunition perhaps you had better bring it along. You might harden your posterior a trifle by soaking in salt water and pounding on a board for a few nights if you think advisable. Be sure and bring Jumbo, don't think he could keep up with the horses but can go with the gals in the car.

Will look for you Wednesday; come directly to the house, I may be home a little late on account of a day at Pendleton but we will be all ready for an early start Thursday morning.

Wrote to DeMille and Sawley, thanking them for their co-operation; told George he probably would be let out after DeMille read my stirring endorsement of him.

Just learned that Pendleton is out so come early Wednesday.

See you all Wednesday, don't fail me Coach.

Bud

Alan wrote to his father before the trip. Significantly, his attention was focused on the horse he would be riding:

[Tuesday, May 11, 1943] Well, here we go at last. Arlene and I are leaving tomorrow for the first vacation since 1940 [three years ago]. We'll be gone one week, so you won't hear from me again until after that.

I enclose Bud's letter, which gives a general idea of what we are going to do. Black Ghost, which he mentions, is an eight-year-old thoroughbred which I have known for about five years. He is very big, strong, and raw-boned, not fast enough for a track winner, though he was raced; very full of power and fire. He always worked very nicely for me.

After the trip he reported on it briefly. The "very wild and rough" country they roamed for a week was in San Diego County, Southern California. Today it is largely farmed, fenced, and paved.

The pack trip with Bud was a great success. The second day out I thought I might possibly not make it through, but I got better during the third day, and after that enjoyed the riding thoroughly. On one occasion we made a series of mistaken short cuts, which so delayed us that we lost a whole day, and missed our supply car, so rode all the next day without grub.

The country we traversed was very wild and rough, and we only saw two residents the entire time — a hermit of 81, and a Swede prospector.

Back at Paramount, Alan was kept captive by *The Rurales* while his agents dangled offers for films he would rather be doing. Lasky Sr. wanted Alan to work on a screenplay about Audubon. Howard Hawks was trying to get him for a picture called *Battle Cry.* Harpo Marx wanted him to write and direct him in a comedy film called *Schweik, the Good Soldier.* But one does not walk out on DeMille and expect to ever work in Hollywood again.

> [June 21, 1943] ... I can't do anything about these things until after *Rurales*, which is the toughest I ever tangled with, and will probably take until doomsday. Doomsday being the day when DeMille is finished with Wassell. If I am still here then, of course we will start all over.
>
> But tonight I am going to the fights with Harpo Marx, under the head of business.

Three and a half years after Alan first started working on *The Rurales*, the script was finished. DeMille had not approved it, Alan still didn't like it, but he was able to say that it was done as ordered and escape to other projects, and a short vacation.

After all that, *The Rurales* was never filmed.

—14—

Useless Cowboy

While the Mark Twain script was stumbling at the starting gate, Alan could not take on new contracts that would interfere. But the delays left schedule gaps, permitting him to start on the serial he had been planning. Even after the film script got going, he still put in nights and weekends on *Useless Cowboy*. All of his novels in the 1930s had been serialized in *Collier's*, so he was comfortable with the style. It was almost as though getting back to magazine stories was a vacation. He outlined his objectives in a letter to his parents:

> [June 13, 1941] I am working along quite unhurriedly on my new serial. It is somewhat of an experimental departure from the things I have done in the past and if my theories are correct it represents the road to considerable fortune. I should not think that you would care a great deal for the content personally, but I think you will like the way it is written.
>
> The new angles of method I am using are first, that I am taking twice as long as I have ever taken before; second, that I am using a much more sensational type of thriller plot than I have ever used before; third, I am taking full time to the careful writing, with the ideal of making every line inescapably real so that the things that are happening shall seem actually to be happening, genuinely experienced by the reader; fourth, at least twice as much thought upon character and character psychology as I have ever used.

The serial was to be a comedy, which was a genre new to him and, as a Western, new to *Collier's*. So rather than write something that *Collier's* might reject outright, he discussed the idea with their fiction editor, as he reported to his parents:

> [June 30, 1941] Max Wilkinson of *Collier's* was out here and spent one evening and an entire day with us, resting up beside the pool at the Tennis club. Max Wilkinson is the one at *Collier's* who never thought I could write. Looking back over the stuff I have written I agree with him. I honestly believe that the "Little Kid" is the only story worth

printing I ever wrote. [It was a short-short story, published in *Collier's* magazine, July 9, 1938.] Too much pressure of haste has prevented me from doing as well as I can. This is now overcome thanks to two years in the DeMille penitentiary and I expect to write much better than I ever wrote before.

After conferences with Max, I am writing an entirely new type of Western serial under the title "Useless Cowboy." This was planned before Max came out, as I think I told you, and my conferences with him did not cause me to change my plans in any way as regards this serial.

His writing of the serial was often interrupted, sandwiched between movie scripts, and sometimes limited to evenings after dinner. As it progressed, he kept his parents informed over a period of months:

[August 14, 1941] ... "Useless Cowboy" now seems to be sufficiently well in hand so that I may be able to dictate from here on in. Up to this point I have been writing long hand which seems to be the best method when it is necessary for me to write with thoughtful care, feeling my way.

[August 28, 1941] ... Today I had a good day on "Useless Cowboy" solving some eleven questions which were a mystery to me when I last left it. Some of the answers will be wrong but I am certain that at least one strong-middle scene which we invented will prove absolutely the ticket and will turn out to make an especially strong point out of the very weakest one in the story. I am sure you are going to be happily entertained by this job which is considerably different from anything I have written before.

[August 30, 1941] ... Wally Heinze, my business manager, has offered to lend me a Dictaphone set. I will pick it up on my way home from tennis today. The principal advantage of this is that it will probably ruin Virginia's shorthand so that she won't be able to get another job and will have to stay with me.

Alan had been away from the magazine market for several years, and was unsure of the quality of the competition. But when he checked, he was encouraged. There wasn't much there. At the same time he was being pressured by *Collier's* to finish his serial, because they needed more material and were still enthusiastic about the subject.

[January 5, 1942] I read some stuff in *Collier's* and frankly was amazed at the tiresome drivel that they print. It encouraged me very much.

[April 29, 1942] After the two weeks [working with the director on *Mark Twain*] which ends about the eighteenth of May, [1942], it is absolutely necessary that I complete "Useless Cowboy." I received quite a long, urgent letter from Max Wilkinson, who is holding the fort at *Collier's*, Littauer now being a Major in the Air Corps. *Collier's* is going to run a slightly heavier magazine now that they have raised the price. This means, Max says, that they will use longer serial installments and hence will need more serials, and they simply don't know where they are going to get them. I have therefore promised Max the serial June 15.

Alan was hoping to steer his career in a different direction, and it was all based on the success of *Useless Cowboy.*

[May 18, 1942] ... If I sell "Useless Cowboy"—and I honestly do not see how I can miss with this one—my notion is to set it up for an inexpensive picture to produce and direct myself. This sounds like a lot of guts and whenever I am appalled by my own nerve, I take a look at the incompetence all around me and become unappalled.

[May 19, 1942] ... I hope I will be able to engineer the financing to produce this. My idea is to push it as an entirely new kind of production, geared to the war. I claim that we are using a fifty thousand dollar subject, a fifty thousand dollar script and producing with brains instead of materials as a laboratory job to show the industry what can be done.

If this worked out it would take care of my next year's expenses and I would be able to devote next year to writing two or three serials ahead as a back-log. This seems to be the only way I can think of to get finances ahead such as would free me to go into the war, inasmuch as the taxes will successfully prevent me from getting enough actual money ahead.

There seems to be considerable doubt as to what is to become of the big magazines in the immediate future. All those full-page good will ads, speaking out for companies who have nothing to sell now, seem to be attributable to only two factors: unused advertising contracts, and excess profits dodging.

However, the price of a serial will probably still buy a family's expenses for a year in a real pinch even if prices go down to pulp rates, which are based on news-stand sales without advertising income. The biggest step the magazines will have to take will probably be the substantial reduction of their circulation.

[June 18, 1942] This story did not have all the work on it that I planned to put; pictures having broken into it very much. While considerable time is charged against it, the major portion of such time was really spent in recuperating from "Reap the Wild Wind" which was on top of "North West Mounted Police"; representing a total of some ninety-four weeks, I think, of heavy harassing by the expert harasser of our time.

Paramount has been trying very hard to get me onto the current DeMille opus and Warners has wanted to put me on a term contract, with Lasky particularly wanting me to start work on his next one; so that stalling everybody off without making anyone sore has not been the least of my worries.

Collier's rejected *Useless Cowboy*! Max Wilkinson, the *Collier's* fiction editor, had followed it all the way, liked the concept, and had pushed Alan to get it done. Then they decided against it! It was the tragic result of their penchant to stick with the tried and true. *Useless Cowboy* was a different type of Western, where the hero is more klutz than superman, and the gutless magazine just couldn't risk that. Apparently they also thought it lacked tension.

Alan wrote to his father of the shocking rejection. Unfortunately, the first page of the letter was lost, or self-combusted; but here is how he starts on page two:

> [July 1, 1942] ... I know how to write tension as well as anybody in the business. Just to be sure I can, I extemporized a couple of tension scenes, and Max cried "that is exactly what we want!" But I intentionally wrote this serial with a calculated ease of style. The hero's life is at stake from the start, and his situation gets worse; but we take it lightly, which is a system we prove in pictures every day.
>
> That is what I believe is right for now. I would not write their way, because I don't believe in it. If I bent to their way, the next step would be that they would have to get a new set of more up-to-date editors, and the first thing the editors would have to do would be to get rid of *me*!
>
> But much more appalling than the stumble of the serial, which I will probably get my money out of anyhow, from someone, is the general picture I got of the state of the magazines. I never saw such jitters. If the magazines are not sunk, at least they think they are, I am now pretty sure.
>
> More of this, including the hysterical condition of the Post, and the degraded condition of Liberty, anon.

Alan rewrote *Useless Cowboy* as a novel, and liked the result. He considered it the best job he ever did. It was published in hardback in 1943 by Farrar and Rinehart.

Aside from that rejection, the year was going fine. *Reap the Wild Wind* became Paramount's leading money earner, both for the year (1942) and for all time. But Alan never sent another manuscript to *Collier's*.

When the novel was released in hardback, Alan sent a copy to his father with the comment:

> [August 10, 1943] We mailed you today a copy of *Useless Cowboy*, which we have just received. The reason it has no jacket is that I promptly took the jackets off all copies I received, due to the depressing nature of the design, which was simply so dull and cheap as to have frightened a Hopalong Cassidy fan. This is the best job I have done, in a light and frivolous sort of way, and might have a chance of being a sleeper, except for the unfavorable subject and camouflage jacket, which make discovery virtually a physical impossibility. So the only fictional cowboy who ever dropped his gun on the floor will probably pass down the corridors of time noticed by none. From this we learn, etc.

On the set of *Along Came Jones*, 1944: Gary Cooper and Alan LeMay (right); William Demarest in background. Seated man on left unidentified. Photograph by John Leroy Johnston.

Alan's agent put the word out that *Useless Cowboy* was available as a film property, and tried to sell it as a package with Alan to write and direct. Columbia, Paramount, and Fox all showed interest, and Columbia was very close to signing a deal, when Gary Cooper preempted them.

> [July 12, 1944] Best news today: Gary Cooper, who has his own producing company now, bought *Useless Cowboy*, for himself. I hope to hear it rumored that the price was a reported $75,000. It wasn't; knock a zero off and you have it. This is peanuts, but also gravy, because I would have given it to him. There are a hundred Westerns available for one of anything else, and hence no price. The gorgeous possibility is that Useless will open a whole new field of outdoor stories, in basic type. There will be a million dollar production, at least, vindicating my departure from the traveled groove, and making a sucker out of *Collier's*.
>
> [July 13, 1944] The deal with Cooper stipulates that I still own the character of Melody Jones. If they make any further pictures dealing with him, without my supplying added material, I get $5,000 a picture.

If I write any more stories about Melody, they have 60 days to make a deal with me. But I cannot write any more until their picture is made, or for two years, whichever is the least. There is some possibility that Melody might become a B-budget series character, like Hopalong Cassidy, after Cooper has set him up; this might result in a small annuity for a while. But the thing that I am most interested in, is the possibility that *Useless Cowboy*, with this ideal star, will open a whole new field of outdoor pictures.

The book was adapted to the screenplay by Nunnally Johnson, and soon was in production. Unfortunately they changed the name. I have no idea why they did this. Every time one of Alan's titles got changed it seemed to lose color. His first Western for *Collier's* was called "There's a Million Cows in the Greasewood," and it was changed to "Cowboys will be Cowboys." Paramount changed *Ghost Mountain* to *Rocky Mountain*, and Columbia changed *Spanish Crossing* to *The Walking Hills*. Not helpful. But Alan otherwise approved, as he explained to his father:

> [December 26, 1944] Gary Cooper is about two thirds through shooting *Useless Cowboy*, under the title "Along Came Jones." I read the script, and it follows the book perfectly, with only the necessary condensation of dialog, to bring it into footage limits for the screen. I went over to the Goldwyn studios and saw them shooting a scene at the Busted Nose ranch, and every detail was just perfectly as I had always imagined it. It was really the biggest thrill I have ever got out of pictures.
>
> Then this morning I received a very nice photo of Melody Jones (Gary), George Fury (Bill Demarest), and myself, by God, all sitting on the ranch house steps; and inscribed to me by Cooper, "with many thanks and my best regards."
>
> There is that about writing for the screen: if you write something for print, and they print it, it just lies there inert, and that is that; but if you write a screen play, it gets up and comes to life, and walks, and talks, and sings, and every darn thing.

In mid–April, 1945, the film was done, and Alan and Arlene were invited to a private showing. Alan called it "a pretty good job," but was very unhappy with the credits. The producer and director each got his name in type that filled the screen, as did "Written for the Screen by Nunnally Johnson." In tiny type below, scarcely readable, it said "From the Novel by Alan LeMay." In many professions such a slight could be overlooked, but in Hollywood the credits get you your next job. Alan vowed to redouble his efforts to get into producing or directing, and in the meantime hired a publicity agent.

—15—

A Year at Warner's

June 1944 to June 1945

For the first time since he arrived in Hollywood five years before, Alan decided to try being a contract studio writer. He was working at Warner Brothers on a two-picture deal to write *San Antonio* for Errol Flynn, and *Calamity Jane* for Ann Sheridan. Warner Brothers offered him a one-year term contract at $1250.00 per week, with a 40 week guarantee, and options out to seven years with pay increases to $2250.00 per week, so on June 29, 1944, he signed on. Freelancing had been valuable for getting his price up fast; if he had started as a contract writer with no film experience his price would have been rock bottom.

But now his price was at a level where taxes took any increases, and the prospect of a modicum of temporary security was more appealing. As a contract writer he would get first crack at the good subjects, instead of, as he said, "being called in as a trouble shooter after the contract men had the subject completely bitched up, everybody sick of it, a $300,000 charge against the script, and a necessity of shooting in five weeks." In addition, Warner's had an excellent record for promoting writers to directors and producers, and that was Alan's real objective.

The term contract may have promised a little more financial security, but it provided no relief from the pressure of rush schedules. The studio could not afford to keep their stable of expensive stars if they were not producing, so keeping them busy was the first priority. Alan was already under pressure when he signed the Warner's contract, as he wrote to his father:

> [June 29, 1944] Raoul Walsh, shooting Errol Flynn in his current production, picked up 3 days on his schedule, so that I had to pick up 3 days on the schedule of San Antonio. This I did by writing 23 pages of screenplay in one day — all living, and in the script. Pressure remained

great, however, until now. I am all done, and the script okayed for production, except for cleaning up details, and handling such requests for
changes as may come from director and stars.

Monday I start *Calamity Jane* for Ann Sheridan.

[June 30, 1944] *San Antonio* is Technicolor set in 1877. Besides Flynn
it has Alexis Smith, Raymond Massey, Zachary Scott, S.Z. Sackal. It
will be exciting, good-looking, mean nothing, cost $1,500,000, and
double its money.

The lyric I wrote on Arlene's idea has been musiced and accepted, and
will be the featured song number in San Antonio. Title is "Pardon Me."

The long studio hours made it difficult for Alan to get his daily work-
outs. When he didn't exercise strenuously he put on weight and lost energy.
He played a lot of tennis on weekends, but his need for exercise was daily.
His problem was solved when his producer on *San Antonio*, Bob Buckner,
invited him to play handball every noon. This was not only a good workout, but an opportunity to communicate informally on film-related issues.
It was a strenuous substitute for golf.

Without the lost time that was common between freelance contracts,
Alan started on *Calamity Jane* in July 1944. The early results looked promising.

[July 11, 1944] Yesterday I had a one-hour conference with Jerry Wald,
producer of *Calamity Jane*. As a writer, Jerry wrote the original treatment in 1940, but it was shelved until Ann Sheridan dragged it out and
battled for it. (Jerry is now about the biggest producer on this lot.) To
my dumbfounded amazement, Jerry cheered every one of the changes I
suggested, and okayed my whole story line for immediate screenplay, I
to work by any method I please. What goes on here?

Am I dreaming, or what?

[July 25, 1944] It looks like Raoul Walsh is out as director of *San
Antonio*; reason unknown to me. But I am not in, though I have been
considered. The budget is now at two million, and they are afraid to
risk me on so heavy a budget. This poses me with a severe problem. I
can't get hooked into an indoor picture because I am the only outdoor
writer they have, virtually; outdoor writers are very abundant, but few
of them can write in girls. And they always throw a heavy budget at
good outdoor pictures — Technicolor, crowd scope, and everything else.
Now, how to break out of this trap?

Apparently there was a custom, if not a rule, that the Office of War
Information (OWI,) the World War II propaganda bureaucracy, was given
a copy of all scripts before production to see that they were not subversive
or detrimental to the war effort in any way. Approval was essential in the
case of war films, where the military contributed scenes of action that the
studios could not themselves create. But when the military was not

involved, compliance was more discretionary. Alan, for one, would not lend his name to revisionist history:

> [August 4, 1944] The OWI wants us to play down the degree of law-lessness in Texas in 1877. The hell with them. I can grudgingly sub-scribe to giving one-sided pictures of other nations, but limitations upon the actual facts of our own history I simply cannot go for.
>
> [August 7, 1944] Looks like this week, too, will be spent on *San Antonio*. The tentative credit reads "Original Screenplay by Alan LeMay and W.R. Burnett." This is robbery, but it will be better for me not to protest. They had Burnett on it for about 20 weeks, and it will not help, politically, for me to insist on showing up everybody as throwing away time and money to no purpose at all.
>
> I may try the noon handball again, but without the dieting. Last time I lost 9 pounds in 10 days, but knocked myself out.

The *Calamity Jane* script neared completion in September with the usual schedule crunch and editing problems:

> [September 9, 1944] Finally completed the first draft of *Calamity* only about 70 pages too long (220 vs. 150). Now comes the hard part, while the producer gets gay, intruding 10,000 ill-considered off-the-cuff ideas, which have to be absorbed in some fashion, or why is he a producer?
>
> [September 12, 1944] I think that what has swamped me is that Dave Butler, director of *San Antonio*, keeps burning up my time with nig-gling little changes, though I am not even on that picture any more. Whereas I greatly need to get forward fast with *Calamity Jane*, lest we lose our priority with Ann Sheridan. She is back from her Pacific tour, and a musical script is already completed for her, by Leonard Lee.

Leonard Lee's musical script was *The Time, the Place, and the Girl.* Warner's wanted to make that next, but Ann Sheridan refused the part, preferring the title role of Calamity Jane. After months of argument, Sheridan was suspended by Warner Brothers, and *Calamity Jane* was deferred indefinitely. (Several years later, Doris Day played Calamity Jane in a musical, directed by David Butler, that won an Oscar.)

This was not an isolated case of studio politics and star power running the show. Alan's next assignment was dictated by Errol Flynn's contract and the Warner Brothers legal department, as Alan explained in a letter to his father:

> [October 25, 1944] I am now working on a job called "The Frontiers-man." I don't know what this is about exactly, we have not found out as yet. It is a tanglefoot that has already bucked down two writers and gotten them fired. But it isn't going to buck me off because I am not going to get aboard it. We will cook some little thing of our own. Mug wump ga boo (the damn fool is chewing gum — Gus)

The reason that I am dictating this is that I sprained my ankle and am supposed to keep my foot higher than my head, making typewriting difficult.

[November 11, 1944] The purpose of this unfortunate purchase [*The Frontiersman*] was to fulfill a pending deal. A contract with one of our stars [Flynn] calls for submitting a property by last Nov. 1. If no property is submitted, the star has a right to go make a picture outside. This, with our man shortage, and our short contract list, would very literally be a million dollar disaster to the company.

So they started in plenty of time to make a satisfactory property out of THE FRONTIERSMAN. The property proved unscriptable. One of our wheel-horse contract writers spent seven weeks on it, and produced nothing but a botch. He ended by tossing the assignment back to the studio heads, with a few well chosen words regarding their sanity. He isn't with us any more.

Next they sent out and brought in a veteran writer with more than thirty pictures to his credit. He struggled for nine weeks, and produced a hopeless mess, then gave up. He isn't with us any more, either.

Sixteen weeks had now been spent, and no script, and the time was up, and nothing to do but submit the original 99 pages. At this point they assigned me to do the ultimate script.

I took a look at it, and perceived to my horror that the job could never be scripted, or if scripted could never be shot, or if shot could never be released, or if released would be a dismal, history-making flop.

Hurriedly I drew up a bill of changes, three pages long, transforming the thing completely into something I could do. This met with cheers from all quarters except the legal department. The lawyers said that my 3 pages could not be called a property; and that if the star (Flynn) accepted the 99 page property, he could not later be given a script so radically changed as I proposed. Squash.

So now I saw that if the star accepted — and who can say what a star will do? — I was trapped. I could script the original and bring in a flop, and be a dead pigeon, or I could tell the heads that they must be nuts, and be a dead pigeon much easier.

But, a complication. Lately 4 producers have been given the old heave-ho out of here (Lasky included). My proper object becomes that of stepping into the place of one of them, as a writer-producer. This I am told I can do. They have said that they are grooming me up for a producer-ship within the next six months. Probably won't happen. Most likely the bunk. But my idea is that I have to keep ramming away at anything that even faintly resembles a hole in the line. Mustn't give up now.

After countless false starts, trying to satisfy the producer, the star, and the legal department, the opposition was worn down and Alan had an acceptable treatment. It was a major change, as it had to be.

Up I come with a whole new property, under the old title. Cheers. The old property, known to the writing staff as "the kiss of death," thrown out, done away with. Green light on the picture, to be done my way.

Al Blum, my business manager, tells me that if I can keep on just like I'm doing, I can quit, in ten years more. Well, we will try. Sure hope this old wreck of a typewriter won't start bleeding at the wheels. Don't know when we'll get another.

As *San Antonio* neared release, the in-house reviews were good. News like this was important in giving Alan more authority in his daily conferences as he wrestled with the script for *The Frontiersman*.

[January 10, 1945] Jack Warner has now seen *San Antonio*, as have his key distribution and audience evaluation men, and all are extremely enthusiastic. They admit now that they were very worried, because of the $2 million cost, and Flynn slipping, and the director never having made a Western before. But now they say it is a cinch; and in the bag, and will make — not gross, make — between $3,000,000 and $5,000,000. So now I am a hero in the very limited way a writer can be in this industry.

While still tied up on *The Frontiersman*, Alan nearly got a crack at *The Treasure of the Sierra Madre,* which was a sleeper that was later to become a Bogart classic. But the timing did not work out.

Last Sunday and the Sunday before I spent studying a novel called "Treasure of the High Sierras." It has been kicking around here for the last eight years, and nobody has known how to screen it; for one thing, no women in it, all male cast. But I had a tip from my agents that if I broke the story I could probably direct it, since it won't be expensive. So I broke it. Then found out that Vincent Sherman is already scheduled to direct it. O well ...I also think Carthage should be destroyed.

By March 1945, Alan had been working on *The Frontiersman* for five months, and the constant struggle with what he had considered from the outset to be bad material was wearing him down.

I am tireder and tireder, and working slower and slower; the third scene from the end of the script has held me up for a week. To apply my mind to setting down anything makes me feel like I am crawling around on broken glass. After coming all this way it is a shame to give up and fold. The time may have come when, if I can set down one more line of any description, it will have to be one more line on the script. I don't know whether there is any possibility that I can finish. But I have to try. Nobody ever understands this.

But three weeks later his attitude changed dramatically:

[April 6, 1945] Well, I finally completed THE FRONTIERSMAN, cut, rewrite, and all, amid gratifying applause. Flynn says, "magnificent achievement — best script I ever saw." Mark Hellinger is very pleased, and suggests we get together on some kind of independent project, outside. No others have seen it, or at least none have reported, except Arlene, who says it is a hell of a good story, and Virginia, [Gus] who says it is the best Western in the world.

Many and many a time I never expected to get it done. But it is done, and no longer contains any trace of the bum property I was stuck with in the first place. I'll get solo original screenplay credit, I should think. Unless something unpredictable goes wrong.

So Monday I go up front to pitch for a break. My agent will go along, to see that I don't give too much away. I will try to sell them an original idea I have, I to write and direct. At second best I will take a chance as producer on something. Failing these, I will try to get free for a lay-off and write my stage show...

Which means that I will have to write my original by Monday, in at least brief treatment form. So I guess I'd better get going at it.

After cleaning up these details, Alan did actually take a break. He and Arlene spent the last week of April at the Smoke Tree Ranch in Palm Springs. While relaxing there he still wrote his father nearly every day.

[April 20, 1945] You asked me about the status of my pictures, as to when you'll see one. This is the dope:

San Antonio, scheduled for release sometime in 1946. All shot, scored, and ready.

Along Came Jones, shot, scored, sneak-viewed and ready to go, release unannounced.

Calamity Jane, production deferred, because of suspension of Ann Sheridan, for refusal to appear in musical, "The Time, the Place, and the Girl."

The Frontiersman, solo original LeMay (very rare credit on a biggie), to be produced immediately following Flynn's "Don Juan." Probably next summer.

But for the moment we are sunning lazily in the prettiest, airiest cottage you ever saw, very isolated.

The rest improved his mood as he returned to the grind at Warner's.

[May 1, 1945] Well, here we are back again, feeling very strong and healthy, and the color of an old boot. I seem to be scripting a very bad new novel by Stephen Longstreet, entitled STALLION ROAD — a phony man and a phony book. It is all about horse people in California, except that in the book California, the horses, and the people are all unrecognizable as such. It is all a singularly fatuous never-never country of Mr. Longstreet's self-isolated head. The story is amazingly weak and pointless, and the background, to a horseman, is a howl.

However, it has one advantage, and that is that it is not a Western, so we will shuck off our coat, roll up our sleeves, and see what we can do.

And the pressure will go on directly, because I should immensely like to finish the script before my option comes up July 1. However, for the present I will attempt daily notes again, at least for a while.

The reason I am anxious to finish before option time is so that if I want some kind of a dicker, for release, or for a better deal, or anything, there won't be a confusing uncompleted job in the fire. I don't know now what I want to ask for then.

At this point (May 1945), the infamous Hollywood strike began to look like it was going to be more than an inconvenience.

[May 2, 1945] ... The strike is completely deadlocked, and may close down production for the summer. It is purely Jurisdictional, no wages, hours, or working conditions involved. If the studios concede to the strikers the opposition (AFL) will close every theatre in the country by pulling out the projectionists. WLB [War Labor Board] decides in favor of the strikers, but AFL is stronger than the government.

No I shouldn't have said AFL. Both strikers and opposition are AFL. The hell with it.

[May 8, 1945] V-E day [end of World War II in Europe], having been built up with a view solely to anti-climax, is not recognizable here as anything but a work day. Could be the studio will go drunk later, but I very much doubt it.

In fickle Hollywood, a good record of credits does not buy any security at all. This is why Alan always seemed to be pushing for the next script, overworked but fearing to turn down the next urgent job, because conditions can change instantly, as they did late in May 1945. Alan described how studio politics and the strike ended his contract with Warner's:

[June 5, 1945] The long delay in communication this time was due to a temporary uncertainty in my immediate affairs, resulting, as of now, that I am entirely detached from Warner's.

This began with a disagreement with Alex Gottlieb about the treatment of "Stallion Road." He thought the story, as I rearranged and modified it, was terrific, and I didn't think it was good enough.

This resulted in my immediate lay-off about two weeks ago, complicated by the imminent arrival of my option date, which was yesterday. The interim was taken up by a great deal of vacillation; you're in, you're out, you're fired, no, it's all a mistake, you're solid, no you're not, he's up, he's down, he's up, ad nauseum. Saturday afternoon Trilling told Hellinger I was built in solidly, and Saturday night he told Alan Miller I was dropped.

Complicating features other than the Gottlieb disagreement: Classification of me as a high-cost-production man, tops chiefly in giant Westerns; a falling box-office making high cost productions defunct; a general retrenchment panic from the same cause; a current Warner's ceiling on writers' prices, so that I was already getting virtually their top price; a general clean-out of the upper bracket writers, such that no top-rating writer has had his option picked up out there this year; a bitter quarrel between Jack Warner and his wife, who has a new boy friend, and whose activities always result in savage explosions at the office (all directors' secretaries were fired the day before my disagreement with Gottlieb, and all producers pared down to one secretary). Etc.

So now I am officially free-lance. I am going out to Universal tomorrow to talk about a writer-director assignment but I think it is just a general conversation, nothing specific. Most especially I am interested in writing an original — working title "Medicine Show" — which I may possibly write as an original screenplay, a serial, and a novel. I think not as a stage musical, which I originally contemplated, but is apparently too involved a project. The screen rights may be in collaboration with Mark Hellinger, who is also detaching himself from Warner's sometime between July and November; he is dynamite, with many high-powered connections.

Which is about all I know about this now.

Stallion Road, which is about a veterinarian, was finally produced in 1947, but not without difficulty. A long parade of writers tried it and failed. Then William Faulkner wrote a treatment that was acceptable, and the author of the original novel, Stephen Longstreet, wrote the screenplay. Humphrey Bogart and Lauren Bacall, fresh from their hit *The Big Sleep*, were asked to play the leads, but they refused, calling it a poor "B" picture, and got suspended. Ronald Reagan, Alexis Smith, and Zachary Scott finally signed on, but the results were not great. Alan did well to stay clear of this one.

The Frontiersman apparently was stopped by the strike. By the time the strike ended, there could have been conflicts with Flynn's schedule, or a reluctance to spend money on a "Big Picture." For whatever reason it quietly disappeared.

—16—

The Walking Hills

This film started out as *Spanish Crossing*, had *Spanish Crossing* as the working title, and then had its name changed to *The Walking Hills* at the last minute. It had nothing to do with a short short story that Alan wrote more than a decade earlier that carried the same name.[1] That story was about a barroom confrontation in a town named Spanish Crossing.

The present screenplay is a completely different story about a group of modern day treasure hunters searching for a wagon load of gold buried long before by the blowing sand dunes (the walking hills) in Death Valley. It was an unremarkable film, but Alan's main objective in writing it on his own was to use it as a vehicle to get his first directing job; in fact, he made its sale conditional upon his directing. So the film had to be kept to a reasonably low budget for a producer to take the risk on Alan's first experience as a rookie director.

Ultimately, Alan was unable to hold out for a deal on those terms because he began to run into financial troubles. His problems resulted from high taxes and too many deferred salary participation deals. In the end, he had to give up on directing the film because he needed the cash from the sale.

During the spring of 1946, Alan's agent did an effective job of promoting the project around Hollywood. Interest was shown by a number of organizations, but each offer had a show-stopping contingency. The big if hovers over every project because filmmaking requires so many different inputs all at once. It needs financing, a distributor for release, commitments from the stars, space on sound stages, a plethora of signed contracts, and a producer to put it all together. It also needs a screenplay, a writer, and a director, but Alan was to provide those.

More often than not, the parts did not all come together, despite enthusiasm over the script. Alan reported on many offers in his letters to his father, but seldom with any confidence that a deal would be made. For example:

[April 6, 1946] Went out and saw Hal Roach Jr., [Hal Roach, Jr. had played on the Riviera Polo Club team that visited Rancho Una Vaca in 1937] and pitched for a writer-producer-director deal. He says he will take it if the releases he is dickering for work out.

The releases worked out, as announced in *The Hollywood Reporter*, and for a short time the prospect was rosy. But nothing happened. At the same time Alan was working on the script and, with less free time to exercise, waging a concerted battle with his weight.

[April 23, 1946] Last week had Hal Roach flirting with idea of setting up an independent company, solely to have me write and direct *Spanish Crossing*, Roach to provide money and space, but release to be MGM. This would triple my income within two years. Guess it blew over.

Diet doctor has me on [a diet], with view to reducing me 30 pounds, down to old 165. Cut off only 12 pounds in 4 weeks. This is at 750 calories a day. This week: Mon, weighed 182, consumed 750 calories, jogged 12 laps; Tues, weighed 183, consumed 750 calories, jogged 25 laps; what goes on here?

Talked to Dr. MacDonald about a rat experiment. My theory:

(1) Senility is in great part caused by densification of the interstitial reticular collagenous tissue which forms a matrix for all body cells. (As in Bogolometz premise.)

(2) Vitamin C is an essential growth element, and in adults specifically is concerned with the maintenance of the collagenous tissue.

(3) Maybe the excess vitamin C recommended in all diets nowadays is occasioning undue prosperity in this reticular tissue.

(4) Maybe rats limited to the minimum vitamin C necessary to avoid morbid symptoms will live longer than those given plenty of salad. He's going to help me set up the experiment.

Alan suggested that I might want to raise a few hundred white mice for this experiment, since I had always had strange pets. The idea faded quickly, and nothing experimental was ever done, but it showed that Alan's acrobatic mind covered far more territory than just Western plots. It might still make a good term project for a bright student. Meanwhile,

[May 1, 1946] Hal Roach is still dickering with MGM for added releases, dissatisfied with their terms. But he says, with such definiteness as can be had at this range, that if he signs, I am in (to write and direct *Spanish Crossing* on a percentage).

Many other deals were offered, usually dependent on something else happening. As he juggled the several prospects, still working to land a director's job while writing the screenplay for *Spanish Crossing*, his extreme dieting was sapping his energy.

[May 2, 1946] Aw, whoa is me, I folded like a shot snipe in the middle of yesterday's work, and only got five pages. So weak and dragged down I could scarcely hold my damn head up, let alone carry the ball. So I had to ease up on the diet some, last night. Still weigh 179 today. But I think I may be able to do my two miles, this PM. This thing is going to take months longer than I thought, which is bad, because my clothes don't fit (after a loss of 16 pounds) and I have 14 pounds to go, so I am caught in mid-stream with nothing to wear. I go around town looking like a man trying to fumble his way out of a collapsed tent.

A few days later, the diet and exercise regimen was canceled as a failure.

[May 6, 1946] Oh, pickles. Came to consciousness with scarcely the strength of a cat today. Doctor was appalled to hear I had been exercising; said the 750 diet was the same for which he hospitalized most people. Forbid all exercise, and took me off the diet for two weeks, to get my strength back. All to do over.

Hal Roach says that if I don't take his proposition, when and if he makes it, whatever it is, he will nevertheless be able to make me a deal on stage space, the key thing right now. You can have star, script, money, and release, and be nowhere today unless you have some in on stage space.

Nothing had jelled by the time Alan finished the screenplay, but a widening scope of potential collaborators was getting a look at it. As usual, responses were favorable but no one could put all the resources together at once. Scripts were being read by Robert Taylor, Fred MacMurray, Pat O'Brian, and others. Hal Roach, Jr., was still working on putting something together. Each of Alan's letters over the next several weeks had some sort of comment about selling a package deal on *Spanish Crossing*. Of all the proposals, the one showing the most promise was from Harry Joe Brown:

[May 28, 1946] ... Harry Joe Brown, who produced and directed scores of pictures for MGM, is now independent, with a tie-up with Randy Scott. He has asked to see *Spanish Crossing*, at the suggestion of Johnny Miles. I released a copy for him.

This turned out to be the contact that worked. With Harry Joe Brown, the pieces began to fall into place. He was a former producer for MGM with a long record going back through *Captain Blood*, and *The Rains Came,* now independent. The proposal required that Randy Scott agree to do it, but he was in the middle of filming at RKO and had no time to read the script. Brown had a Zane Grey story, *Twin Sombreros,* he wanted Alan to script for Randy first, after which they would make *Spanish Crossing* if the bank would agree to Alan directing.

Scott's schedule, and a long list of other complications, dictated the deferral of *Spanish Crossing* until after the Zane Grey picture. Alan accepted a participation deal on the *Twin Sombreros* script, and started work on it immediately. He had a loose agreement with Brown on *Spanish Crossing* and so withdrew it from the market. He was happy to postpone the contract negotiations with Brown until after he finished *Twin Sombreros* because he was optimistic that a good job on that would improve his negotiating position.

The weeks dragged into months, with Randy Scott fulfilling three other commitments, and Alan finishing *Twin Sombreros*, which he usually referred to as *Twin Hats*. It was a participation deal, however, so Alan was not getting paid. Once more he had to fall back onto his family as he wrote to his father:

> [November 11, 1946] Now that TWIN SOMBREROS is wrapped up, such as it is, I have returned to waiting out a deal on SPANISH CROSSING. Pretty good chance of a United Artist release, produced by Sam Bischoff in color, Randolph Scott starring, and LeMay directing. I could have got a deal several times if I had not insisted on directing.
>
> Meantime, due to deferred salary for the second half of the year and having put the earlier part of the year on SPANISH CROSSING, and the government being what it is, I am now stony broke. If my most favorable deal on SPANISH CROSSING goes through I will get about $50,000 next May. But nothing meanwhile. Can you let me have $15,000 for six months?

The anticipated United Artists release was suddenly put on hold for several months by a row that broke out among Chaplin, Selznick and Pickford, the three owners. Nothing could get through the quarreling board. In the meantime Alan "graciously accepted an assignment (that means my agent got me a job, thank God)" scripting *Tap Roots*.

By June 1947 Alan still had no firm contract on *Spanish Crossing*, but he reported that Harry Joe Brown's deal appeared to be close. It fell through two weeks later because Randy Scott refused to ever work with Brown again. There was no reason given, but that's Hollywood.

So Alan graciously accepted another day job at Paramount while working nights on a full screenplay of *Spanish Crossing*, now under the title of *The Walking Hills*. He had also been working on setting up his own company, and at this point had financial backing but no star.

As 1947 came to a close, he wrote a Christmas Eve letter to his father summarizing his plans and accomplishments:

> [December 24, 1947] This has been a fairly good year for me. I worked 32 weeks, enabling me to break even with the government. The other 20 weeks I variously advanced my novel to sixty pages, closely outlined and rough-drafted a play in collaboration with Bill Holm, and actually

completed the new version of SPANISH CROSSING, under the new
title of THE WALKING HILLS.

This latter has gone on the market and my agents are happily offering
it at a price which will very nicely represent all I need to make in
1948 — if they get it. They swear they are about to get it. But I want to
see the certified check.

I also have coming early in 1948 the ten weeks' salary I deferred on
THE GUNFIGHTERS in 1946. This is certain. I also have 5% of the
net profit on THE GUNFIGHTERS coming, for working on deferred
salary. THE GUNFIGHTERS has turned out to be a great astonishing
sleeper, and is a cinch to net half a million on a nut of only three-
quarters of a million, which is very fast ball carrying these days.

So even if THE WALKING HILLS does not come through, I figure
I have held my own again. And, with THE WALKING HILLS, I have
at least come closer to writing my way out of this trap than I ever have
before. So I will simply try to come still closer in 1948. I can't come
closer forever without knocking one of these years over.

I also completed TAP ROOTS for Walter Wanger. This went
through a sneak preview the other night with the utmost acclaim. It is
probably the best picture I ever worked on.

In the course of this year we adopted Mark Logan LeMay.

I also stained the floor of the back porch and my woodshed, and
painted my woodshed, and built a new shade garden near the back porch.

And that is all I did in 1947.

* * *

During this period, Alan was still dreaming of escaping from Hollywood, and in fact wanted to put some distance between his family and the
concentrated targets of civilization. He got as far as systematically scoring
possible destinations, but not quite as far as going there.

[January 2, 1948] ... I personally believe an atomic war with Russia to
be quite possible within the next seven years. I do not see how Los
Angeles, with its tremendous air concentration, can rate much better than
target number three. I would feel much more comfortable if my family
were not so high on the list for irradiation. Too, I expect the breakdown
of communications under atomic bombardment to cause dreadful conditions of famine and other forms of death in the affected areas; notably
this area, which can survive about a week with the railroads out. The
pictures of skull-faced women, carrying toothpick babies as they pick
over the garbage dumps of Europe impress me very much.

That this could happen here may indeed be very improbable — but I
don't know that. And I believe in trying to do something about foresee-
able possibilities. What I should like is a few acres someplace in a tacti-
cally remote community, with a hoard of basic food elements sufficient
to give me time to get a little primitive agriculture going. Say basic sus-
tenance for one year.

Among the places I have been considering are Peru, Chile, Papeete (Tahiti), Pago-Pago (American Samoa), Hilo (Hawaii), and Honolulu. But I have struck off Peru, Chile and Tahiti because I feel certain that Arlene would never be happy or feel secure under a foreign flag.

I very seriously considered Pago-Pago, which at least has a naval base such that you can get medical attention. But there are no educational facilities for the children.

This last objection also applies to Hilo.

That leaves Honolulu. I do not think Honolulu will be considered as strategic in the Russian war. Well-placed friends assure me that I hold this view in common with the army and navy; this time we are going to fight across the top of the world. But Honolulu has many of the same disadvantages as Los Angeles. The over-crowding is very bad, and the housing situation compares to our own. Everything except fish, poi, sugar, pineapples, coconuts, beef, and pekaki leis has to be imported, and eggs are $1.60 a dozen. Household help, which used to be a great attraction there, is now $1.00 an hour, same as here.

But lately we have had another thought. What about the stern and rock-bound farms of New England as an atomic refuge? It looks to me as though Pinhook [the farm of Alan's sister and brother-in-law near Groton, Massachusetts] is about as safe as anyplace I can think of. The hills and atmospheric drift should make Pinhook safe, even if Boston was atomized, which I scarcely expect. And it would be nice to have the family more nearly together again.

Alan never acted on these ideas, but this letter supports his previous essays on worry (see Chapter 4) to show that he valued a strong defense against all dangers, real or perceived.

The Walking Hills was finally produced by Harry Joe Brown, and starred Randolph Scott and Ella Raines. The credits are interesting, because the producers are listed as Harry Joe Brown *and* Randolph Scott. The surprising co-producer credit may explain why Randy reversed himself on never working with Harry again. The writing credits were: story by Alan LeMay, screenplay by Alan LeMay, and additional dialogue by Virginia Roddick (his long-time secretary, Gus). Alan did not object to sharing credit, he merely objected to sharing credit with those he saw as hindrances that had been fired off the picture.

The film was released through Columbia in 1949 and one review called it "a terrific little treasure hunt movie." It was obviously not high budget, and ran only 78 minutes. Alan had finally given up on his objective of directing the film as part of the deal. It was directed by John Sturges, who had good credentials and later directed *The Magnificent Seven.* One review said he did "extremely well with this little sleeper."

—17—

The Business of Filmmaking

It was all about the money. Alan did not like writing for films. He appreciated the medium for its ability to show spectacular scenes, but he did not adapt well to being saddled with a parade of collaborators, nor to being edited by producers and directors. He knuckled down and endured the frustrations because he could make a lot of money very fast, although wartime taxes took a huge percentage. He had spent so many years worrying about money, being broke and borrowing, being self-employed without a safety net, that making money nearly became an obsession. Here is his early opinion of Hollywood in 1940, as expressed in a letter to his parents, after he had been at Paramount for barely five months:

> [October 31, 1940] The only thing that can be said for it is that there is a certain amount of money in it. My new business manager functions primarily by seeing that we are personally broke at all times. Probably he has other functions, but I wouldn't know what they are. I have an allowance of $12 a week, a little less, if I remember correctly, than I made in a lumber camp at the age of seventeen. The business manager collects the money and dispenses it in the necessary channels, such as rent, and the actual money we ever see is very little. However, he undertakes to carry all expenses, commissions and tax reserves, and pay himself (he gets about 4%) and set aside $1,500 a month savings. This is better than I can do without him.
>
> Incidentally, my pay goes up to $750 tomorrow in accordance with the terms of the time limitation agreement I made when I took on this job. We are in fairly good shape. The manager believes that he could finance us for about a year of independent writing on what we now have. This is comforting because I should not be at all surprised if Paramount would attempt to do away with the raise in pay, in which case I will, of course, walk out.

Salaries were always quoted per week, which is appropriate considering how quickly writers were hired and fired. And inflation makes the numbers look unreasonably low. The Consumer Price Index (CPI) was 15 in 1941, and 205 in 2007, meaning that wages and prices from 1941 should be multiplied by fourteen to get 2007 rates. Thus the $750 salary would translate into $10,500 per week in modern dollars, and his $1500 per month savings would add up to a 2007 value of more than $250,000 per year, (before taxes) *if* the work were steady. And with Roosevelt's wartime increases, income taxes became confiscatory.

As a writer of novels and short stories, Alan was accustomed to sharing the credit with no one. But there is much more to producing a film than there is to publishing a story, so the writer in Hollywood becomes a smaller frog in the pond. After nearly two years in pictures, Alan understood how the system worked, and he could see that he was in the wrong end of it. He decided that what he really needed to do, both for profit and for artistic control, was to produce his own films. While still at Paramount, he explained the system to his parents:

[April 6, 1941] The more I see of this, the more I am sure that the people who are doing the work are not getting the money in this. Aside from the capital profit and the studio overhead, the producers, associate (assistant) producers, and the directors are getting the money in the order named. As thus:

Pictures are principally sold on the basis of a percentage of total take which the exhibiting houses kick back to the studio. The stronger the picture, the higher the percentage, e.g., *Philadelphia Story* cost 30% kicked back by the exhibitor from his take. This is a high percentage. The picture did well above average business, but the exhibitors could not make money at this price. NWMP [*North West Mounted Police*] got 40%—super-high; but does such a business that the exhibitors are making money. Lesser pictures pay on down as low as 15% or 10%, and the worst play for a small flat price from the exhibitor.

The amount which the exhibitors pay to the producing company is known as the Gross. NWMP will take nearly twelve million, grossing thereby around four and a half million.

"Cost of negative" is what it takes to write, prepare, and photograph the picture, cast, salaries, etc. This is 62% of total cost, the rest going into distribution and promotion. Cost of negative on NWMP was $1,425,000; bringing total cost to 2-¼ million. Thus NWMP doubled its money, and showed a profit of $2,250,000.

Leaving out some complicated details, in which DeMille puts up $100,000 temporarily as an income tax dodge (but gets back first $100,000 of gross)—DeMille's deal is for *50% of profit*, paid to him partially in advance in the form of salary, the rest as it is made (trailing out over several years). Thus DeMille will make $1,125,000 on NWMP.

Of this, DeMille will pay Bill Pine (Associate Producer) 10% of what DeMille himself gets. Thus Pine gets $112,500.

Cost of script was about $72,000. Most of this was wasted or overhead, for I myself wrote between 96 and 98% of the actual shooting script for a little less than $12,000.

Entire detail of production — everything from schedules and props to background business and chalk marks for the actors to walk on — was worked out by assistant directors; mainly by Eddie Salven, who probably gets $125 a week and not over $150. Entire coaching of actors and supernumeries was done by Eric Stacy (probably $175 a week, not over $250); Eddie Salven; and Eddie Maxwell, (maybe $100 a week). All business and accounting detail was handled by the business manager (small salary). All trick film work and special effects by Edouart Fascio; scene and set design by staff artists; camera work and lights by camera men and electricians — all on low pay. All this, including my salary, which came to one half of one per cent of the profit, came out of negative cost, however, not out of the profit, which was shared by the company and the producers.

The above is a pretty good general picture of the financial breakdown, except that the producer in this case directed it himself. A salaried first director would have been highly paid.

The producer, who profited so handsomely, made the decisions, all the way. Otherwise he confined himself to dealing out the nastiest insults he could think of to everybody but the stars, who were big enough to walk out.

The Associate Producer ($112,500) communicated the Producer's wishes to the people who carried them out, and nagged everybody, and yessed the Producer.

Now, I have not been to the trouble of finding out how all this worked merely to have something to beef about, or to demonstrate social injustice. I am convinced that the greatest contribution to the success was that of the writer. The writer constructed the screen story, wrote the dialog for the stars (Cooper's useless until a writer tells him what to say), described the sets, specified the camera movements, delineated in the most complete detail every movement that anybody made upon the screen. Excellent but low paid technicians then brought it to the screen.

I do not feel the need of the producer to stand by my shoulder making decisions in the form of continually cursing my work. That was all he did. Accordingly I do not need the producer. Yet he took all the profit, a lion's share of the credit, and I took a relatively tiny wage.

So now I begin to have a theory about how this perhaps ought to be done. A Class A script is conceded to be worth $75,000 (ready to shoot, I mean). Hollywood writers seldom prepare a shooting script independently, however, because they never get enough money ahead. Non-Hollywood writers just don't know how, any more than I did, before the last 94 weeks I have spent in apprenticeship.

But I do have enough money ahead to give me considerable latitude. I also have another advantage: I have serial and book markets for every story I construct, which other screenwriters do not, with but few exceptions.

After two more successes on the screen — if I can get them, and I think I can — a course such as this will be open to me:

I schedule my time, say, to produce one picture every 16 months. I spend ten months on my story, which will be in screenplay outline first, then developed into a smash serial and as promising a book as possible. I convert this to screen play in one month, I dicker one month, and make a profit-splitting deal to produce the picture myself. One month to prepare to shoot, three months shooting.

My advantages in making the deal are that I go to the company with a complete script, ready for quick action, with no element of uncertainty, and no initial script cost. That is, I have $75,000 in my hand in script form, and a sure shooting script already in the bag. They get this for nothing except a split of the *profits* if any.

I have lost not one minute of my time; because ten months is what I intend to put on my next serial anyway. More time is the next necessary step to better work.

And, failing the production contract, I will certainly get something for the script — at least $25,000, and perhaps the $75,000.

It's the old story — if you can't beat 'em, join 'em!

Once in production I am confident of great success, because I feel that the success of a picture *really* depends upon its script, and there I am upon my own sure ground. As producer, I can assure that dumb direction will not prevent the story clearly reaching the screen.

Producers, predictably, take a different view. Former producer Lawrence Turman, producer of *The Graduate, The Flim-Flam Man,* and others, wrote a book entitled *So You Want to Be a Producer* (Three Rivers Press, 2005) in which he said:

> The producer is the person who shows up on set only when there's trouble, and then causes more trouble, cell phone in one hand, bull-whip in the other. His or her range of responsibilities might include, but not be limited to, arranging for a film's financing, commissioning and shaping the screenplay, hiring the director and actors and crew, approving the shooting schedule, making product-placement deals, helping with marketing and publicity and fielding the endless day-to-day problems that come up at every turn.
>
> The producer does all the hard work on a film and gets none of the glory. But it's the producer, and only the producer, who accepts the Academy Award for best picture.

In Alan's drive to become a producer, there was a catch 22: he needed a successful record *as a producer* to obtain the financing needed for producing an expensive "A" picture. Most producers had worked their way up through cheap "B" pictures, but Alan had started at the top with DeMille, had a reputation for writing big outdoor pictures, and was not willing to go through the cheap-picture apprenticeship. This hurdle kept him from producing his own films for several years.

In the meantime, he built his reputation as a screenwriter. The Hollywood publication *Box Office* is the authority on ratings, its strength resulting from its distribution to almost every motion picture exhibitor in the country. Monthly and yearly they rate the pictures, the stars, the directors, the producers, and the writers based on the box office draw reported by the exhibitors. The ratings are in comparison with the normal or average business for each show house. The writers are rated in two categories, one for original story and one for screenplay. When the annual ratings came out in November 1941, Alan was rated number one in the industry in original story (170 percent of "average") for *North West Mounted Police*, and also number one in screenplay for the same production. Alan modestly, (or realistically), said the award was "a fluky thing ... if it were repeated a few times it would begin to mean something."

After two and a half years in Hollywood, Alan could analyze his market and explain what it meant to his own future. It was a week after the assault on Pearl Harbor when he wrote the following letter to his parents. It shows a total preoccupation with his job, and remarkably, has no mention of the new war with Japan:

> [December 14, 1941] Hollywood is still using about seven hundred picture scripts a year, although this number is falling somewhat. The reason it is falling is that the steady effort to get away from double features is producing some gradual effect. The production of what are called stream liners, which are a cross between a short subject and a feature picture, is being used to wean the masses of public away from the double feature with very good effect. We may get down to about four hundred pictures a year, which will be a great thing for everybody except those who write the worst of the scripts.
>
> Nobody has seven hundred good stories a year, nor four hundred good stories. The cheapest productions, about one hundred and fifty of them, use the same stories all the time, hashing and re-hashing them according to simple formulae. This still leaves a great dearth of scripts with any idea behind them and any really competitive talent in the development of them.
>
> The haunted look that all producers have comes from a great number of causes such as the knives they are always sticking in each other, but one of the main causes, I think now, is the lack of decent scripts that they can take out and shoot.
>
> When a producer is under contract to produce six pictures a year or

three pictures a year or two pictures a year, the difficulty of getting hold of something that he can actually take out and shoot and call a picture, haunts him night and day.

If it is possible that a creditable and shootable script can go begging around here, this is something I need to find out. The impression persists among writers that hundreds of good stories go begging, but I think I see where this impression develops.

The average producer does not have much imagination and when a treatment of a few pages is offered him, he less readily sees an imaginative thing that he can make of it than simply the memory of other pictures something like it that he has seen.

This gives him the impression that in buying a good workable treatment that really could be developed and made, he is making a sucker of himself by buying a re-hash he thinks he has already seen. On the other hand if it does not remind him of things he has seen he does not think it is any good at all. [This perfectly describes today's endless parade of re-makes, sequels, and me-too copy cats, both in movies and in TV.]

I think this accounts for the fact that good workable treatments are not sold around here, while terrific prices are paid for novels that have no screen possibilities whatever. The producer has simply accepted the public ballyhoo in place of the imagination which he himself does not have. This same difficulty may also apply — I may learn — to a fully developed script under my name. But I do not believe it, and will have to try it and fall down at it before I am convinced.

It should also be noted that a movie made from a novel seldom compares well with the original book. The picture usually seems shallow, and sometimes contains little of the original story. A practical reason for this is that the number of scenes, the detail, and the character development possible in a 300-page book greatly exceeds what can be shown in a couple of hours. So why do the studios buy novels when the associated films are unrecognizable derivatives? One answer is that the public acceptance of a good novel will carry over to the gate for the film.

But a no less important reason is the plagiarism risk. Warner Bros. paid $100,000 in 1994 for the rights to *The Searchers,* purportedly with a plan to make it into a sci-fi space odyssey. (Mercifully, that idea died.) A version like that could hardly be called plagiarism, but the theory is that it is cheaper to buy the rights than to pay the lawyers to prove it is not a derivative.

* * *

Through the latter part of the war, and the devastating union strike, the studios had seen their profits eroded by excessive taxation and union featherbedding. Alan wrote to his father about the financial problems of

Hollywood, but with his survivor's cunning he suggested that he might be able to take advantage of the changing situation to attain his goal of becoming a writer-producer.

[September 19, 1947] You probably heard nothing about the British ad valorem tax on American films, but it has created a major diastrophism in my industry. I looked up ad valorem but was unable to understand what it means. Actually, however, it is a 75% tax upon anything American films earn in the United Kingdom. The stroke is so severe that the American producers have shut off all export of films to England. (GUNFIGHTERS fortunately got in before the tax.)

The blow is more serious than it sounds. The rule of thumb has been that you try to get back your cost domestically, and make your profit on the British return. Other outlets, such as re-dubbed foreign language, don't amount to much. Actually, as nearly as I can find out, the lost British market has represented about 20% of our total take.

The psychological effect of this blow on the industry is for the time being more important than the actual loss. The effect is much worse than the simple removal of the promise of profit. For one thing the blow coincides with an expected recession of unpredictable depth in the domestic market. Many pictures which have in the past shown a profit or broken even, may expect to sustain severe losses in the present situation.

First actual effect has been the suspension or entire folding of most of the independents. These are the companies which, while they release through the major companies, make their pictures on their own hooks, without the major studio's facilities and contract players. Although greatly handicapped by lack of stars, the independents have been able to avoid much of the top-heavy costs which afflict the major studios; and have consequently been able to do some very profitable work. The field of the independents has been of special interest to me because it is the one in which the hired help, such as the writers and actors, can obtain participation in the profits, principally by deferring a portion of their salaries until such time as the picture upon which they have worked comes into the black. The independents are now dead. Nobody will lend them the money to shoot with, and nobody wants deferments.

The majors, on the other hand, now suddenly feel the enormous weight of their inflated costs. The inflation in picture costs have been of several kinds. One of the high costs is the huge salaries paid the stars and other quality help; raised to high levels by legitimate competitive bidding for people who have proved they can bring the money back through the box office. The high fixed costs with which the majors are stuck, partly comes from their necessity of carrying, on long contracts, these high-salaried people. Their great strength, amounting almost to monopoly, carries a corresponding penalty of enormous fixed cost.

Another important element in high picture costs is the labor situation. More than in any other industry, the Unions have been able to seize jobs and hold them for ransom. The extremely high returns upon pictures have made this possible; if one studio would balk, another would seize this opportunity to get ahead; and if all existing studios would balk, I myself would go across the street, make the pictures for which the public seems forever thirsty, and make one hundred million in a year simply by acceding to exorbitant demands.

A laborer makes a base pay of about $96 a week in pictures. But more important than this is the minute specialization the Unions have achieved in cutting up the jobs into little pieces. We have between 140 and 160 union classifications; none of which may touch any of the tools or work of any of the others. The man who plugs in the cord between the camera and the sound board can make as high as $48 a day; nobody can touch his cord and he touches nothing else, although anybody can do his work who can plug in a toaster. The $96 laborer is limited to opening and closing the big door. Usually there is nothing else there he can touch, but the door has to be opened and shut and nobody else can touch that. If a flower is to be put in a vase a green man must be present on full time. He cannot, however, move the vase. And so on, incredibly.

The loss of the British market affected everyone in Hollywood. It not only wiped out the independents, but it drove the majors into a mood of conservatism that caused the cancellation or postponement of a number of high-budget projects. Alan's job on *Davey Crockett* was shelved, leaving him once again among the unemployed.

This should have been the time for him to relax and take an extended rest. He was bone tired from his self-imposed schedule, his diet, and his lack of exercise. Instead, he viewed the situation as an opportunity. He saw a parallel between the present downturn and the Depression in 1929 that had allowed him to break into the slicks.

He was convinced that as a writer-director he could make films that would clear their costs and make a good profit in the domestic market alone. "Clear in this country" was his battle cry. He would use the situation to break into directing, and he had two prospects in mind.

Thus the actual result of the British *ad valorem* tax was not to permit Alan to take a rest. Instead, it drove him to start work on two stories at once, on a double-time schedule, without any assurance of getting paid for either one. There was no further mention of a vacation.

—18—

Independence

Alan finally achieved independence from the big studios in May 1949, by forming his own company with George "Dink" Templeton: Arfran Productions, Inc.[1] Their first film was backed by independent producer N. Peter Rathvon; Alan claimed that to get the money he had to insure himself for a million dollars and agree to die if anything went wrong, but none of that was true. The screenplay was adapted from Alan's novel *Thunder in the Dust*, and was ultimately re-titled *The Sundowners*.

Alan and Dink had lined up the key actors, and had nearly lost some of them during the inevitable waiting for the attorneys. When the legal maneuvers were finally wrapped up, Alan made the announcement to his father:

> [June 1, 1949] The papers finally did come through at long last, and we still have the essential part of the cast on the hook — Robert Preston, Chill Wills, John Barrymore Jr., Cathy Downs, and John Litel. Supported by two of the boys who worked in Old Man Coffee — Don Haggerty, my sidekick, and Jack Elam, the heavy; and by Al Overholt, at Dink's insistence, and over his own dead body. [Alan used Al Overholt as his screen name.]
>
> I would not have played in this one, except for one thing: Jack Elam, the comptroller who is trying to become an actor because he is going blind, has worked tirelessly for us without pay, on our books, budget, and certain technical arrangements such as insurance and union contracts. He is tops when it comes to knowing pictures from the CPA side. His salary as an actor is low; and he will get Al Overholt's pay, less taxes, under the table. I cannot be brittle about a few hours misery in front of the camera, when it means several hundred dollars to Jack.
>
> Well, I have fixed it so Al Overholt has only two-three lines, and little to do but ride.
>
> Now we have reservations on the plane to Amarillo for Friday morning and also Saturday morning. Looks like Saturday to me, and then only if all goes perfectly well.

Conferred with Al Colombo, our music composer yesterday. He still insists THUNDER is the best western script he has ever seen in his life.

A call to the phone. I learn that Fox is trying to power us out of our cameraman, Win Hoch, with every chance of succeeding. This will be a very bloody blow, if it lands; it could easily be a conclusive disaster.

Rathvon's attorneys took three and a half weeks to draw the money contract, and our attorneys took two and a half weeks more to read it and adjust it. I estimate the total work involved did not exceed two man-days. For this they split $3,500. Yes, I am in the wrong racket.

Loss of Win Hoch will be just one more expensive trouble attributable to the obstructionism of the legal mind. [Winton Hoch, the highly-respected camera man, did stay with LeMay-Templeton for this film.]

On the whole, I doubt that there is any possibility that I will ever break even on this project. Might lead to future opportunities, of course. I feel it to be an interesting phenomenon, however, a curiosity indeed, that Dink and I should be handed a third of a million ($386,000) with which to go and film my story in the wilds of the Panhandle.

Alan and Dink spent two weeks prowling the wilds of the Texas Panhandle, scouting locations. They were impressed by the wealth of suitable backgrounds, and the cheerful assistance of the Texans that they met. The magic glamour of Hollywood could still open a lot of doors in the outback.

[June 13, 1949] Back from Texas, where everything was handed us on a platter, and we got everything we wanted, including many irreplaceable things free. The Palo Duro Canyon exceeds all expectations; you should see the waterfalls we found.

Texas people are wonderful. We were helped particularly by Jack King, theatre owner; Gene Howe, editor (son of the Sage of Potato Hill); John Curry, cattle millionaire, whose ranch home we will overrun, in the canyon below the park; Cal Baird, 68-year-old man-killing sheriff; and Don Harrington, oil multi-millionaire.

Some of these people took days at a time driving us over the country, or flying us over it in their private planes. It is breath-taking and bewildering to find yourself among such friendly people, after ten years in the Hollywood shambles.

Now we have to explain to Rathvon why, when John Curry drawls, "Tear out anything you want to fellows; it's all yours —" there isn't any way to hand him a 27-page document to sign, full of liability releases and/or commitments to pay damages in case the party of the second part...

How to make these tarantulas understand that neither we nor all Hollywood has anything the owner of a 250,000-acre cattle ranch, with 82 oil wells on it, could possibly want? They will say, "He likes money, doesn't he?" Should I say, "He doesn't know. He's always had so much

> more than he can use, he may think it's a nuisance." Or maybe I should
> say, "You like to breathe air, don't you? Sign this sheaf of papers, and I
> will send you a box of it." ... No, no good. I guess I will just sit quietly
> here at my typewriter, and peck out 23,000,000 words, and let Dink
> do the hand-tooled explaining.

Alan set a brutally tight schedule because he was determined to meet
the budget on his first film as an independent. By the third week in July,
they were still on schedule, and $15,000 under budget. By the middle of
August, they were home with the film in the can, and the editing had
started.

> [August 15, 1949] Rough-cut of "Thunder in the Dust," re-titled "The
> Sundowners," is said to be sensational by the backers, the technicians,
> and such others as have seen it. Sourpuss Comptroller (Rathvon's) says,
> "I have been in this business 20 years, and this is fantastic!" (At the
> price, he means.)
> One day in Texas, which seemed a typical day to me, the thermome-
> ter was 128, in the sun. On a different day, it was 118 on the side of the
> camera. Don't know what it was in the shade — wasn't in any.
> We seem to need some sunset plates, to back credits, etc. Would you
> like to send me some?

The plates referred to above are still photographs used for backgrounds. Alan's father was a very skilled photographer, and sometimes
used his talents for providing background shots, or for scouting locations.
His long history of vacations and trips with his camera provided a huge
library of stock shots, including many sunsets. He also attended some of
the filming and wrote newsy letters to the rest of the family when Alan's
letter writing took a back seat to the crushing schedule of location filming.

A worn clipping from the *Amarillo Globe-News*, Monday, June 6,
1949, carries Alan's penciled "Finally made it, by God!," a triumphant
comment to his father on his ten-year struggle to become a producer.

As the editing started the backers were already pushing to do another
film at once. Alan had a story in mind, under the preliminary title of *Death
Before Snowfall*. They lined up John Barrymore, Jr., to be the star. As the
script progressed the title was changed to *Night by a Wagon Road*, and then
to *Deadfall*, and finally to *High Lonesome*. Progress was swift because Alan
had no collaborators or daily studio story conferences to slow him down,
although there were still interruptions from *The Sundowners*.

Editing of *The Sundowners* went quickly, and it was scheduled for
release on January 30, 1950. Reviews in the theatrical trade papers were
very favorable. It appeared that this first effort was a guaranteed success.

And the starry-eyed Texans came through with incredible hype of their own. On January 19, 1950, *The Hollywood Reporter* said that Texas Gov. Allen Shivers had declared January 30 "Panhandle Pioneer Day" to coincide with the world premiere of the Eagle-Lion release of *The Sundowners* in Amarillo. The city's streets were roped off from regular traffic on that day to permit local cow punchers to parade 15,000 cattle through Amarillo's modern business district. Mayors from twenty surrounding cities joined Mayor Gene Kline of Amarillo in a gigantic parade to promote the film. Taking advantage of the square dancing craze, Eagle-Lion staged a competition among 500 couples from Amarillo and nearby towns to precede the premiere.

The Herring Hotel in Amarillo hosted a *Sundowners* cocktail party, followed by the World Premier Dinner, a four-course gourmet extravaganza priced according to entrée at $1.25 to $2.00! The special souvenir menu featured a John Barrymore Club Steak, a Chill Wills Roast Beef, and a Robert Preston filet mignon.

The shooting schedule of the second LeMay-Templeton Technicolor film *Deadfall* (to become *High Lonesome*) was rearranged to allow John Barrymore, Jr., and Chill Wills to make personal appearances during the week of January 30–February 5, 1950 in Dallas, San Antonio, Houston and Fort Worth.

Alan was elated with the results. In Dallas, *The Sundowners* was held over a third week, and in Oklahoma was running ahead of *Tulsa* in 98 percent of the houses. The big studios were said to be showing it to their production staffs as an object lesson in what can be done under $400,000 on a picture no Hollywood producer would attempt under $1,200,000. The actual cost was $360,000.

Location shooting on *High Lonesome* was much the same crushing schedule as *The Sundowners,* but even tougher on Alan because he was directing. The crew of 60 was headquartered in the tiny town of Marfa, which created housing problems and meant that the only place for Alan to rehearse his actors was in his room, sitting on the bed. Here is his description of a typical day's schedule in a letter to his father, November 11, 1949:

> 6:00 A.M., call.
> 7:00 hit the road. (54 miles, 22 on dirt, to our principle location.)
> 9:30 turn the camera.
> 6:00 P.M. wrap it. (We carry lights and generator. But we do not always wrap so early. Last time, our first day was smeared by a curious crowd of 5000, all carrying crying babies, so we worked until 5 A.M. the next morning, and lost a day.)

8:00, get back, we hope, bathe and dress.

8:30, highballs for some section of the crew, or the department heads.
Don't drink there, myself, but do this for morale. If a hard wrap, most
of the crew won't be in for another hour.

9:00, confer with Hollywood on the phone, mostly as regards the
rushes, which we ourselves never see.

9:30, or after, dinner.

10:00, rehearsal, about two hours, covering next day's work, and its
alternatives, sitting on bed.

12:00, office, signing of releases, vouchers, local contracts, requisitions,
checks, expense sheets, etc. Wrangle with Dink over fielder's choices in
plans, and decisions on same. But mainly trouble shooting — union
renegotiation, local lawsuits, insurance dickers,— and principally above
all, the unforeseen.

1:00 A.M. or 2 A.M., or sometime, lay out all set-ups — we shoot about
16 to 20 a day — for day after tomorrow, because the heads will have to
have them before they can load efficiently tomorrow night.

6:00 A.M., up again, all radiant and smiling, full of peppy inspiration
for all, and starry-eyed with creative imagination. Yes, I fall a little
short in a few of these requirements.

This schedule allowed for only single-track concentration, and was the
reason why Arlene was invited to please stay home. Alan later commented:

[November 11, 1949] Every once in a while a road guard comes to one
and says, "Jesus Christ and the President are out here, and want to
know if you can take a minute to shake hands with the Governor of
Texas." And one is swept with despair.

The schedule of shooting, an unusually brutal one, was necessary
because the cast would be gone for their personal appearances at *The Sundowners* premieres for a week. Dink had set it up, which their distributor,
Eagle-Lion, could not have done. Alan knew that it amounted to about
$500,000 to $750,000 gross, and his word was on the line that the cast
would be available, so he had better be on schedule.

There was no chance that Alan would get home for Christmas, so he
invited his father to either stand in for him in California, or stand in for
his family with him in Marfa. His father opted for Marfa, and was immediately immersed in the daily activities. His letters to the rest of the family,
excerpted below, give a vivid picture of what it means to go on location.

[John LeMay to family, January 3, 1950] I got up this morning at 5:45
and went down to breakfast at 6:25. Found Alan there just finishing. At
6:30 he and Dink and a number of others beat it out and started for
location, calling to me to follow the seven o'clock station wagon. Which
I did. The location is in Pinto Canyon, a wild and beautiful spot 40
miles from Marfa via a dirt road all the way. About half the way is fairly

good driving. The rest is narrow, rough, crooked, and in places very steep. After being certain that I couldn't miss the road I dropped back from the car I was following because the dust, illuminated by my headlights, obscured the frequent bumps and hollows in the road...

About 8:45 I got a couple of gorgeous sunrise shots. At about 35 miles I overtook the biggest of the lighting equipment trucks, a huge, ten ton affair with a trailer almost as big and heavy, that had just begun the descent into the canyon over the very narrow, rough, gullied, hairpin turn infested path dug out of the canyon wall. Couldn't pass, so I trailed along behind, stopping occasionally to enjoy the view and allow the truck to get out of my way....

[At the location] were two old adobe buildings, one was a trading post, the other had been used as a schoolhouse, very tiny, and is now designated as "the ruin." An end wall had been removed from each to permit photographing the interiors. Cactus and thorn bushes had been removed from a considerable distance to facilitate out door shots. The camera men were unloading and setting up the huge Technicolor camera. The lighting crew were getting out and setting up about six sunlight reflectors. These are four foot square flat affairs covered with aluminum foil mounted on adjustable tripods, used to illuminate the shady sides of the actors' faces. During the shooting a man is stationed at each reflector to adjust the angles. The sound crew of two men were setting up their microphone boom and control mechanism — very clever and elaborate stuff. The electricians had parked their generator truck (1250 KW) a quarter of a mile away and were running the cables up to where the shooting was to take place. The property men were setting up a buggy and a buckboard and placing various properties where they would be instantly available. The costume man and the make-up man were checking up on the actors. The horsemen were trying out their mounts. And Alan and Dink and the first and second assistant directors all appeared to be very busy indeed.

It was after ten o'clock before everything was set up to begin shooting and the morning clouds had cleared away so that there was sufficient light. Scenes are not shot in sequence but as the light conditions and the arrangement of the equipment permit. The morning scenes shot were mostly of men on horseback.

At noon a hearty buffet luncheon was served to all.

After lunch the sky had clouded up so that there was not enough light to continue with outdoor scenes, so they went to work on some interiors. That meant taking the big Technicolor camera off it's very fancy, rubber-tired wagon, and setting it up on a low platform. It takes four men to lift the thing. The lighting crew put away their sunlight reflectors and set up a forest of flood lights of various styles and sizes, from huge, searchlight-looking affairs to baby spots, all of which were hooked up to the cables from the generator truck. It seemed impossible to get all that lighting equipment into a position where it could bear on a scene in that little old school room but they did it.

Later, Alan's father wrote:

[January 5, 1950] End of the third day, and all is well. The picture is
running on schedule, and Alan's tension is markedly reduced. This huge
gang of workers is working very efficiently and in close cooperation.
Alan is doing a swell job in handling the actors, never losing patience or
raising his voice even when a "take" has to be repeated as many as
fifteen times to get every detail of the action and every inflection of the
voices to his satisfaction. And they love him.

Young John Barrymore is doing a swell job, is trying very hard, and is
taking Alan's direction gratefully. The girl, Lois Butler, who is in many
scenes with John, is a charming kid with a lot of ability, is working just
the same way. So is everyone else from seventy year old Basil Ruysdale
(a very competent actor) to Clem Fuller and Frank Cordell, stunt men
and expert horsemen. In fact, we seem to have here a large group of
very likeable and even intellectual people. Yesterday I found myself for
about an hour in a discussion of religious beliefs and their effects in
motivating human conduct with Jack Elam, the villain of the play. The
other girl in the picture, Christine Miller, has not been used in any of
the scenes as yet but has been learning to ride under the tutelage of
Clem Fuller....

Yesterday they sprayed the side of a hill with black paint because it
was reflecting too much light from the wrong direction. Today they
were working inside the trading post with lights mounted in every
available spot not occupied by the camera and the sound recording
equipment. Big searchlight-like floods shot their beams thru some of
the doors and windows while others were draped with black canvas and
one door had a huge translucent screen mounted a few feet back thru
which the direct sunlight was filtered. And it isn't just a matter of setting up a lot of equipment. They have to set it up and see what it does,
and maybe work hours before they get it to suit them....

Alan and Dink are trying very hard to finish this location tomorrow.
At noon Alan told me that they were two and a half hours behind
schedule. At three o'clock he said that they were gaining and he thought
they might make it. Then another change in scene ate up a lot of time
and I do not know now how the matter stands. They worked until
seven o'clock before they knocked off for the day. Fortunately the
weather, though pretty cold, is on the whole favorable....

Finished up the work in Pinto Canyon about 7:00 P.M. Am glad that
there'll be no more of that 41 mile drag over those rough and crookedy
dirt roads....

The barbeque and other takes at Burton Mitchell's ranch Tuesday
and Wednesday were completed, plus a few takes not previously scheduled. That brought them almost up to schedule. Then the two days at
the Antelope Springs Ranch were condensed into one except for a couple of takes that can be done at Clay Mitchell's where they are working
now, putting them ahead of schedule for the first time....

Last night the crushing news came from Technicolor in Los Angeles, that the camera in which I reported several days ago the film "jumped the sprocket" had been acting up some more and considerable footage had been unusable. It seems to take several days to process the films and report back to us here, so we do not know as yet the results of Tuesday's work and seq. Late last night Alan told me that from reports that had just come in it would not be necessary to go back to Pinto Canyon, which was a great relief. It would have been just too bad to move all that heavy equipment down into that place again....

A new camera was received from LA by air last night, and they should have no more trouble. This sort of thing is almost unknown with Technicolor who have the best possible equipment constantly in care of thoroughly trained experts....

The big barn dance scenes at Antelope Springs were very colorful indeed, with about 50 local people, men, women and children, costumed in their grandparents clothing, and trained by a young man from Alpine who is a promoter of square dances. Technically a wonderful break in a story which itself is pretty grim.

[January 17, 1950] ... The worries we had last week, over film spoiled by a defective camera, have not as yet proved as serious as we feared. Yesterday they retook a Pinto Canyon scene that went bad in a place on Fletcher's ranch and avoided a trip back into the Canyon. We have still to hear from the takes of the two days at Nopal Ranch and the one day at Antelope Springs. It seems that the defective camera was erratic, sometimes functioning all right and sometimes spoiling the film. Everyone says that they never heard of such a thing with Technicolor....

I am looking forward to tomorrow when the battle along the fence will be shot, if it doesn't rain, and the indications are favorable at the moment. The most spectacular scene of the picture should develop when several acres of tall, dry marsh grass is fired to destroy the fence, which though of wire is supported by well-dried wooden posts. Bulldozers have been used to make fire breaks to restrain the fire, which breaks are well out of range of the cameras of course. To use this fire scene they had to get the permission of about half a dozen state and national conservation agencies, and they are providing all the safeguards against the spread of the conflagration demanded....

Tomorrow should end the outdoor shooting except for some panoramic views of spectacular scenery without actors. The rest of the picture will be inside shots....

In a scene the other day John Barrymore exposes his back, while Abbie is fitting a shirt to him, revealing a mass of almost-healed scars from a beating which he says his uncle gave him with a trace chain (prior to the opening of the picture). Harry Ray, the make-up man, had done an outstanding job on that back, so good that a visiting lady was shocked and indignant, protesting that no one should be allowed to maltreat a boy that way even for a picture and threatening to bring the matter to the attention of the authorities.

Top: Alan (left) with Dink Templeton on location for *High Lonesome*, 1950.
Above: Alan with Lois Butler and John Barrymore, Jr.

Top: Alan at the "Death Fence." *Above:* Filming at the trading post.

[January 20, 1950] On Monday some re-takes of scenes spoiled by
the bum camera were made. Also the "drag scenes," in which Coon-cat
(John Barrymore Jr.) is dragged on the end of a lariat by a mounted
horseman to bring him into submission. A stunt man was used where
the kid is lassoed and pulled off the horse on which he was planning to
escape, then a rubber dummy took the rougher part of the dragging
(very lifelike) and John himself got a little of this very rough stuff.
Then some scenes were shot against a background of several hundred
head of bawling cattle....

   The ten actors, plus a lot of local extras, and 50 technicians have put
on a marvelous exhibition of smooth, efficient cooperation, partly due
to the fact that every man was hand-picked for his job, and partly to
the quiet but firm management of George [Dink] Templeton as producer, and Alan's smooth, easy direction. Members of the staff who
have worked for many top directors have told me that they do not come
any better than Alan. They all love him.

   These 16 to 20 hour work days, plus the responsibility, have been
quite a strain on Alan, but he has held up well, and now, near the end,
he is more relaxed and is getting the joy of accomplishment out of it.

When the location shooting of *High Lonesome* wrapped, Alan and
Dink left immediately for Amarillo to attend the premiere of *The Sundowners*. And just as soon as they could gracefully leave those festivities
they were on a plane to Quebec. Alan's father went along to photograph
prospective locations for the next LeMay-Templeton film, which was still
just an idea in Alan's mind. He was eager to get going on another project
while the investors were enthusiastic.

   It took two months to complete the editing and cutting of *High Lonesome*. There were more than two hundred scenes in the script, and each
was shot an average of three times, sometimes more than a dozen. The
editor used his judgment as to which takes and how much to use, and put
together the "rough cut," which was then viewed and reviewed and revised
until everyone was satisfied that they could do no better. Finally the music
score and the titles and credits were added and it went back to Technicolor
to print the exhibition films.

   It was released immediately, and did well at the box office, but was
not a critical success. The reviewers compared the film unfavorably to *The
Sundowners*. They thought the cast was weaker, and needed at least one
star. They did not like Barrymore's acting, which they blamed in part on
the directing, and they thought that some aspects of the plot were poorly
developed, which they blamed on the cutting. But the bottom line was
good; the picture made money for the investors, so they were eager to back
another LeMay-Templeton production.

   And the next one had already started. Alan had scouted the locations in Canada and talked to the Mounties about their participation. They were eager to help, and the locations were spectacular, so Alan started on the screenplay for *Quebec* with his usual rushed schedule.

But despite the enthusiasm, there were problems with the backers. LeMay-Templeton had to make alternate arrangements, and thanks to their recent record of being on time and under budget, they were able to get new financing quickly, as Alan wrote to his father:

> [May 25, 1950] I held off writing until I could find out what we were going to do. Rathvon never did get back from Europe. I am inclined to think his money ran out. Dink was in Quebec making final deals when I learned that Rathvon would not meet Dink in New York May 10 as prearranged.
>
> I consulted Dink on the phone, then went to Y. Frank Freeman, Paramount head. He communicated with the New York home office, and Dink flew there.
>
> After two weeks and a half on the hook, Paramount finally has lined up with us, and Quebec goes as a Paramount picture, I producing, Dink directing.
>
> This is thought to be the record for speed in setting up a deal with a major. There are many other fabulous things about this, but the most fabulous right now is the amount of work now on our necks to get going.

Unbelievably, less than a month after closing the deal with Paramount, they were deep into the filming on location in Canada. The schedule had required Alan's self-imposed long hours for writing the script, and would not have been remotely possible at a major studio, with their co-authors and producers kibitzing.

The film was considerably more complex than *High Lonesome*. They were shooting "very big stuff," using the Royal 22nd Regiment of Paratroopers for extras. There was a lot of night shooting which was made late by the daylight lasting until 10:00. Some nights they were still shooting at 2:00 A.M. But with another killer schedule, in less than four weeks it was "in the can."

An exhausted Alan wrote to his father:

> [July 21, 1950] We got home day before yesterday after a few days in New York and a few days cleaning up final affairs in Quebec. Principal photography was completed three days under a thirty-day schedule with nothing left to shoot in Hollywood that we know about yet.
>
> Since you have not mentioned it, I guess you did not read about the disastrous tragedy that overtook us the night of July 1, when two Paratroopers of the Royal 22nd Regiment were drowned during the shooting of a scene. We were shooting night for night, using an old

abandoned commercial dock. The action represented rebel canoe men landing in force in the face of sharp cannon fire and scaling the dock. We had previously shot the cannon firing from the ramparts of the Citadel. The effect of the cannon balls falling in the water among the canoes was represented by charges of black powder mixed with photoflash powder. A charge submerged at three to four feet sends up a column of water ten to twelve feet high. There were also charges fastened to the timbers and pilings of the dock itself.

First we made three scenes on the shallow water side of the dock. The third of these showed a canoe being blown over by a charge which it carried below water upon an outrigger. I worked in these three scenes, once within a few feet of a very shallow water charge and these passed without any event.

We then went to the deep water side of the dock. It was high tide and the water was about forty feet deep, but without current or eddies in the pocket where we were. Nine canoes carrying four men each charged the dock in a mass. There was a great confusion of explosions and waterspouts. Close to the dock — inside fifteen feet — some of the boys stood up in the canoes apparently preparatory to landing on and scaling the dock. Several of the canoes turned over, and it was at once apparent that some of the boys were in trouble. Byron Munson, whom you remember, and a local man dived in and rescued three boys who were floundering. After the landing had been completed, it was believed that two of the boys had gone down and a roll call proved this to be true.

We immediately went to work with drag hooks and pulled up one man within twenty minutes and the other two and a half hours later. The pulmotor which was standing by took no effect.

Military and civil inquiries followed, taking up a full day. An unfortunate confusion arose due to the fact that the boys in the canoes had understood that the explosions were to occur after the canoes had passed the charges. The charges had gone off among the canoes on the previous shots and were controlled by an electrical switch panel. However, this misunderstanding may have led the boys to think that something had gone wrong or that they had been tricked into a dangerous situation. The Army unfortunately took this view in its prepared statement and announced that a panic had occurred resulting in the loss of the two men.

Personally I think that there was no actual panic, but that some misapprehension existed as to how well the men could swim if at all. The two boys apparently took each other down within two strokes of the dock, and a boy that Byron pulled out from a depth of five feet, and sinking, was within arm's reach of the piling.

Many of the newspaper reports were erroneous and unfavorable, due principally to the fact that we had to hold off until the Army statement came out and then again had to hold off until after the Inquest. However, the Inquest gave us a clean bill of health as to any possible negligence.

We had a power launch and a row boat standing by, and life preservers and hand lines showered the water immediately.

After the Inquest I still had a miserable two days in which I went to Remesky to attend the funerals.

This probably would have been a commercial disaster as well as a tragedy had we not been so close to the end of the picture. The three days by which we undercut the schedule was not intended. But we were racing because something might at any time have happened to our use of the soldiers, our use of the Citadel, our use of the church, or simply a bad weather situation for our high proportion of outdoor shooting.

I have only seen about four reels out of about forty-five that we brought back, but I am convinced that we have a very big and very beautiful picture with some very fine performances in it. In size it is a good deal like DeMille; in fact we used more men in full costume than DeMille used in "The Unconquered." A check of wardrobe hand-outs shows that we used 1,777 bits and extras, figuring by the scene, not by the day. DeMille, in "The Unconquered," counted the same way, used 1,100.

The sets of course are actual and absolutely unbeatable and the exteriors particularly are very lovely. Some of the interiors, too, are unique, particularly the interior of the Governor-General's quarters in the Citadel; the vaulted stone underground works; the crypt of the church; the church itself, which dates from 1734 and the exterior and interior of the House of Parliament itself.

We are very tired from the heavy blow that the tragedy caused us and the strain that it entailed. However, we are rapidly recovering.

After the years that it took for Alan to gain his independence in Hollywood, achieving about as much autonomy as can be had when working with outside investors, he cannot be blamed for comparing his accomplishments to those of his old mentor/tormentor, DeMille. But it does show his perennially competitive nature.

The strain of *Quebec,* following the rushed production of two other films without a break, brought Alan to the point of admitting that he needed a vacation. He had lost a great deal of weight, and looked gaunt (something he had never been able to accomplish by diet and exercise). The hard-driving Dink Templeton was also worn a bit thin, and the two partners agreed to back off to a more reasonable schedule of two films a year. They made plans for a World War II story, with South Pacific locations to be shot in Florida, on a schedule that gave nearly six months for creating a script and setting up the business deal. By previous standards, this seemed like a more relaxed project, if they could get the cooperation of the U. S. Navy.

—19—

Working with the Military

The next story envisioned for LeMay-Templeton was to be about the Consolidated PBY "Catalinas." They are large, lumbering amphibian aircraft with two big radial engines on a wing held high on a pylon to keep it out of the spray. With a 115 mph cruise speed they were a simple target to shoot down, but survived in the South Pacific by flying mostly at night. For this duty they were painted black. They had a great record for saving pilots downed in the water, and when armed with makeshift bomb racks actually sank more Japanese shipping in the South Pacific than any other type of aircraft. They were called the Black Cats, and they deserved their own movie.

A story such as this cannot be filmed without the cooperation of the U. S. Navy, because they must provide aircraft, airmen, extras, background shots of the hangars, airstrips, and other locations, all to fit the script. This cannot be done with just library shots. The Navy is eager to help because a favorable film is good publicity both for recruiting and for getting funding through Congress.

Under the working title of *Black Cat Patrol*, Alan started on a treatment. The setting was to be the South Pacific, with production to be done on location in the Florida Keys or Guantanamo, Cuba. But before he could proceed very far with the treatment he needed to know what he could expect from the Navy. He had not worked directly with the military before; the government's participation in *The Story of Dr. Wassell* had been handled by the staff at Paramount. This time he had to make the arrangements in Washington himself. A series of phone calls located the right officials. They said that the first requirement would be the Navy's approval of the story, which was to be presented in three pages. That done, he went to Washington.

> [Alan to Dad, September 15, 1950] ... We obtained prompt and liberal cooperation in Washington, largely due to the groundwork laid by Bill Faralla.[1] We obtained priority upon our subject for ninety days, extensi-

ble; and preliminary cooperation which comprises the cooperation necessary to complete an accurate survey. This was rather an achievement for we had no release — an absolute necessity according to regulations. This was waived. Our chief power derived from two admirals in key positions in relation to what we are trying to do. We also had a highly political type of introduction to Dan Kimball, Undersecretary of the Navy, who comes from this area. He urged us to let him know the minute we hit a snag so he could clear it for us. But we didn't hit any and our heaviest gun thus remained in reserve.

We were then accredited to the Navy Air Reserve in Florida. Here we found all the most important components that we will need, including five serviceable PBY's in part-time duty, and adequate personnel in part-time reserve training. We toured as far as Key West in a PBY; I, in fact, co-piloted one way, holding course for 120 miles. On one occasion, searching for location, we also used a Coast Guard surface boat.

After extensive search we found what we needed on the doorstep. It is Hurricane Harbor on Key Biscayne — reachable by a causeway and only about twenty-five minutes from the hotel we will use. It is a very lovely little lagoon set in the heart of a coconut plantation. [Hurricane Harbor today is in the middle of town, surrounded by streets down to the water.] It is only about two hundred feet across, but deep enough for the PBY's. You will see them land in the open sea, taxi up winding water to the lagoon, and then be ramped up into hiding among the coconuts for repair. You'll see this if we make the picture, I mean. This spot represents a small, far-advanced Black Cat hide-out, like those the Japs went crazy trying to find.

All this is very elegant, but two headaches developed that may very easily make the project impossible. In the first place I am going to have severe and perhaps disabling trouble pleasing the Navy with a story, and the full cooperation which we will later need, inasmuch as the Navy is bringing all the production elements, depends upon everybody's being perfectly delighted. The Navy bruises very easily, in fact is bruised all over already, and lets out a scream of self-pity if touched anywhere. All Navy personnel, at any grade whatever, they very quickly let me know, must be shown as the very highest possible examples of charm and infallibility. Further, the Navy publicity policy is sighted solely upon enlistment.

Jim Henderson, the former Black Cat navigator who is collaborating with me on this subject, has been writing a series of enlistment scripts for the Navy and is able to tell me what they conceive to be good for enlistment. As I see it these are the things they wish to sell:

1. Comradeship of the most touching order, such that once you have joined the Navy you will forever be surrounded by nothing but bosom pals.
2. Continuous sociability aboard a series of floating men's clubs, or possibly boys' clubs, and at exotic shore installations composed chiefly of recreational facilities.

3. An educational system envied by Cal Tech, such that anyone who
    enlists is guaranteed to come out an advanced electronics scien-
    tist.
4. One long series of vacations in selected beauty spots of the world.

Anathema from this point of view are:

1. Work.
2. Danger.
3. Physical discomfort.
4. Social unpleasantness.
5. Shortage of any type of equipment necessary to make life bril-
    liantly successful and altogether lovely.

Unaware of this viewpoint, I started off by making just about the
foulest guess I ever made in my life. My story treatment, which preceded us to Washington, missed the mark by about one hundred and
eighty degrees on the nose. My disagreement with the Navy as to what
was good for it turned out to be complete. My ridiculous notion was
that what the Navy needed was public appreciation and solicitude with
a view to funds and power. The Jap being of no use as a heavy (everyone knows he's licked) I chose as heavy the public lethargy and fat-
headedness as expressed in the Navy budget between wars. I based my
theme upon the unfair demands made upon the Service personnel at the
outset of every war. Stalin sends them to the cellar, but democracy takes
its blood sacrifice by sending too few young men, obsoletely armed, to
meet destruction while waiting for support. I expressed this by developing the case of a young pilot who courageously concealed battle fatigue
and horror psychoses as best he can in order to stay in action; and is
permitted to do so because in the desperation of the situation, and in
the absence of any replacement for him, he must be regarded as expend-
able. He ends discredited and detested, his concealment of what is the
matter with him having been too successful with those immediately
around him; and his solution is to kamikaze, making the enemy pay for
it with just one ship more.

Now how could I have been any farther off the mark than that? I was
quickly made to know that the Navy's unbroken record of flawless successes is achieved by means of superlative equipment, superb training,
and native brilliance. The interesting actions in which the boys participate, always in an atmosphere of warm comradeship, are of a refreshing
nature purely. No one ever experiences fatigue of any kind, let alone
battle fatigue, perish the thought! If anyone ever did experience a trace
of it, it would immediately be recognized and the victim would immediately be subjected to measures of the utmost solicitude.

Any possibility of full cooperation depends upon my script's fitting
into all that. One factor which conceivably might not fit into the pattern could be the audience. Oh, it can be done all right — ANCHORS
AWEIGH with Kelley and Sinatra is a fair prototype. Whether I know
how to do it is another matter.

The other unfavorable factor is that of time, of course. This is the second time in a row that we have hit into a tourist season. We made reservations for seventy people at a suitable and accessible hotel, but these have to be confirmed Dec. 1. By that time the script must not only be completed, but accepted by the Navy and we must have financing and release. A script completion date of Nov. 1 is therefore very late, and every day thereafter makes the prospects more dim.

I have devised a new story which may possibly accomplish something toward compromising with the Navy at least. But it still is not a musical about comradeship. About all I can guarantee is that the script will be very bad, from lack of time.

* * *

Alan's other approach to independence, to write scripts on his own and then sell them to the studios, was designed to give him the time he needed to get the quality that his present schedule precluded. This had met with some success. He had written a story on his own called *Ghost Mountain,* and sold it to Warner Brothers. They filmed it with Errol Flynn under the new name of *Rocky Mountain.* It had been rewritten, of course, as screenplays always are when the cast is established. That was the part that Alan hated. He seldom liked his own films when others were through changing them. He particularly disliked seeing his material rewritten by writers he didn't respect. But here is one of those rare cases where he agreed with the rewrite, and went out of his way to tell the writer so, as he reported in a letter to his father on October 5, 1950:

> [Enclosed is] a trade paper review of ROCKY MOUNTAIN, which I originally wrote as GHOST MOUNTAIN. Winston Miller is a very good, relatively young writer who put a final polish on the script because I was not available when they sent for me to do it; it needed it. He made some excellent improvements particularly in the ending and stream-lined it and took some clutter out. But everything I cared about is still in there and so is 90% of my own dialogue. I called up Miller and told him that he was the first collaborator whom I had ever had whom I appreciated. He really improved it. I was also able to say that this was the first picture I ever had my name on that I enjoyed looking at.
>
> It begins to look as if I had missed the boat with BLACK CAT PATROL. I got it onto the market just a little bit late, so that the majors are all loaded with war plane pictures. However, it is still breathing a little.

At the same time, he was struggling with the schedule on *Black Cat Patrol,* Alan had the burden of the final revisions of *Quebec.* The effort had been too much for too long, and Alan was becoming worn out and discouraged. The LeMay-Templeton films were outstanding examples of what could be done on tight schedules with low budgets, and they were making good money for the backers. But Alan's pride of accomplishment was tempered by his critical evaluation of the product. Having his own company had not turned out to be the panacea he had envisioned.

> [December 7, 1950] We sneak-previewed QUEBEC, and then made enormous revisions, including the removal of 700 feet; the insertion of no less than 23 commentaries to explain what is supposed to be going on; and put in some shots out of TAP ROOTS. We then sneaked it again with not entirely satisfactory results, but sent it to answer print, believing it to be the best we can do with the stuff. I do not believe it to be a very good picture. Don Haggerty and Nikki Duval put in performances that really shine, but the rest of the cast runs from adequate to lousy. Nobody can understand a word that Corinne Calvet says. Photographically the picture is very beautiful, and the production very big, but the story is choppy, episodic and dull, and the actors uninteresting.
>
> This picture rounded out my growing conviction that the LeMay-Templeton set-up does not promise to make the kind of pictures that I am interested in making.
>
> I have therefore traded my interest in John Barrymore, Jr.'s contract to Dink for his interest in the BLACK CATS; and LeMay-Templeton is now inoperative.
>
> I put a four-page prospectus of the BLACK CATS In the hands of MCA, and every major studio in town is very much interested in it. I have no doubt that I will be able to sell the subject advantageously if I get a good script. I am working on that now.

Alan wasted months, without pay, trying unsuccessfully to create a script that would sell to both the Navy and the public. In the end he pleased neither, and the project was shelved.

To add to his concerns, Alan was running out of money again. There were plenty of promised profits on deferred payment deals, but no cash flow. The LeMays reduced expenses a bit by firing the couple that did the cooking and house cleaning, and hiring one girl to cook and take care of the downstairs. They reduced the gardener to half price for the winter, and put their Monaco Drive house on the market. But Alan needed to go back to a job that had a regular paycheck, at least for a while.

He signed on at Republic Studios, on a four-week guarantee, to write a treatment on a story about flight nurses in the Korean war. It was not the prestige appointment he might have hoped for; while Paramount and Warner's were known for big Technicolor pictures, Republic was better known for black-and-white "B" pictures. Alan said their motto was "Always a good seat at a Republic picture."

The *Flight Nurse* assignment was most interesting in terms of the research. There was no assigned story line other than the general subject. Alan was to get a story from the source. He went after it like an investigative reporter, and immediately got to see the right people. He didn't explain how he did this; we can only imagine that his experience with the Navy, his résumé of successful films, and the magic word "Hollywood" opened doors wherever he went. It was a quick trip, but adequate for creating a treatment, as he recounted to his father:

> [June 20, 1951] ... I immediately took off for Travis Field, north of San Francisco — and thence to Honolulu; and I just got back yesterday. I talked to 38 nurses and various surgeons and pilots, and came back on an Air-Evac C-97 (DC-6) with two nurses and 59 patients, mostly wounded.
>
> The wounded in the "police action" are very badly mauled. Nurses who were in France say they got mostly boys with a wound, nothing like these. The Chinese have no riflemen. These wounded are blown all to hell with mortars — many big holes in them, many amputations; or else are shot in many places by the short range burp guns. Many psy-

Lt. Gloria Rapp, USN, flight nurse, and Alan LeMay. June, 1951.

chos, also; we had seven of them in our load, three of them violent, all under restraints. I suppose in former wars they were just thrown in the brig and dishonorably discharged, instead of hospitalized.

The girl in the picture is Lt. Gloria Rapp, USN, nurse assigned as my aide at Hickam Field, Hawaii. The flight nurses are light-hearted, high-spirited, well-adjusted, and screened not only for competence, youth, and stamina, but for good looks.

June 30 I turn in a treatment, which goes up to Main Wheel (and chief owner) of Republic, and nothing happens unless he decides to go on with it. So the financial strain is momentarily relieved, but not solved.

While Republic management considered the treatment, Alan stayed on to start a Stephen Foster biography called *I Dream of Jeannie*. Management pondered until the end of summer, but then Alan reported:

> [September 17, 1951] I have a green light from the Pentagon on my Flight Nurse story, and I have also turned in a rough script on the musical about Stephen Foster. Now I am waiting for a studio decision on which they want me to go ahead with, if any. Waiting while on salary, fortunately.
>
> Decision rests with Yates, chief owner and prop. of this trap. He is in court. Seems Roy Rogers, who left this studio (don't know on whose request) got himself an enormous TV deal. 50 shows a year, or something fabulous like that. But the TV contract says that if Republic should release the old Rogers films to TV the deal is off. So, yes, Republic dumped a couple hundred old Rogers films into TV, along with about five hundred other hunks of spoiled celluloid, and Roy's deal is stone cold dead in the market. So now Rogers is suing Republic for $240,000.

While that issue was tying up management, Alan finished the Stephen Foster script, and at the end of October 1951, finally got a go-ahead on the *Flight Nurse* project. Unlike Paramount, who had staff people to arrange coordination with the military, at Republic it was in Alan's lap.

> [October 29, 1951] Went back onto "Flight Nurse" and went to Washington, where I researched MATS (Military Air Transport Service), who fly Airevac, and from whom we will have to borrow the planes. Lined up MATS and the Surgeon General's Office for full cooperation, completing mission in one week, instead of the two allowed for it, and bringing back a fourteen page (single-space) research report, and a borrower's who's who in Washington.

Republic had no intention of sponsoring a research trip to the war zone, but MATS (probably with Alan's urging) insisted that Alan visit Tokyo and Korea, on guest orders. Alan was delighted, and left for Tokyo on a MATS flight November 5, 1951. He got back from Japan the week before Christmas, and was excited about all he had learned.

[December 18, 1951] The trip to the Far East proved to be the most interesting trip I ever took. I was out there only two weeks and a day, of which six days were in Korea. But though I would have liked more time, I was so lucky in my coverage that I could have found no specific need for staying longer.

Stops made: *On Honshu*, Tokyo (only two days), Fuchu, Tachigawa, Nagasaki, and Beppu.

On Kyushu, Ashiya, Fukuoka, Itazuki, and Brady. (How did that Irishman get in there? I could find nobody who knew.)

In Korea, Taegu, Taejon, Kimpo, Seoul, Pupyong Ni (farthest forward air strip), X Corps HQ, 17th Infantry, 1st Batt. Aid station, and front lines, Punchbowl, 1st Marines and front lines, Heartbreak Ridge. I talked to 94 people enough to put down some sort of note of what was said.

Korea is a thousand miles of knife ridges, running about 2000 feet high, sides from too-steep-for-a-jeep to vertical. These follow one after another, with nothing but narrow defiles between with creeks at the bottom. Tanks can only operate up and down these creek beds. The "plains" around Seoul, very limited in extent, are rolling, to say the least — about as flat as our Alleghenies.

We are fighting on a basis of total air supremacy. The lines run along the knife-tops of the ridges, facing enemy lines on the next ridge, within rifle shot, but a days march taking in the vertical down-and-up-again. You can look up at an angle of 45 degrees and see the bunkers on the point of Heartbreak Ridge, and hear the rifles, and identify the P-51s making an air strike just beyond — but it takes 10 hours to get down from there carrying a litter. Between the ridges the line is held by elements totally pinned down by snipers, who look right down their throats. As in the case of Fox Company of the 17th Inf., who live flat on their bellies in their fox holes.

Right behind the ridges lie perfectly open troop concentrations and truck parks, and farther back the planes stand in open lines along the strips. No camouflage, earthworks, or dispersion — making it a very queer-looking war indeed. The amount of damage that could be done to us by 500 planes with 1000-pounders would be fantastic.

They can't get through to us, yet. While I was there a bomber mission against us was turned back into Manchuria with the loss of twelve enemy bombers. But it cost us five of our dwindling jets. Our Sabrejets, inferior in all respects to the MIGs, are the only plane we have that can fight them. The Sabre pilots are getting pretty tired of being outnumbered two and three to one, with more coming all the time, and the enemy shooting better every day. In November we lost 21 jets while killing 19.

So I get home to read that we will be tooled up to build jets in about another six months.

When he returned to the script revisions, he found that he had to nearly start over. He felt that he had learned too much, too late. He said that he knew nothing until he went to Korea. As he struggled through a new rough draft of *Flight Nurse*, the Foster musical was completing shooting with everyone completely happy, which Alan considered to be an ominous sign.

The participants always seem to be happy with their results at this stage. The cast of the musical was completely unknown, topped by Ray Middleton, Bill Shirley, Muriel Lawrence, and Eileen Christy. The reviewers described the lead singers as having little past film experience and, as it turned out, virtually no future. The minstrel-show blackface aspect, coming just two years before *Brown* v. *Board of Education*, raised the hackles of those who chose to be sensitive, but didn't keep the crowds away. The film made money, but was no classic.

The day that Alan completed the *Flight Nurse* draft, Republic cut him loose, and he immediately took a salaried job at RKO to rewrite a pirate story about Blackbeard. A week and a half later, Republic wanted him back. But he was unavailable, as he explained:

> [March 21, 1952] I am about to do the rewrite on "Flight Nurse" on my own time at night, probably for free. This due to they [Republic] can't hold a writer for rewrite while waiting for okay, and Yates, the boss, was in Europe; so when I finished the rough draft, amid cheers, they very promptly disassociated my feet from the trough. So a week and a half later they wanted me back, but I was already working at RKO. Pretty silly. I figure they spent $20,000 making me the only expert on Airevac in Hollywood.

Alan worked nights and weekends, and got a script that was okayed by the Department of Defense with very kind words. Republic management was also happy, and shooting started in August 1952. Erd Brandt, the *Saturday Evening Post* editor, came to call when he was on the West Coast, and Alan discussed with him a Korean story to be contracted on the basis of a first installment and outline. His mind was still overflowing with ideas from his trip to the far east. (And he still wouldn't speak to *Collier's*.)

When *Flight Nurse* was released it was well received, but suffered at the box office for lack of any star drawing power. The big names in it were Joan Leslie and Forest Tucker, about right for a Republic "B." The loss of enthusiasm for the Korean war was another factor. Alan's short story, "A Gift from Korea," was rejected; his agent said it was very good, but the public was sick of the war. This was particularly unfortunate for Alan because his research trip had given him so many ideas for stories that now would not be written.

— 20 —

Television

Television credits are conspicuously absent in Alan's list of accomplishments. This is not because he did not see television coming, nor because he did not see its possibilities. As early as 1941, he was anticipating the impact of a technology that was still unknown to most people.

Alan never claimed to have technical capabilities, but here is one more example of his analytical approach to a situation, and his appreciation for the technical details. By understanding the characteristics of television transmission, he saw an opportunity for capitalizing on its limitations.

[Alan to Mother and Dad, November 26, 1941] I become more and more interested in television. Its technical advancement is now amazing, and includes the transmission of color. No technical or financial difficulties now stand in the way of an immediate inception of television broadcasts in all our big cities, except the defense effort, which prohibits the making of consumer sets.

Stations in key cities are at present broadcasting one hour a week, for the purpose of holding their wave length in accordance with law, although there is no appreciable number of receivers out for them to broadcast to. They are using the interlude to advance technically and are making terrific strides.

A television receiver costs about a hundred eighty dollars now [equivalent to more than $2500 in 2010 dollars], but this is dropping. After the war there will undoubtedly be a tremendous upsurge in the television industry.

The great limitation of television is that its waves do not follow the curvature of the earth, so the range of a station is only that circle which can be reached in a straight line, possibly forty miles. The programs cannot be transmitted over telephone lines as in radio, but require a "co-axial" cable which is a bundle of insulated wires about as thick as a man's leg and about as expensive to lay as a road. Consequently we are ages away from a national hook-up in television, which for the present must operate by means of stations in the centers of dense population.

In this limitation lies the great opportunity which I see.

I propose to prepare television programs upon technically specialized film and sell them to every city in the country. This will about duplicate the use of transcribed programs in radio now, except that it will not have the competition of any national hook-ups.

Very special presentation is necessary in order to present a play or a show upon the little television screen which in the lower priced receivers is about the size of a magazine. But I think I can solve the proper use of this little screen; and by operating upon film I will have enormous advantages over the direct broadcasting from live actors which is all they are doing now. The cutting of the film, enabling instant shift of spectator viewpoint and the availability of any type of background will give my canned programs the edge.

I am certain that television is going to kick the hell out of the movie theatre business, and is also going to do the magazines a lot of no good. This will not bother me if I am a leading exponent of the new medium.

As an expedientist I am forced to appreciate that the holding up of television by the war has given me such opportunity as I have to achieve this. It is essential, in order to carry out this plan, that I be myself in a producing position by the time the market displays itself.

I am working on that now.

So television was one more reason why Alan wanted to establish himself as a producer.

He also wanted to learn more about its technical aspects, and announced in 1947 that he and Bill Holm and George Toley were going to build a television set. Holm was a theoretical physicist. Toley was a tennis coach. Alan was overworked as usual, TV sets were far too complicated for amateurs, and the project was never seriously started.

Alan's approach to getting into television on the ground floor was to produce his own pilot film. The problem of getting backing when he had no experience as a producer was the same as it was in the motion picture industry, so it took years to get there. In 1949, Alan was finally able to put himself in a producing position by just going there and doing it himself. He went on location in the California Mother Lode country and shot a two-reel short, *Old Man Coffee*, with his own money. It had been intended as the pilot for a TV series, but it was not picked up.

By 1951, the TV boom was well under way, and Alan was analyzing the financial aspects of it:

> [Alan to Dad, August 27, 1951] Television may really amount to something terrific, pretty soon. National sponsors are still scarce and weak, but increasing. Good price for a top-liner half-hour commercial carrier (2300 feet) is now $1250. I can make it for that. A little higher, and *I* will get paid, too.

Better bet seems distribution to stations for local sponsorship, dept. stores etc. The stations make two to three times the price they get for a national or chain program. Present price they pay for film is the same as their minimum rate, and runs from $75 to $600 an hour; average about $75 a half hour. Only about 100 stations now functioning plus 380 that are supposed to be.

But about 1400 licenses have been placed, and 2300 proposed. Uncertainty as to color situation the main reason for hesitating expansion. Once this is resolved, you'll see the gold rush, with anticipation of 2000 in two or three years. Underselling at an average of $50 a half hour and servicing only half the stations, you see $50,000 a film! Most to come in over a period of two to three years. Charge off half to distribution cost, lavish $20,000 on the film; take a profit of $5,000 each on 26 films a year: $130,000 a year.

No hurry. Not one single agency yet exists devoted to distribution for local sponsorship.

And the vast consumption of footage leaves the competitive field wide open, forever, from sheer lack of talent to meet the demand.

Predictions made "forever" are usually overstated. But a half century later Alan's forecast is holding true: there remains a lack of adequate talent to meet the demand.

In the late 1950s and early 1960s, Alan wrote a few episodes for Western series that were produced by others. He wrote episodes for *Cheyenne, Sugarfoot, Bronco,* and a couple for *The Wide Country,* but nothing with impact. He also proposed a series of one-hour shows to be called *Passport,* based on true events from the inexhaustible files of the State Department. He outlined a half dozen episodes and wrote one called "Man Without Existence" but it did not sell.

Alan had been an important player, first in the magazine and book trade, then in the motion picture industry, but he never achieved that position in television. His forte was the "Big Outdoor Film," and that was not for the small screen television in his lifetime.

—21—

Racing

During World War II Alan had, by necessity, driven a motorcycle, and although he hated the cold nights driving home in the rain, on sunny weekends he found it to be a lot of fun. When the war ended he gave the motorcycle to me and bought a new Ford. It was not fun. The early postwar "Detroit Iron" was heavy, mushy, and a chore to drive. Alan kept saying he wanted his '41 Plymouth convertible back.

The awful driving characteristics of the American sedans spawned the sports car craze of the '50s, but when I bought an MG-TD, Alan thought it was silly. He had a low opinion of British engineering, and said it looked like something from the '30s, which it did.

Then one night my wife, Mary Ann, and I went to Alan and Arlene's house for dinner, and we began discussing cars. Alan had been driving over the winding Sepulveda Pass every day to Warner Bros., and said he couldn't keep the damn Ford in one lane. He even tried running one front tire low so that the car would pull to that side and take the backlash out of the steering. I told him that precision cornering was a major feature of sports cars, and finally talked him into trying my MG. After dinner we took it over Sepulveda Pass to the Valley, Alan driving, and he was convinced. We turned off onto Ventura Blvd., where we found a foreign car lot. He bought a used '51 MG-TD and drove it home.

Alan became an instant enthusiast, and went with us to several sports car road races. People were racing stock sports cars just like his and having a ball. He had to try it. He joined both the California Sports Car Club (known as the Cal Club) and the Sports Car Club of America (the SCCA), went to races regularly, and finally entered the next race on the schedule.

He had thought he could just drive to the track and race, but it was a little more formal than that. "Scrutineering" (tech inspection) was the first hurdle. The car had to be inspected to see that it was "stock" and had all the latest safety items. Alan had to buy a helmet, new seat belt, new tires, and a few other things. The bill for all this was surprising, but he accepted it as a one-time expense. That also was too optimistic. Every race something major wore out or needed upgrading. Maintenance between races usually took all week even if there had been no race damage.

The MG didn't have enough power to get in trouble, and Alan went from rookie to expert in a couple of races. But he was more than a little upset by the other "stock" MG's that powered past him on the straights. Between-race maintenance turned into engine tear-downs, port polishing, and a variety of engine refinements allowed within the definition of "stock." The MG was out of commission for repairs or modification most of the time between races, so Alan bought a Jaguar XK-120 to drive to work.

It did not take long for him to decide that since the Jag was much faster than the MG, he should be racing that. His first race in the Jag was at Santa Barbara, and again he was getting passed on the long straights by supposedly identical cars. On lap three, he was driving beside another XK-120 and was keeping up until he got to the engine redline speed, but when

Alan in his 1951 MG-TD. Fun to drive, but not fast enough for Alan. Photograph by FAE Foto, Studio City.

he shifted, the other car shot ahead. Well, he thought, if they could run the engine past redline, then he could too. On lap four, he was again beside a similar XK-120 and held the throttle on full as the tachometer swung into the red zone. He planned to shift when the other guy did, but instead the engine exploded. What he got from that race was a very expensive connecting rod, bent into the form of a "C," that sat on his desk as a trophy.

With a new engine, he raced the Jag at Palm Springs and burned out the rings in the Saturday heat race. Someone said that pure castor oil would plug the leaks and make the engine last for the Sunday race. So Saturday night we went from pharmacy to pharmacy in Palm Springs buying out their inventory of castor oil, down to the 4-oz. bottles. The Jag had a huge 12-quart oil system so it took a lot of little bottles. Alan finished out of contention in the Sunday race, and left it to me to drive the limping Jag home. It was stop-and-go traffic all the way, shivering in the open cockpit, and with the oil pressure warning light complaining at me any time the engine dropped below 3000 rpm. A trip to remember.

The lesson taken from the MG and Jag experiences was that racing "stock" cars was too restrictive. Alan needed a true race car that could be modified to the extent necessary to win! What had started as a casual hobby was rapidly becoming an obsession.

Alan moved up to the "under 1500 cc modified" class with the purchase of a Lotus Mark IV powered by a highly-modified MG engine. He raced it at Stockton, winning the novice event his first time out. The press report[1] emphasized the fun-friendly-family aspects of sports car road racing in those days:

> The Under 1500 cc Novice event was taken by 55 year-old Alan LeMay, driving his first race in his Lotus MG. His pit crew was made up of his father, who is 82, and his son, 26 ... a family affair!

Harry Hanford, the mechanic who had done so much work on the car, and had years of racing experience, drove the Lotus-MG in the main event, and came in third. For Alan this was not good news. If Harry couldn't win in the car, then what chance did he have as a rookie? He was not thrilled with a good competitive drive, he would be satisfied only with a win. The car needed more power.

The endless between-race modifications improved the car, but were a drain on Alan's funds, and both his and my time. My list of home chores was suffering from neglect, and Alan's usual prolific story output dropped off. But the tempo escalated, and the next major modification was an engine change. Out went the MG engine, in came a new midget Offenhauser. The engine was not completely developed, and Alan's father spent many hours at the factory, testing the new engine on the dynamometer to get it to run well on gasoline.

In Alan's first race with the new engine (Hansen Dam, June 1955), he got overly aggressive when someone passed him on the back stretch, and he stepped on the throttle so hard that it jammed wide open. Carrying the full speed from the end of the straight, with the new engine in full song, the car had no chance to make the turn. Photographer David Iwerks was ready with an unusual motor-driven Leica; he saw what was coming and clicked off a great three-shot sequence that was featured in *Road & Track*.[2] The crash crumpled the nose sheet metal and bent the suspension, but we were able to straighten it all out for the next race.

Alan was rather proud of his reactions during the crash. As he described it, the first picture shows the steering hard over for the turn, but the car powering straight ahead with bad understeer. In the second frame, he has straightened the wheel to avoid a rollover, and his right hand has swept up the right side of the instrument panel, killing all four electrical switches. The last frame shows a courteous follow through, getting the car and hay off the track and out of traffic.

Alan drove many more races: Palm Springs, Paramount Ranch, Willow Springs, Torrey Pines, and on and on. Between the SCCA and the Cal Club there was a race about every two weeks. But the competition was getting tougher with each race, and Alan continued to look for ways to squeeze more speed out of the car. He considered making a new streamlined body. He did everything he could to reduce the weight. He got special lightweight driving shoes. He dieted. He said, "On race day, skip breakfast. Before you get in the car, empty everything out of your pockets. And just before the flag drops, spit!"

While his interest was focused on the sport, Alan began to write about it. His plans are revealed in a letter to his editor at Harper & Brothers[3]:

> I am writing my road-racing story. It should be ready late in March, unless the Pan-American is run next spring, which is highly doubtful, and I decide to drive it. If it is, and I do, this would take at least another month.
>
> Object would be an inside look, only. European Grand Prix drivers call the Pan-American the toughest race in the world, and I would be silly to think of winning it. It runs nearly 2000 miles, cut up into five legs, run one leg a day. For fast time a co-pilot is necessary. Much of the route is mountainous, and nobody has ever been able to memorize the thousands of blind turns. The co-pilot reads to the driver, through ear-phones, a carefully prepared estimate of the speed at which he can go into each successive turn and conceivably stick. But I would not carry a passenger on this one for anything in the world.

The caption in *Road & Track* said "A Lotus makes a dusty Group, single caption detour into — Lotus Land?" Reproduced with permission of photographer David Iwerks.

> Too bad. I have got hold of a really fast (164 mph) 3-litre Monza Ferrari somehow....

The beautiful, sleek Ferrari was the ultimate reality check. It was designed for the professional racer, and worked well in the hands of drivers like Mike Hawthorne, Boris Said, and Phil Hill. But it required a rather high skill level for anyone to drive it off the lot.

We rented time on a paved glider airport at El Mirage Dry Lake, set up turn markers, and spent hours in practice. In one session Alan drove until he got heatstroke that laid him low for a week. He loved the tremendous power and acceleration, but never felt that he mastered it. In the "main event" races he was competing with drivers who were mostly young men who had been racing Go-Karts when they were seven. There were few that kept racing past 40; Alan had never driven a race car before he was 50, and was typically the oldest driver by a large margin in any race he entered. He liked the saying, "Old age and treachery beats youth and enthusiasm," but it doesn't usually work that way in a high-powered race car. This was reality, and it was a bitter pill.

For a novice driver, the Ferrari was intimidating. Each of us who tried it was convinced that we were not ready for this level of car. Fortunately Alan came to the same conclusion, and got rid of it before anyone got hurt. He also had gotten enough of a taste of the maintenance bills to know that he did not want to try a better model of Ferrari. The sport had become expensive and non-rewarding, with no support or encouragement from his family. Arlene never supported it; Molly and Mark were too young; Jody had no time to travel to the races; Alan's father returned to Wichita; and my own interest was diverted entirely to our new twin baby girls, so Alan's rooting section was gone.

The surly but beautiful 3-liter 1954 or 1955 Ferrari 750 Monza. Photograph by John LeMay.

Alan always raced to win, not just to race. And he wanted to win in the top class, not in mini-sedans. But not everything he wanted was possible at that point, so without further comment he gracefully retired.

He lost interest in his racing story and scrapped it. He said he found the subject to be shallow, and not worth his time. The only drama was in the deadly crashes, and there was no way to avoid the obvious plot twists. There have since been a few good movies made, such as *Grand Prix* and *LeMans*, in some cases featuring excellent actors such as Steve McQueen, James Garner, Yves Montand, and Paul Newman, and showing outstanding race footage which was greatly admired by those who love race cars. But in the end the films were rated as clichéd and predictable, and they were a disappointment at the box office.

Alan had that one right.

— 22 —

Legacy

During the winter of 1951–52 Alan had good income from screen-writing assignments on *Flight Nurse, I Dream of Jeannie,* and *Blackbeard the Pirate,* plus some deferred payment deals that began to pay off. This left him with enough cash to leave Hollywood and write on his own as he had wanted to do for years. He sounded burned out and ready to leave when he wrote to his father in July 1952:

> My sole object now is to get out of pictures and become a writer. All I want of this business and this town is out of it. I finally saved enough expense money to run until the first of the year without salaried assign-ment, and I have refused several jobs since I left RKO. So now I have five months for my first try.
>
> But I do not leave pictures, — if I make good my escape, I mean — I do not leave defeated. I claim the following records for my decade-plus in Hollywood:
>
> > Writer who wrote most big pictures,
> > Writer with most millions expended on scripts,
> > Writer whose pictures had greatest total gross,
> > Writer whose pictures showed highest net returns,
> > Longest continuous performance without ever bringing in a loss, and
> > Writer most empty-handed at the end of it.
>
> I have directed one, produced two, written seventeen, or maybe it's eighteen; and now come out wherein I went, if I can find the way out, except that I am now totally unknown, and can start over at the bottom. But the industry is hurt too — theatres dark all over the country — so I claim a draw.
>
> Either the people running this business don't understand it, or else I don't understand it — and in either case I'd better swim for it. Writing has changed since I've been gone, and nobody knows whether I have anything, not even myself. But if I fail this time I will try again later.

He had not, in fact, forgotten how to write a novel. On a somewhat more leisurely schedule than he had endured in films, he wrote what is

163

generally considered to be his finest: *The Searchers*. Alan wrote it as a serial entitled *The Avenging Texans*, and it ran in five installments in *The Saturday Evening Post* starting November 6, 1954. Harper & Bros. bought it immediately to be published as a hardcover novel.

I can remember him telling me that he sold the film rights with the stipulation that he didn't have to write the screenplay and he didn't have to see the film. Of course, the contract didn't actually say that, but it was clear that Alan's frustration with Hollywood had not faded.

Evan Thomas, Alan's editor at Harper's, was enthusiastic. In an internal Harper's memorandum, Evan wrote[1]:

> Here is the unrevised LeMay frontier novel now entitled THE SEARCHERS. I should explain that the author is adding some new material and doing some reorganizing, mainly to give us a better understanding of the main character, and to change the present serial-type organization. (*The Saturday Evening Post* is doing this as a five-part serial, though it will be a hundred pages shorter than even this manuscript.) Stuart Rose of the *Post* says that this is the best novel he has read in his time there. There was considerable competition and large bids from a number of publishers. So we have had to promise to give this a big push as a straight novel. Jack and Mike and I are all very keen about this.

The story has two heroes: Amos and teenage Martin. Evan Thomas at Harper's made it clear that he approved of the manuscript as written, but suggested that the character of Marty could be strengthened if Alan agreed. He said in a telegram,[2]

> Glad to read any part of manuscript as it comes. Don't forget that we consider this already a fine novel and would be proud to publish as is. Don't worry too much about subjective since pace and story quality are essential to this novel. I suggested some subjective writing simply as possible means of deepening reader association with Martin and one or two others. I know you won't let revisions weaken terrific theme of kind of courage that is finest gift of man.

Given the opportunity to add a hundred pages, Alan made extensive changes, adding material on Marty, and developing the Indian culture more extensively. An entire episode in which Martin accidentally marries an Indian girl called Look was added. Harper's was in a hurry to meet a book contest deadline, and Alan had taken a short rush screenplay job for Republic, so he was again saddled with a crushing schedule. He took it seriously, and it affected his health. He wrote to Evan Thomas,[3]

> Oh murderation! I've had it now! Within twenty minutes of mailing Saturday's letter to you my eyes started to fail. Blind spots appeared on the page, and within two hours I couldn't even see to drive home.

Today I can see to drive, and believe this thing is improving. One eye, anyway. This never happened to me before. I can't proof a page yet....

As I have told you, I must report at Republic today — within the next hour — but I will complete the next few pages in the next few nights, if only I can find a secretary to take it down and read it to me, so I can do it by ear.

He was nearly finished six weeks later when he wrote[4]

The present last-of-its-kind detour is finishing very slowly. I am fast running out of horse without running out of track. I have sat in this same office and run off 36 pages in a day; yesterday I got two. I can tell when I'm really tired and not fooling myself by blood pressure fluctuation: Six months ago, $^{124}/_{68}$, now $^{186}/_{2}$, It's been almost that high before, and returned to normal in a few days when the pressure went off.

Stripped down to its framework, the novel appears pretty simple, which supports one of Alan's maxims: "It ain't what you tell, it's how you tell it." So without the character development, nuances, and ambiguity that made it great, here's the plot of the novel:

Amos Edwards (called Ethan in the film version) returns from the Civil War to visit his brother, Henry Edwards. It is hinted that he loves his brother's wife, Martha, but neither has the slightest intention of acting on that. Indians have stolen some cattle from a neighbor, and Amos joins the hunt for the culprits along with Marty, a teenager adopted by the Edwards years ago when Indians killed his family. The searchers are led far from the ranch before they realize they have been duped into leaving the women and children vulnerable to a killing raid. The men return to the Edwards' ranch to find a smoking ruin, the adults massacred, and two young daughters, little Debbie and teen-age Lucy, missing.

Amos and Marty lead a party to rescue the two girls, and soon the others give up and return home. Ethan and Marty continue on, and on. Early in the search, Amos finds Lucy raped, murdered, and mutilated by the Indians. His obsessive quest is seen to be driven by his need to avenge the murder of his brother's wife. He considers the possibility of little Debbie being killed in a rescue raid to be acceptable, or even inevitable. Marty is dedicated to preventing that outcome.

After several adventurous years they catch up with Scar, the original abductor, because he finally yields to the persistence of these men who just keep coming on, and on, past all reason. Scar has long since adopted Debbie as his daughter. In the final encounter, Amos is killed by a squaw and Debbie escapes, to be found and rescued by Marty.

Both the novel and the film were well accepted. Neither won any awards at the time, although the novel briefly touched the *New York Times* bestseller list.[5] But after more than 50 years, *The Searchers* is still popular at retrospective film festivals, and frequently reappears on television. It is widely acclaimed as John Ford's best film, and John Wayne's best also (although Ford liked *The Quiet Man* better). But, as Alan would have bitterly expected from Hollywood, the credit usually went entirely to John Ford.

What sets the story apart from the typical Western is the complexity and ambiguity of the theme of racism, and of the dual heroes. Giving the hero some anti-hero characteristics has been recognized as a trend in Western fiction in the 1950s, and it was accomplished here by splitting the traditional hero into two main characters.[6] At this late stage in Alan's writing career, he took advantage of his independence to escape the Western formula, as he had done with humor in the stumble-bum hero of *Useless Cowboy*. Much of the character development is ambiguous and, despite Ford's treatment, is too subtle to be fully appreciated when viewing the film for the first time. That could be the reason why it has aged so well. Neither main character in the novel wore the white-hat/black-hat uniform of a traditional Western character.

Even more important to the film's longevity is its depiction of the culture war between the Indians and the white settlers, here given a racist spin at a time when the country was embroiled in that issue, sometimes violently. The Indian raiders are shown as heartless killers, murdering women and children, raping, and taking scalps. This does not sit well with some reviewers who see the Indians as simply defending their own territory from the white invaders. But both the novel and the film, in fairness to the Indians, portray them with historical accuracy as friendly traders, helpful scouts, brilliant horsemen, and valiant warriors where appropriate. LeMay even has Charlie MacCorry, speaking as a Texas Ranger, say, "Half the Indian trouble we get nowadays is stirred up by quick-trigger thieves and squaw men poking around where they don't belong."[7] Indians who have viewed the film praised it as being their fairest treatment yet in a Hollywood Western.[8] But as Alan knew from both his research and his family's experience, the Indians were not a monolithic culture. There were definitely good Indians and bad Indians.

The worst Indians were the Dog Soldiers of the Northern Cheyenne. The appellation was from the Indians themselves. They denigrated dogs but admired soldiers, so by the words of their own people the Dog Soldiers were despised as the vilest element of tribal society, but were admired for their effectiveness, skill, and bravery as soldiers.[9] Most prairie Indians in the 1860s were content to abide by a fragile truce, trading with the settlers and limiting their predations to thievery and cattle rustling for food. But the Dog Soldiers, young bucks enraged by the takeover of their ancestral lands, killed, burned, kidnapped, raped and pillaged. Their objective was to get rid of the invaders completely, by killing all they could and terrorizing the survivors.

In the late 1860s, Indian war parties were particularly active on the western frontiers of Kansas and Texas. The problem was exacerbated by the government giving rifles and ammunition to the Indians, which they were required to do by treaty, "for their fall hunt." On August 3, 1868, a large allotment of arms was given to the Indians at Fort Larned, Kansas.[10] Just ten days later about 200 well-armed Cheyenne Dog Soldiers, joined by some Arapahoe and Sioux, began a series of raids in Cloud County, Kansas, and along the Solomon and Saline rivers. They killed or wounded about 40 settlers: men, women and children alike. They attacked while the men were out working the fields, when the women and children were vulnerable at their house. At each farm the Indians did as much damage as possible, stealing what they wanted and destroying the rest. They killed the men, took women and children captives when they could, but killed the children if they caused any trouble. In short, they acted just like the Indians in the opening raid in *The Searchers*. The women were treated horribly; the phrase "a fate worse than death" appears frequently in the contemporaneous accounts. The captives were used as work slaves and trade items among the Indians, and sometimes were ransomed back to their own people. Most were treated as hostages to be killed instantly in case of an attack by rescuers.

One such captive in the Kansas summer of 1868 was Sarah White, age 18. Her father was killed and she was captured in a raid by Dog Soldiers, just eight miles west of Concordia.[11] Their home was destroyed, but Sarah's mother and six younger brothers and sisters escaped. Two months later in a similar raid, 25 miles south of Concordia, James Morgan was badly wounded and his bride of one month, Anna, was captured at their farm on the Solomon River. The farm was destroyed. The following March, Custer and his troops recaptured Sarah White and Anna Morgan by cleverly capturing several Dog Soldier Chiefs and negotiating a prisoner trade. Custer optimistically wrote in his report, "This I consider as the termination of the Indian war." Sarah had been with the Indians for seven months, Anna for five months. Both had been beaten, raped, and starved. Both were pregnant. Sarah recovered, but Anna went insane.[12]

Indian attacks were still a fact of prairie life when, later that year, the Rev. Nels Nelson homesteaded a farm near the new settlement of Denmark, Kansas. He had only been there but a short time when on May 30, 1869, his farm was burned out by a band of about 60 Indians.[13] Nelson and his family escaped, but three other settlers were killed. Nelson had watched in horror from the other side of the Republican River as a 12 year old neighbor boy was run down by thirty screaming Dog Soldiers and was shot twice in the head. There was no help from the military, who arrived late. But then they stayed in the vicinity for the rest of the summer, easing the fears of the nervous farmers.

Sophia Karen Jensen certainly knew of the recent Indian attack on the Danish settlement and her friend Nels Nelson when she nevertheless left Denmark and followed him to Kansas, arriving April 20, 1870.[14] Within the year she met and married Alan's grandfather, Oliver Lamay, and started a family homestead on the prairie west of Concordia, in Cloud County, Kansas. The mood of the settlers was cautious, but not fearful.[15] They believed the local news that the Indians had been confined to the reservations and that the few roaming bands were more of a curiosity than a deadly threat. And since the Civil War had ended, the settlers expected to be protected by the returning Army and the Kansas State Militia. These expectations were supported by the campaign of the railroads in their aim to foster development. Alan's father later wrote of those times[16]:

> To induce people to move into the huge tracts of unoccupied but essentially productive farm lands, railroads were necessary and to induce investors to build railroads, large grants of land were made to them to extend their lines. The roads conducted advertising campaigns not only to the eastern states but also to the land-hungry people of Europe, and they came arunning. My Mother, Sophia Karen Jensen, daughter of a large family of peasants in Denmark, joined a group of families bound for Kansas, about 1870. This group took up claims, largely in Cloud County, just north of Jamestown, and along the Republican River.

To a large extent the relaxed feeling of security was valid, and the few roaming bands of Indians were not a serious threat. But not all of the Indians were ready to concede defeat. They donned their war paint one more time for the last raid in Kansas.

The last Kansas raids were a series of attacks on settlers in September 1878. The campaign was led by Chief Dull Knife of the Northern Cheyenne.[17] They had been interred under miserable conditions on a reservation in Oklahoma, and wanted to return to their homeland in the Black Hills of South Dakota. Dull Knife led a group of 89 men, 112 women, and 134 children off the reservation. They were able to steal away at night undetected, and could very probably have made the entire trip to the Dakotas without being found. But instead they blazed a bloody trail of destruction as they went. They murdered out of sheer rage, burning out the white settlers, killing men, women and children, and taking scalps.

The raids started at Sheet's cattle camp on the Salt Fork of the Cimarron River, just north of the Oklahoma–Kansas boundary. Two people were killed outright, two others seriously wounded, and a baby mortally wounded. The band went on to the Payne ranch where the Indians shot Payne, his wife, and their baby. A cattle herder was caught out by himself and was chased down and killed.

At one point, south of Dodge City, a troop of United States regulars was joined by enough Barber County scouts to outnumber the Indians. They were able to surround the band in a canyon and thought they could contain them over night. But the Indians crept away in the dark, showing once again that they could have sneaked back home quietly if they were merely homesick. Instead they continued killing and burning their way north until they were finally defeated and captured in Nebraska. These were the Indians that Alan had given such favorable treatment in his first novel, *Painted Ponies*. The death toll in Kansas from Dull Knife's campaign is variously reported between 75 and 100 settlers.

There were countless other Indian wars and raids at that time, from Texas to the Dakotas, many involving the capture of white women and children. Few captives ever returned successfully to white society, either because they did not want to come back or because they were reviled as contaminated. Feelings ran high, and the white settlers, in many tragic cases, did not accept them back graciously.[18]

This is all a matter of record, and was well known to Alan. It particularly affected his attitude about Indians because his father and grandparents (Sophia Karen Jensen and Oliver Lamay) had been so close to the action. They were homesteading west of Concordia when Alan's father, John LeMay, was born in 1873. John was five during these last Indian raids, and was attending the little one-room school in Concordia. That is where he met his future wife, Maude Brown, who had recently arrived with her family from Indiana.

Writing to his editor at Harper's about *The Searchers* manuscript, Alan said[19]

> These are not things my own people did, or that happened to them.
> But the story is about the kind of people that some of my family were.

* * *

During those years, the situation in Texas was about the same as in Kansas.[20] The dangerous Indians were Comanche instead of Northern Cheyenne, but the settlers had all the same problems with them. Alan did extensive research on the Comanche and their Texas abductions as well as the Northern Cheyenne in Kansas.[21] It could be said that in *The Searchers*

Alan was motivated by the Kansas raids, but put the story into a Texas setting because cattle wrangling is more entertaining than sod busting.

Many reviewers of Ford's film have claimed that the novel was based upon the Fort Parker Massacre of 1836 and the abduction of Cynthia Ann Parker.[22] This small Texas outpost was attacked by a huge war party, estimated at 500 Comanche warriors, joined by some Kiowa and other tribes. The surprise attack was initiated by subterfuge behind a white flag of truce. The men were away in their fields, so the Indians had little opposition. They killed five men and captured three women and two children. One of those captured was Cynthia Ann Parker, age nine. Her abduction enraged the Texans, who were able to bargain for the release of four hostages, but Cynthia Ann remained with the Indians. She was recaptured by a company of Texas Rangers and Militia in 1860 at the battle of Pease River[23] after living as an Indian for 24 years.

The end of that story was tragic. Back with the Parker family, Cynthia Ann was not treated well and was never happy. She missed the children she had with Comanche Chief Peta Nocona. One of her sons was Quanah Parker, who became a famous Comanche war chief. It remains controversial what became of Peta Nocona, whether or not he was killed at the Pease River when Cynthia Ann was recaptured. Cynthia Ann survived until 1870, when she became sick and stopped eating. It was variously reported that she starved herself to death or that she died of a broken heart.

It is easy to suppose that *The Searchers* is based on Cynthia Ann Parker — she was nine when captured, and Debbie in *The Searchers* was about the same age, and they both were objects of long searches. But the similarity ends there, and it was not Alan's intention to base his novel on that history, or any other single event. Alan described Debbie in a letter to Evan Thomas[24]:

> [She was a] little girl who — like many others in a score of recorded instances — seemed to turn into a wild thing in the years through which the Comanches held her captive, raising her as their own.

In June 1958, Alan responded to a letter from a fan asking what he knew about the Cynthia Ann Parker story, and suggesting that he write a novel about Cynthia Ann. He wrote back with a recounting of the known facts of the case, and concluded with[25]:

> As for a novel about Cynthia Ann: I question if the most laborious research would add more than a few pages to the above — and those few would be the only ones in the novel that could be called "every bit of it true." What you would have, then, in effect, is my own novel THE SEARCHERS, which represents about all I have to contribute on this

particular subject. But thank you for your thoughtful suggestion, and thank you again for your letter.

In another letter, Alan responded to a Texas high school senior who asked why he wrote *The Searchers*[26]:

> As to why I wrote it: a great deal has been written about historic injustices to the Indian; I myself once wrote a book highly partisan to the Northern Cheyenne [*Painted Ponies*]. I thought it was time that somebody showed that in the case of the Texans, at least, there were two sides to it, and that the settlers had understandable reasons to be sore.
>
> The book took me about a year and a half. I wrote about two thousand pages, mostly no good, to get the two hundred pages we used.

And later in 1960 he wrote to a fan who thought she might be related to the Edwards family[27]:

> I am sorry to say that the families in my story are all fictitious. The name Edwards was suggested to me by the Edwards Plateau. The locale is indeed regional to Fort Worth, intended to vaguely resemble, more or less, parts of Palo Pinto, Parker, Wise, Jack, or Young Counties interchangeably. But I do not knowingly use the names of real people in fiction because I don't know what the real people said.

There were too many other cases of women and children being captured which were a better fit to the description of the raid in *The Searchers*. The Cynthia Ann Parker case was by far the most famous abduction, and that is undoubtedly the reason why so many reviewers, unfamiliar with the many Plains Indians abductions of that era, seized upon it as the inspiration for the novel. I would suggest that these same reviewers, especially those who complain that the Indians were misrepresented, are not familiar with the Dog Soldiers or Chief Dull Knife's Last Raid in Kansas. Alan had, as usual, done thorough research and was an expert on the Comanche, the Northern Cheyenne, the Kiowa, and the several other tribes important to the events of that time. He had a wealth of data to work from, as he stated in a response to another fan letter[28]:

> I have dug up some 64 cases of white children kidnapped in this period, but I believe these to be only a small minority of the actual total.

Sarah White, Anna Morgan, and Susanna Alderdice, for example,[29] were better prototypes for Debbie Edwards than Cynthia Ann Parker. They were captured in assaults on small farms while the men were away, much like *The Searchers*.

Sarah White's farm, in fact, was just a few miles from the Oliver Lamay homestead, and on that sparsely populated prairie, the Whites and Lamays probably knew each other. But in Cynthia Ann Parker's case, Fort

Parker was not an isolated home, but a defensive stockade for several families where the Indians got inside by trickery. No similarity there. Nor is there similarity in their captivities. LeMay's Debbie was adopted by Scar and raised as his child. She viewed him as her father, avoiding the miscegenation stigma. Cynthia Ann Parker married Chief Peta Nocona, had children with him, and longed to be back with him after her recapture.

The Edwards' home in *The Searchers* was not a fort, but was more like the White's or Lamay's, a typical homestead on the Kansas or Texas frontier, (at least in the novel). In the film, John Ford put it out in the desert of Monument Valley, which again was nothing like Fort Parker.

Why did Ford use Monument Valley for the homestead? Because he liked it. He preferred location shooting, and had a particular love for the stark beauty there. He apparently thought no one would notice that it was nowhere near Texas; it is actually in Utah, just north of the Arizona border. It is also a really bad place to homestead or to raise cattle because they would starve. Ford thought that the scenery, as filmed by Winton Hoch, was worth it. He was right. The scenic beauty became a feature that helped sell the film. But Alan LeMay would have balked at sacrificing reality to that extent.

Much of the credit for the "big picture" look of the film must go to Hoch. He had photographed several of Ford's previous westerns in Monument Valley, including his classic *Stagecoach*. Ford respected Hoch's talent and did not micromanage his camera work. The Ford/Hoch technique can be recognized as framing the scenes like portraits, maintaining camera position as the action moves within or through the setting. Hoch's work was so reliable that retakes were rare. Ford was known to shoot most scenes just once, giving film editors fewer choices and thereby maintaining control over the final cut.

Hoch's talent had been clear to Alan years before when he was signing the crew for his first independent production, *The Sundowners*. Alan believed that for *The Searchers*, Win Hoch could have made the cattle lands of west Texas look majestic, while preserving reality at the same time.

An acknowledged basis for the film's classic status is the complex character of Ethan Edwards, played by John Wayne. (His name was Amos in the novel, but Ford changed it because it made him think of Amos 'n' Andy.[30]) Ethan/Amos is a hero, but also a killer. He is likeable, but turns vicious as an Indian-hating bigot. He shocked audiences when he shot bushwhacker Futterman in the back, along with his two accomplices. The more typical Hollywood characterization would have contrived a face-to-face gunfight. But this is frontier reality as portrayed by LeMay, where the objective in real life is to dispose of the bad men without risking the outcome for style points. It shows Amos as being pragmatic rather than evil.

But Ethan/Amos is also an anti-hero because of his racism. The novel partially excuses this by showing that since the Indians had savagely massacred his family, he had justification. The primary motivation of Amos throughout the entire story is not the rescue of Debbie, but vengeance for the rape and murder of Martha, his brother's wife, in the Indian raid. Alan named the original serial version of the story *The Avenging Texans*, not *The Rescuing Texans*. Alan explains Amos' motivation quite clearly at the end of Chapter 7, at a point where we have been introduced to the characters, and their motivations can be understood. In Marty's thoughts, "the key to Amos' life suddenly became plain ... Amos was — always had been — in love with his brother's wife."

In contrast, Ford shows Ethan's love subtly without comment in an early scene, before we know any of these people, by the way Ethan and Martha look at each other, and the way Martha caresses Ethan's coat. This was too subtle for some early critics, who missed the message entirely. And at the end of the film, when Ethan catches Debbie, Frank Nugent wrote an all-important line: Ethan looks at Debbie cowering under his pistol and says, "You sure favor your mother."[31]

So the motivation for Ethan to suddenly change from hunter to savior is that Debbie reminds him of Martha. Ford thought Nugent's line was too obvious and re-shot the scene with no dialogue. Ethan boosts her up in the air as he did in the early scene when she was a child, and then lowers her into his arms and finally says "Let's go home, Debbie."[32] Most viewers saw this with welcome relief, that not only is Debbie not murdered, but Ethan is a hero after all. We wanted to like him, and now that is OK. It is considered one of the great moments in film.

It is also credible that Ethan's scalping of Scar has sated his appetite for revenge, and he is no longer in a murderous mood. But for some of the early critics, this was too subtle and they chided Ford for pulling a Hollywood switcheroo with inadequate motivation, just to give Wayne a measure of salvation at the end.[33] Ethan's motivation becomes clearer on a second viewing, but can be missed by the casual viewer who sees the film once as just another Western, and forgets the plot as he leaves the theater. This could be one reason why the film earned no awards when released, but became a cult favorite a decade later.

Of the two main characters, LeMay developed Marty as the hero, made Amos/Ethan ambiguously evil but clearly obsessive, and killed him at the end. Ford made Ethan the hero (he had to — it was John Wayne), but then went out of his way to make him a more incorrigible bigot. Ford portrayed Marty as part Indian so Ethan could display irrational intolerance by chiding him about it. It placed Ethan in conflict with the rest of the family who accepted Marty unconditionally, and thus by implication showed that the family would accept Debbie back from the Indians (most real frontier families in similar cases did not.)

Ford and Nugent also made it clear that Ethan wanted to kill Debbie just because she probably had been "defiled" by the Indians. But the novel is more ambiguous, primarily showing that Amos considered the possibility of her death in a revenge raid against the Indians to be an acceptable risk. Here again the novel is more true to history; there are many recorded cases of white hostages being killed during rescue attempts, but none of relatives killing their kin for having lived with Indians. They were shunned, yes. But not murdered.

Ford made a number of other changes for the purpose of darkening the character of Ethan and amplifying the specter of miscegenation. In the novel Debbie is adopted by Scar as his daughter, but Ford made Debbie Scar's wife. Ford hired Henry Brandon to play Scar specifically because he has blue eyes, showing that even Scar was part white and the product of miscegenation.[34] LeMay had given Amos a couple of speeches about the pioneers extending the frontier of civilization and buying 18 years of peace with their lives,[35] lending Amos some justification for his actions. But Ford and Nugent took those comments away from him and gave them to Mrs. Jorgenson, a deliberate move to rob Ethan of any idealistic motives.

LeMay made the Indian maiden Look a very sympathetic character: not attractive, but cheerful, helpful, and clean. She is in a very difficult position, having been accidentally bought by Marty to be his wife, but is making the best of it. In Chapter 16, Marty says to the threatening Amos, "It's my fault she's here — not hers. She's done all she possibly could to try to be nice, and make herself helpful, and wanted. I never seen no critter try harder to do right." The entire episode with Look was not in the original serial, but was added by Alan in support of Harper's suggestion to deepen Marty's character.

Ford portrayed Look the same way, and then contrasted her civility with Marty's crudeness by having Marty kick her down an incline when she affectionately snuggles up to his bedroll. Surprisingly, most film critics interpreted this as Ford's bad attempt at humor. But it is so universally viewed as *bad* humor that it is more likely Ford's backhanded way of dehumanizing the guffawing Ethan and humanizing the Indian girl. It is certainly not funny when she is later killed in a raid by white soldiers.

Alan liked to put his fingerprints on a story, and there were several in the novel that did not get into the movie. There was no cameo appearance of Al Overholt (Alan's adopted screen name). The book mentioned a town called Una Vaca, and the Jorgenson's cattle brand was the Lazy

Lightening, which was Alan's registered brand for his Rancho Una Vaca herd. And in the final scene, Marty is able to locate Debbie in the vast badlands by following the vultures making "Circles in the Sky." The first story Alan ever sold was entitled "Circles in the Sky."

While Alan would have done a number of things differently in the film, it was just as well that he did not write the screenplay. He had had enough of directors and producers assuming artistic control, and despite the wide acclaim given Ford for the brilliance of his changes, Alan's opinion would most likely have been his standard "if I had wanted it that way I would have written it that way." Ford was generally known as being on a par with DeMille as a tough man to work for. In several biographies, he is variously called an Irish egomaniac, a binge alcoholic, a tyrant, a curmudgeon, and a bully, with adjectives such as dour, sadistic, and dictatorial. All that aside, many actors said that Ford brought out the best in them. At this stage in his career, however, Alan had seen enough of that side of Hollywood, and he did not have to put up with it anymore. So it is well that he wasn't asked to. Frank Nugent had written scripts for Ford on a half dozen films before *The Searchers.* He was accustomed to Ford's rants, and knew how to do what Ford wanted, so the collaboration worked well for them.

* * *

Despite his happiness at being free of Hollywood, Alan did one last screenplay for his old friend Jesse Lasky. It was an adaptation of Zane Grey's *The Vanishing American*; the film was released under the same title in 1955. Alan got solo screenwriter credit, but was not enthusiastic about it, and I don't remember his ever talking about it. It was classed as an "A" picture, but the cast and crew were not famous names.

He also wrote a couple of war stories. "Missing in Action" was published in *The Saturday Evening Post* on December 8, 1956, but "A Gift from Korea" did not sell.

In the fall of 1954, Alan spent a month "among the Kiowa Indians, and other remote places"[36] in preparation for his next novel, *The Unforgiven.* As with *The Searchers*, he wrote it first as a serial. It ran in *The Saturday Evening Post* in seven installments, starting March 16, 1957, under the title "Kiowa Moon." Edited into a novel, Harper & Brothers immediately published it in hardcover as *The Unforgiven.* It was later published in the U.K. as *The Siege at Dancing Bird*, and Hecht-Hill-Lancaster bought the film rights. Burt Lancaster and Audrey Hepburn starred in the film which was directed by John Huston.

The story has been called a mirror image of *The Searchers*, because Indians are trying to recapture one of their own who was raised by a white family. The story has more emphasis than *The Searchers* on the irrational hatred of the Indians by the implacable white settlers. The Zacharys, a good white family, are ostracized by their neighbors for taking in a helpless baby, Rachel, who was left behind by a fleeing Indian band. The Zacharys claim she had been a white hostage. But they are unforgiven by half-crazy old Abe Kelsey, who had lost a son to the Indians and wanted the Zacharys to swap Rachel to get his son back. They refused, so Kelsey spread the word that Rachel was Indian, and hounded the Zacharys as Indian lovers.

There are no significant good Indians in the story. The Kiowa are portrayed as worse than the Comanche.[37] They more resemble the Dog Soldiers of the Northern Cheyenne. They were not even fighting to defend their lands; they were away from their homelands raiding for glory, loot, and sport. The demise of the Wild Tribes was said to be inevitable because the land was being taken over by the white settlers, "a race that fed a thousand people upon the land the Wild Tribes needed to feed one."

The style of writing in *The Unforgiven* reverts back somewhat to Alan's early Western jargon. Compared with *The Searchers*, the soddy is more primitive, the people and their lifestyle are more primitive, and they use many more words that don't appear in modern dictionaries. This is sometimes humorous, always colorful, and adds to the realism.

The first few chapters of the novel give a vivid portrayal of life under frontier conditions, setting a mood with the relentlessness of the wind and the loneliness of the women. The physical description of the soddy closely echoes that in his father's autobiographical notes.[38] The discussion of the cattle drives is a history lesson of how they were formed, how they were run, and how they ended. Like a gold rush, there was always the promise of great riches, but the more usual outcome was disappointment and poverty.

The novel was modified for film by writer Ben Maddow, produced by James Hill, financed by Hecht-Hill-Lancaster, and directed by John Huston. It starred Audrey Hepburn as Rachel and Burt Lancaster as Ben. Besides the usual simplifications needed to reduce a novel to a two-hour film, there were a number of changes made for the sole purpose of emphasizing the theme of racism.

In the movie, Old Zack (father of Ben and Cash) was killed when he led an attack on a Kiowa village, rather than the novel's version of drowning at a river crossing in a cattle drive. This turned Cash (Audie Murphy) into an implacable Indian hater. Rachel had been orphaned in a previous battle, and was saved by Zack who brought her home to Matthilda who had just lost her own baby girl. This change pretty much made the whole war with the Kiowa a problem of Zack's doing, even though his ongoing attacks on the Kiowa camps were arguably justified by their raids to recapture Rachel.

Rachel was adopted by the Zacharys, and in the film always knew she was adopted. She just didn't know she was Indian. That part was known by mother Matthilda, brother Ben, and no one else. There is no doubt that she is in fact Indian, but it was denied publicly. Abe Kelsey's dying claim that Rachel is Indian was clear and convincing in the film, but in the novel he was just taken off to be hanged as a horse thief and we still weren't sure. The family's version, that Rachel was left behind accidentally by fleeing Indians, but was white, still has the ring of possibility.

Rachel loves Ben more than as a brother, and in the film, between them there was the looming impediment of miscegenation, but not incest. The novel kept Rachel thinking she was Ben's blood sister. So learning she was Indian was, to her, good news/bad news. If she was Indian she could marry Ben, but.... Thus the film emphasized the racism issue as the only block to romance, and left out the incest.

Younger brother Cash was characterized as putting race ahead of family. Again the film changed to emphasize irrational racism. This justifies the casting of the non–Indian-looking Audrey Hepburn as Rachel — she looks white, she sounds white, she was raised white, she has always been a member of a good white family, but she is instantly despised by Cash when he learns she probably had Indian parents. Bigotry beyond reason! The character of Johnny Portugal (John Saxon) is also turned into more of a race issue, just to keep racism in the forefront.

In the film's final battle, the Indians are stereotyped as incompetent to the point of silliness. They lose several warriors in repeated attacks on a piano, right in front of a fortified wall bristling with guns, because of their superstitions about musical medicine. The piano was a film contrivance, completely out of character with frontier soddy living. A soddy is always cramped for space. Please don't bring home a baby grand!

And in line with the most trite portrayals of cowboy versus Indian battles, every shot by a white person brings down an Indian, and usually his horse as well, while the Indians can't hit a thing other than a stray fatal shot to Matthilda. In contrast, the novel shows the Kiowa as clever and resourceful, and the whites killing very few.

The film closes with Rachel demonstrating her fidelity to the white side of the conflict by shooting her own Indian brother. This is a very mechanical resolution of the racism issue, leaving it settled by violence. The novel in contrast ends with a gentle character revelation: Ben burns unread an old Indian parchment that would settle Rachel's parentage once and for all, demonstrating that her race means nothing to him.

Racism is pattern recognition gone awry. To deny pattern is to fail to learn. But stereotyping is only useful in the absence of experience, and

learning trumps stereotyping. Animosities develop for good reason between
cultures, and race becomes involved as a convenient identifier of culture.
The settlers were not necessarily racist who despised Kiowa any more than
Americans were racist who despised Nazis. It was a conflict of cultures
learned from actions.

But to despise Rachel as an Indian, ignoring her lifetime of non–
Indian living, is knee-jerk racism, and that certainly existed also. Alan's intent
is expressed in a letter to his editor[39] responding to a critic who had searched
for "some bit of universal meaning" in *The Unforgiven*. Alan replied:

> I thought I had made an exceptionally exact and detailed exploration of
> an historic race-hatred, in terms of the tragic events that generated it.

The film clearly portrays that theme, but Huston argued with his producer for even more racism. The bickering ended in compromise, and Huston
did not like the results. You can't blame him. The production cannot com-
pare with the Ford/Hoch job on *The Searchers*. There are fits of bad over-
acting, and for a big outdoor film the camera work is spotty. For example,
in a dust storm, shooting day for night, the dust nearly blocks visibility
in front of the camera, but just beyond the fan-blown dust strip the distant
scenery is clear and so is the sunny blue sky with puffy white clouds.

These and other shortcomings can probably be attributed to the well-
publicized production chaos that plagued the filming.[40] Rick Height and
the financiers waged a constant battle with Huston, who wanted to make
a statement about racism in America. Height's company wanted to tone
it down to be more commercial and less controversial. Neither was satisfied.
Hepburn broke her back in a fall from a horse during rehearsals, and production was suspended for several months. Huston left the company early,
did not participate in the final edit, and did not like the outcome.

I should add that most reviewers liked the movie better than I did,[41]
but I doubt that they had read the book, which was judged by many to
be better than *The Searchers*.

* * *

Even though his novels sold well, Alan was still able to live beyond
his means. He had received about $35,000 (estimated; that is what the
Post paid for his "Kiowa Moon") from *The Saturday Evening Post* for "The
Avenging Texans," (the serial version of *The Searchers*). Harper & Brothers
had followed immediately with a $5,000 advance for the novel,[42] and C.
V. Whitney bought the film rights for $60,000.[43] Then *The Unforgiven*
earned Alan another $35,000 from *The Saturday Evening Post*,[44] another
$5000 advance from Harper's, and $75,000 for the film rights from Hecht-
Hill-Lancaster on January 28, 1957.[45] Thus the two stories paid Alan about

$215,000, plus royalties, in a three-year period. Even with high taxes, this should have been a very good living.

But the race car episode was expensive, and in 1959, to settle his tax bill, he grudgingly took on a six-week treatment for Harold Hecht on *Taras Bulba* at $2,500 per week "on the strict understanding I was under no circumstances to write the screenplay."[46] He ran into trouble finishing the treatment because of a Writers Guild strike. They ordered him to stop work or be expelled,[47] reinforcing his low opinion of Hollywood.

Alan's last novel, *By Dim and Flaring Lamps* (Harper & Brothers, 1962) is set in the time of the Jayhawkers, Bushwackers, and the lawless days in Missouri leading up to the outbreak of the Civil War. There were no Indians, no theme of racism other than the reality of slavery, but a colorful portrayal of the aristocratic south breaking down as families split over secession. The locale follows the Mississippi and Missouri Rivers, and the narrative brings back the great riverboats that Alan had written about in New Orleans 30 years before.

Alan in his Pacific Palisades office, c. 1962. The tacky venetian blind is an apparently-staged salute to non-conformity.

During this period, he worked from his office in Palisades Village. It was within a mile of his home in Pacific Palisades, and he walked or jogged to the office most days. His normal working day was 12 hours. He would start at 6:00 with a four-hour stint, which included rewriting yesterday's product. Then he would take four hours off mid-day for a workout at the local gym, lunch, and a nap. Starting again at 2:00, he would write until 6:00, and then walk home for a drink, dinner, and social time, with *no* story conferences.

It was, for him, a very relaxing schedule. He responded well to the rest and exercise, and wrote some of the finest material of his life. He still smoked heavily and had coughing fits from his "chronic bronchitis," but claimed that he was in the best condition he had been in in years. Then one morning he walked down to the local bank to cash a check, and he could not endorse it. His right hand was paralyzed.

Tests revealed a brain tumor. The only recommended treatment was surgery, and they were not very good at it in 1964. Alan knew that, but decided that the gamble was a better bet than the no-chance alternate. Arlene said his last unsedated words were, "OK, pull the trigger!" He survived the surgery, but the tumor could not be removed completely. He lingered for a few months, and died at home on April 28, 1964. Honoring his World War I service as a "shavetail," he was buried in the military cemetery at Fort Rosecrans on Point Loma, San Diego.

Alan LeMay had lived during an era that had been perfect for him, through the Roaring Twenties, the polo and ranch days of the thirties, the Big Studio film era of the forties, and finishing with a very active retirement of sports car racing and, most of all, returning to the independence of writing as he wanted. It was a huge scope for one lifetime. As he said many times, usually when his luck had gone against him, "Me ... who have seen what I've seen ... been where I've been ... done what I've done..."

Despite this rich, full life, and his prodigious output of stories in both print and film, he is best known for that single novel *The Searchers*. And he is often given little credit for that.

For example, Gary Arnold in "Hero's Welcome for *The Searchers*" in the September 23, 1979, *Washington Post*, noted that reviewers had neglected "the seminal, utterly indispensable importance of Alan LeMay's original novel" and identified that as a symptom of "the disparity in status between superior Western fiction and superior Western filmmaking." Arnold further commented on the lack of recognition given to writers:

> ... the filmmakers felt impelled to sacrifice certain elements whose loss you profoundly regret once you become aware of them. LeMay devised stunning climactic and concluding episodes. They leave emotional

reverberations that the movie never quite equals, despite the combined eloquence of Ford's pictorial genius and Wayne's towering physical presence at the fadeout.

When the film's final portal image closes, it appears to exclude Ethan Edwards from the society he has struggled to revenge, protect and restore. The movie ends with a lingering impression of Wayne's Ethan Edwards beyond the threshold, a proud, lonely man. But there's also an unseen, forgotten man lingering out there in the cinematic ether: the storyteller who imagined *The Searchers* in the first place.

It is partly true. Alan LeMay never won an oscar. They don't give an Oscar for a career of reliable performances that never brought in a loss. But the writer is not forgotten when his name keeps coming back to the screen in glorious Technicolor, over and over for more than fifty years, proclaiming

FROM THE NOVEL BY ALAN LEMAY

Alan LeMay c. 1962.

Appendix: Story List

The following list of Alan LeMay's novels, short stories, film and TV credits is probably not complete. It is certainly missing stories that were not published, and screenplays that were never filmed. It also does not include all of the numerous republications in various anthologies, collections, foreign languages, big print editions, and such. Many reprints had changed titles, and these are included where known. A few older anthologies are listed because they may provide a second source for finding stories that are more than a half-century out of print. The installments of serials are listed as separate items to document the issues of the magazines in which they appear.

There are a number of titles listed for *Collier's* between 1928 and 1933, where no issue is known. These were included in a listing by year, apparently typed by Alan or his secretary in 1937 (the last entry). Most of the titles on this list have been confirmed with specific issue dates, although those dates indicate that publication was frequently delayed, sometimes by as much as three years. It is possible that *Collier's* bought some stories that they never used, or published them with different titles.

Alan developed several characters (Bug Eye, Whiskers Beck, and Old Man Coffee) that were used in a number of different stories. These are noted with some of the titles.

Alan LeMay's only confirmed pseudonym is Alan M. Emley. It first appeared for reasons unknown in the November 1929 article listed below, and then was used frequently for pulp stories, starting in 1935 after he had established a name in the slicks. An unrelated Alan M. Emley wrote a pseudo-scientific book called *Solar Psychology* in 2003.

30 Dec 1919. "Circles in the Sky." *Detective Story Magazine*, pp. 62–75.
2 Mar 1920. "Out of the Swamp." *Detective Story Magazine*.
9 Jun 1922. *I Am Villon* (stage play). *Aurora Dramatic Club*.
30 Jun 1922. "Hullabaloo." *Adventure*, pp. 77–80.

10 Jul 1922. "The Brass Dolphin." *Adventure*, pp. 164–166.

20 Dec 1922. "Ghost Lanterns." *Adventure*, pp. 106–110.

1924. "Mr. Pringle Saves a Life." *Top Notch*.

1924. "Pirates of 1922." *Sea Stories*.

1924. "Refuge." *Western Story Magazine*.

1924. "Yard Crock." *Sea Stories*.

20 Sep 1924. "Needin' Help Bad." *Western Story Magazine*, pp. 128–129.

10 Nov 1924. "The Three Missing Men." *Adventure*, pp. 131–135.

1925. 35 articles on contract. *Dough* (a magazine for bakers).

1925. 3 issues on contract. *The Earthmover* (a trade magazine).

1925. 1 issue on contract. *National Guardsman* magazine.

10 Mar 1925. "Mustang Breed." *Adventure*, pp. 125–131.

30 Jun 1925. "Terlegaphy and the Bronc." *Adventure*, pp. 49–55.

1 Jul 1925. "His Better Idea." *Top Notch*.

30 Jul 1925. "Top Horse from Hogjaw." *Adventure*.

10 Oct 1925. "The Legacy Mule." *Adventure*, pp. 89–98.

30 Oct 1925. "Whack Ear's Pup." *Adventure*, pp. 39–49.

20 Nov 1925. "The Contest Man." *Adventure*; also in *Selected Western Stories* (Popular Library, 1949) pp. 110–127.

10 Dec 1925. "Help, Bug Eye — I Cover the Town." *Short Stories*.

20 Dec 1925. "Strange Fellers." *Adventure*, pp. 29–41. Reprinted in *Adventure's Best Stories*, 1926.

20 Feb 1926. "Long Rob from Rapahoe." *Adventure*, pp. 64–72.

8 Apr 1926. "The Fourth Man." *Adventure*, pp. 41–50.

23 Nov 1926. "Baldy at the Brink." *Adventure*, pp. 132–138.

23 Dec 1926. "Two Old Men." *Adventure*, pp. 48–55.

1926. *Painted Ponies* (novel). Doran.

1 Jan 1927. *Painted Ponies* (serial, part 1). *Adventure*, pp. 24–51.

15 Jan 1927. *Painted Ponies* (part 2). *Adventure*.

1 Feb 1927. *Painted Ponies* (part 3). *Adventure*.

15 Feb 1927. *Painted Ponies* (part 4). *Adventure*.

15 May 1927. "Bug Eye Neerly Starves." *Adventure*, pp. 48–53.

1 Jun 1927. "The Dedwood Coach Brakes Down" (Bug Eye). *Adventure*.

1 Jul 1927. "Play-Actin' fer Gents." *Adventure*.

1 Aug 1927. "Bug Eye Loses Hisself." *Adventure*, pp. 110–116.

1 Sep 1927. "Old Father of Waters" (serial, part 1). *Adventure*.

15 Sep 1927. "Old Father of Waters" (part 2). *Adventure*.

1 Oct 1927. "Old Father of Waters" (part 3). *Adventure*.

15 Oct 1927. "Old Father of Waters" (part 4). *Adventure*, pp. 112–146.

1 Nov 1927. "Old Father of Waters" (part 5). *Adventure*, pp. 124–142.

15 Nov 1927. "The Bells of San Juan." *Adventure*, pp. 134–142 (Whiskers Beck).

1 Dec 1927. "Facts and Figgers on Cayuses." *Adventure*, pp. 156–157.

1927. "I am in Jail, Bug Eye." *Adventure*.

1927. *Rivermen Die Broke*. Paperback version of *Old Father of Waters*.

1928. *Old Father of Waters* (novel). Doubleday Doran.

1928. *Pelican Coast* (novel). Doubleday.

1928. "There's a Million Cows in the Greasewood" (article). *Collier's*; see 8 Feb 1930.

1 Feb 1928. "The Cross-Eyed Bull." *Adventure*, pp. 75–77.

15 Mar 1928. "Bug Eye Gets Hisself in Jale." *Adventure*, pp. 77–82.

1 May 1928. "Bug Eye Among the Soo." *Adventure*, pp. 42–50.

15 May 1928. "Hank Joins the Vijiluntys" (Bug Eye). *Adventure*.

1 Jun 1928. Hank's Other Pardner (Bug Eye). *Adventure*, pp. 124–132.

10 Nov 1928. "Bug Eye's Wandering Partner." *Short Stories* V. 125 #3.

25 Dec 1928. "Are You There, Bug Eye?." *Short Stories* V. 125 #6.

1929. "Brothers in Violence." *Collier's*.

1929. "Dead Man's Horse." *Collier's*.

1929. "One of Us Is a Murderer." *Short Stories*.

25 Jan 1929. "There's No Justice, Bug Eye." *Short Stories* V. 126, #2, pp. 83–92.

23 Feb 1929. "Loan of a Gun." *Collier's*, pp. 12–13, 54, 56.

18 May 1929. "The Wolf Hunter." *Collier's*, pp. 28, 60–62.

1 Jun 1929. "The Young Rush In" (Whiskers Beck). *Collier's*, pp. 14–15, 44.

15 Jul 1929. "Hank Arrives Back Ware He Cum Frum" (Bug Eye). *Adventure*.

Nov 1929. "Consistent Characterization" (article). *The Author and Journalist*, (by Alan M. Emley) Vol. 14, #2.

7 Dec 1929. "Sentenced to Swing." *Collier's*.

10 Dec 1929. "Help, Bug Eye — I Cover the Town." *Short Stories* V. 129, #5.

14 Dec 1929. "A Shot in the Dark." *Collier's*, pp. 20–21, 67–69.

1930. "Gambler's Suicide." *Complete Stories*.

1930. "Guns in the Cards." *Collier's*.

1930. "Gunsight Trail" (book). Farrar and Rinehart.

1930. "One of Us Is a Murderer" (novel). Crime Club (Doubleday, Doran).

1 Jan 1930. "Facts and Figgers on Women by Whiskers Beck." *Adventure*.

1 Feb 1930. "Facts and Figgers on Sheep by Whiskers Beck." *Adventure*.

8 Feb 1930. "Cowboys Will Be Cowboys" . *Collier's*, pp. 30, 54–55, probably changed from "There's a Million Cows in the Greasewood."

22 Feb 1930. "Just a Horse of Mine." *Collier's*, pp. 14–16, 30.

8 Mar 1930. "Under Fire." *Collier's*, pp. 10–11, 43–44.

22 Mar 1930. "Old Thunder Pumper." *Collier's*.

25 Mar 1930. "The Jungle Terror." *Short Stories*.

26 Apr 1930. "Battle of Gunsmoke Lode." *Collier's*, pp. 30, 61–63.

1 May 1930. "The Creeping Cloud" (serial). *Complete Stories* (Tonapah Range).

31 May 1930. "Tombstone's Daughter." *Collier's*, pp. 14–15, 32, 37.

5 Jul 1930. "Trail Driver's Luck." *Collier's*; reprinted in Bantam, *Western Roundup*, 1948, and *The Cowboys*, Fawcett, 1985.

26 Jul 1930. "One Charge of Powder." *Collier's*, p. 18.

27 Sep 1930. "To Save a Girl." *Collier's*, pp. 10–11, 62–64; reprinted as "Lost Dutchman O'Riley's Luck" in *The Big Book of Western Action Stories*, Barricade, 1995.

18 Oct 1930. "Kindly Kick Out Bearer." *Collier's*, pp. 22–23, 64, 68, 70.

8 Nov 1930. "Horse Laugh." *Collier's*, p. 26.

30 Dec 1930. "The Scourge of Kodaung." *Far Eastern Adventure Stories*, pp. 10–48.

1931. "The Bloodhound Failed." *Collier's*.

1931. "Lynch Law." *Collier's*.

1931. "A Flea Can Grow Bigger Than a Man." *Collier's*, and Carolyn Wells Anthology.

1931. *Bug Eye*. (Book, a rewrite of the Farrar and Rinehart *Wandering Partner* Shorts).

10 Jan 1931. "The Jungle of the Gods," Part I. *Short Stories*, pp. 4–30. Part II *Short Stories*, pp. 116–143.

31 Jan 1931. "The Braver Thing." *Collier's*, pp. 14–16, 30, 35.

1931. *Gunsight Trail* (book). Farrar and Rinehart.

7 Mar 1931. *Gunsight Trail* (serial, part 1). *Collier's*.

14 Mar 1931. *Gunsight Trail* (part 2). *Collier's*.

21 Mar 1931. *Gunsight Trail* (part 3). *Collier's*.

28 Mar 1931. *Gunsight Trail* (part 4). *Collier's*.

4 Apr 1931. *Gunsight Trail* (part 5). *Collier's*, pp. 18–20, 53–54.

11 Apr 1931. *Gunsight Trail* (part 6). *Collier's*.

18 Apr 1931. *Gunsight Trail* (part 7). *Collier's*.

25 Apr 1931. *Gunsight Trail* (part 8). *Collier's*.

2 May 1931. *Gunsight Trail* (part 9). *Collier's*.

6 Jun 1931. "The Biscuit Shooter" (Old Man Coffee). *Collier's*, pp. 7–9, 56–57.

27 Jun 1931. "Mules." *Collier's*, pp. 18, 34.

1 Aug 1931. "Horse for Sale" (Old Man Coffee). *Collier's*, p. 13.

22 Aug 1931. "Saddle Bum." *Collier's*, pp. 14–15, 49–50, 52.

19 Sep 1931. "Delayed Action." *Collier's*, pp. 7–9, 38, 40.

24 Oct 1931. "Six-Gun Graduate." *Collier's*, p. 12.

7 Nov 1931. "Neat Quick Case" (Old Man Coffee). *Collier's*, pp. 17–18, 48–51.

1931. *Winter Range* (novel). Farrar and Rinehart.

19 Dec 1931. *Winter Range* (serial, part 1). *Collier's*, pp. 7–9, 36, 38.

26 Dec 1931. *Winter Range* (part 2). *Collier's*, pp. 26–28, 38.

2 Jan 1932. *Winter Range* (part 3). *Collier's*, pp. 14–15, 44–45.

9 Jan 1932. *Winter Range* (part 4). *Collier's*, pp. 16–17, 44–45.

15 Jan 1932. "Soldiers of Misfortune." *Complete Stories*.

16 Jan 1932. *Winter Range* (part 5). *Collier's*, pp. 14–15, 43–45.

23 Jan 1932. *Winter Range* (part 6). *Collier's*, pp. 24–25, 47–48.

30 Jan 1932. *Winter Range* (part 7). *Collier's*, pp. 14–15, 32–33.

6 Feb 1932. *Winter Range* (part 8). *Collier's*, pp. 14–15, 54–55.

13 Feb 1932. *Winter Range* (part 9). *Collier's*, pp. 20–21, 34, 36.

1932. "The Cook was a Serious Thinker." *Collier's*.

1932. "The Nester." *Collier's*, possible title change; see 11 Feb 1933.

1932. "Luck." *Collier's*, co-author with Lyman Bryson.

15 Feb 1932. "Have One on Me." *The Popular Complete Stories*.

20 Feb 1932. *Winter Range* (part 10). *Collier's*, pp. 18–20, 45–46.

1 Mar 1932. "Today's Raw Bronc" (part 1). *Adventure*, pp. 134–135 (with Gil Strick).

9 Apr 1932. "Eyes of Doom." *Collier's*, p. 16 (co-author with Lyman Bryson).

15 Apr 1932. "The Raw Bronc" (part 2), "Breaking Him to Stake." *Adventure*, pp. 65–67 (with Gil Strick).

16 Apr 1932. "Thanks to a Girl in Love" (Old Man Coffee). *Collier's*, pp. 9, 30, 33–34.

14 May 1932. "Bronc Fighter's Girl." *Collier's*, pp. 7–9, 47–49.

15 May 1932. "The Raw Bronc" (pt. 3), "Unfinished Business." *Adventure*, pp. 91–93 (with Gil Strick).

18 Jun 1932. "A Girl is Like a Colt." *Collier's*, p. 18.

1 Jul 1932. "The Killer in the Chute." *Adventure*, pp. 24–35.

27 Aug 1932. "And Him Long Gone." *Sat. Eve. Post*, pp. 14–15, 65–66. Reprinted in *Western Triggers*, Bantam, 1948.

15 Oct 1932. "Pardon Me Lady." *Collier's*, pp. 22–23, 28.

1933. "Murder Range." *Novel Selection.*

1933. "Kiss Her and Let Her Go." *Collier's.*

Jan 1933. "Range Bred." *Cosmopolitan*, pp. 72–73, 98, 100, 102.

28 Jan 1933. "Spanish Crossing." *Collier's*, p. 26.

11 Feb 1933. "The Nester's Girl." *Collier's*, pp. 14–15, 36–38.

1933. *Cattle Kingdom* (novel). Farrar and Rinehart.

4 Mar 1933. "Cold Trails" (serial, part 1). *Collier's*, pp. 7–9, 28, 30 (Old Man Coffee) version of *Cattle Kingdom.*

11 Mar 1933. *"Cold Trails"* (part 2). *Collier's*, pp. 12–13, 59–61.

18 Mar 1933. *"Cold Trails"* (part 3). *Collier's*, pp. 18–19, 33–34.

25 Mar 1933. *"Cold Trails"* (part 4). *Collier's.*

1 Apr 1933. *"Cold Trails"* (part 5). *Collier's*, pp. 24, 34, 36–37.

8 Apr 1933. *"Cold Trails"* (part 6). *Collier's*, pp. 18–19, 38–39.

15 Apr 1933. *"Cold Trails"* (part 7). *Collier's.*

22 Apr 1933. *"Cold Trails"* (part 8). *Collier's*, pp. 20–21, 44–46.

29 Apr 1933. *"Cold Trails"* (part 9). *Collier's*, pp. 20–21, 42–44.

6 May 1933. *"Cold Trails"* (part 10). *Collier's.*

Sep 1933. "The Fiddle in the Storm." *Cosmopolitan.*

30 Sep 1933. "A Passage to Rangoon." *Collier's*, pp. 7–9, 34–35.

18 Nov 1933. "They Sometimes Come Back." *Collier's*, pp. 7–9, 51–53.

Nov 1933. "Fiddle in the Storm." *Cosmopolitan.*

1933. *Thunder in the Dust* (novel). Farrar and Rinehart.

2 Dec 1933. *Thunder in the Dust* (serial, part 1). *Collier's*, pp. 7–9, 38–40.

9 Dec 1933. *Thunder in the Dust* (part 2). *Collier's*, pp. 18–19, 29, 32.

16 Dec 1933. *Thunder in the Dust* (part 3). *Collier's*, pp. 20–21, 37, 39.

23 Dec 1933. *Thunder in the Dust* (part 4). *Collier's*, pp. 22–23, 30, 33.

30 Dec 1933. *Thunder in the Dust* (part 5). *Collier's*, pp. 18–19, 36, 38.

6 Jan 1934. *Thunder in the Dust* (part 6). *Collier's*, pp. 16–17, 47–49.

13 Jan 1934. *Thunder in the Dust* (part 7). *Collier's.*

20 Jan 1934. *Thunder in the Dust* (part 8). *Collier's.*

27 Jan 1934. *Thunder in the Dust* (part 9). *Collier's*, pp. 20–21, 39–41.

3 Feb 1934. *Thunder in the Dust* (part 10). *Collier's*, pp. 28, 39–42.

10 Feb 1934. *Thunder in the Dust* (part 11). *Collier's*, pp. 22, 28–30.

24 Feb 1934. "Out of the Whirlpool." *Collier's*, pp. 7–9, 41–43.

May 1934. "Gun Fight at Burnt Corral." *Cosmopolitan.*

May 1934. "Lawman's Debt" (Emley). *Dime Western*, pp. 70–77.

Jun 1934. "Hell on Wheels" (Emley). *Dime Western*, pp. 103–109.

20 Oct 1934. "After the Hounds." *Collier's*, pp. 22–23, 54–56.

1935. *The Smoky Years* (novel). Farrar and Rinehart.

12 Jan 1935. *The Smoky Years* (serial, part 1). *Collier's*, pp. 7–9, 50–52.

19 Jan 1935. *The Smoky Years* (part 2). *Collier's*, pp. 13, 36–38.

26 Jan 1935. *The Smoky Years* (part 3). *Collier's*, pp. 20–21, 51–53.

2 Feb 1935. *The Smoky Years* (part 4). *Collier's.*

9 Feb 1935. *The Smoky Years* (part 5). *Collier's*, pp. 17, 34–38.

16 Feb 1935. *The Smoky Years* (part 6). *Collier's*, pp. 20–21, 34, 36.

23 Feb 1935. *The Smoky Years* (part 7). *Collier's*, pp. 22, 30–31, 34, 39.

2 Mar 1935. *The Smoky Years* (part 8). *Collier's*, pp. 22–23, 41, 44.

9 Mar 1935. *The Smoky Years* (part 9). *Collier's*, pp. 20–21, 50–51.

15 Mar 1935. "Halfpint of Hell" (Alan M. Emley). *Dime Western*, pp. 115–125.

16 Mar 1935. *The Smoky Years* (part 10). *Collier's*, pp. 20–21, 60–62.

23 Mar 1935. *The Smoky Years* (part 11). *Collier's*, pp. 18–19, 39–41.

May 1935. "Death on the Rimrock." *Western Fiction*, pp. 6–95. Reprint of "Winter Range."

May 1935. "Hands of the Law" (Emley). *Popular Western*.

Sep 1935. "Shoot to Kill." *Complete Western Book Magazine*, pp. 4–108. Reprint of "Gunsight Trail."

Sep 1935. "Blood Moon" (Emley). *Popular Western*, pp. 102–109.

1935. *Deep Water Island* (novel). Farrar and Rinehart.

21 Sep 1935. *Deep Water Island* (serial, part 1). *Collier's*.

28 Sep 1935. *Deep Water Island* (part 2). *Collier's*.

5 Oct 1935. *Deep Water Island* (part 3). *Collier's*, pp. 14–15, 39–40.

12 Oct 1935. *Deep Water Island* (part 4). *Collier's*.

19 Oct 1935. *Deep Water Island* (part 5). *Collier's*.

26 Oct 1935. *Deep Water Island* (part 6). *Collier's*.

Oct 1935. "The Blessed Mule" (or "The Miracle Mule"). *Complete Western Book Magazine*, reprint of "The Legacy Mule," 10/10/25.

2 Nov 1935. *Deep Water Island* (part 7). *Collier's*, pp. 20–21, 41–43.

9 Nov 1935. *Deep Water Island* (part 8). *Collier's*.

16 Nov 1935. *Deep Water Island* (part 9). *Collier's*, pp. 28, 68–72.

Nov 1935. "The Killer." *Western Novel and Short Stories*, pp. 112–121. Reprint of "The Killer in the Chute," 1 Jul 1932.

Nov 1935. "Empty Guns" (Alan M. Emley). *Thrilling Western*, pp. 91–98.

Dec 1935. "Fight Back or Die." *Complete Western Book Magazine*, pp. 6–86. Reprint of Cattle Kingdom.

1936. "Prelude to Empire." *McCall's*.

Jan 1936. "The Man from Arapahoe." *Complete Western Book Magazine*.

Jan 1936. "From an Old Timer in the Black Hills." *Wild Western Novels*, pp. 103–115. Reprint of "Bug Eye Loses Hisself."

Jan 1936. "A Cowboy in San Juan" (Whiskers Beck). *Western Novel and Short Stories*, pp. 80–87. Reprint of "The Bells of San Juan."

Feb 1936. "Gunnies from Gehenna" (Alan M. Emley). *Popular Western*, pp. 95–100.

Feb 1936. "Strange Capture." *Western Novel and Short Stories*, pp. 92–101. Reprint of "The Dedwood Coach Brakes Down."

Mar 1936. "Outlaw Cavalcade." *Western Fiction*, pp. 6–92. Reprint of *The Smoky Years*.

Mar 1936. "Iron Paws." *Best Western Magazine*.

Apr 1936. "Hard Boiled" (Emley). *Popular Western*, pp. 41–49.

May 1936. "Death Rides the Border." *Western Novel and Short Stories*, pp. 6–88. Reprint of *Thunder in the Dust*.

Jun 1936. "Uneasy Lead" (Emley). *Thrilling Western*, pp. 105–112.

Jul 1936. "Wild Horse Valley" (Emley). *Smashing Novels*.

Sep 1936. "Grey Rider" (Emley). *Thrilling Ranch Stories*, pp. 76–93.

Sep 1936. "Next Door to Hell" (Emley). *Western Action Novels*, pp. 100–108.

Sep 1936. "When Outlaws Pay" (Emley). *Smashing Western*, pp. 111–118.

Oct 1936. "Guns Flame in Peaceful Valley" (Emley). *Texas Rangers*, pp. 83–91.

24 Oct 1936. "Dark Tropic Sea" (serial, part 1). *Collier's*.

31 Oct 1936. "Dark Tropic Sea" (part 2). *Collier's*, pp. 14–15, 52, 54–55.

7 Nov 1936. "Dark Tropic Sea" (part 3). *Collier's*.
14 Nov 1936. "Dark Tropic Sea" (part 4). *Collier's*, pp. 18–19, 44, 47.
21 Nov 1936. "Dark Tropic Sea" (part 5). *Collier's*.
28 Nov 1936. "Dark Tropic Sea" (part 6). *Collier's*, pp. 16–17, 62, 64.
5 Dec 1936. "Dark Tropic Sea" (part 7). *Collier's*, pp. 20, 56–58.
12 Dec 1936. "Dark Tropic Sea" (part 8). *Collier's*.
19 Dec 1936. "Dark Tropic Sea" (part 9). *Collier's*, pp. 22, 55–56, 58.
26 Dec 1936. "Dark Tropic Sea" (part 10). *Collier's*.
Dec 1936. "Bandit Blood" (Emley). *Thrilling Ranch Stories*.
Feb 1937. "Nester Lead" (Emley). *Thrilling Ranch Stories*, pp. 117–122.
Mar 1937. "Death Rides the Trionte" (Emley). *Thrilling Western*, pp. 56–72.
20 Mar 1937. "Ghost at His Shoulder." *Collier's*, p. 20; reprinted in *Dealer's Choice*, Barnes, 1957.
1937. *Empire for a Lady* (book). Farrar and Rinehart.
Mar 1937. *Empire for a Lady* (serial, part 1). *McCall's*.
May 1937. *Empire for a Lady* (part 2). *McCall's*.
26 Jun 1937. "Revolt of a Cowgirl." *Collier's*, p. 68.
Jul 1937. *Empire for a Lady* (part 3). *McCall's*.
3 Jul 1937. "Man with a Future." *Collier's*, p. 26.
7 Aug 1937. "Night by a Wagon Trail." *Collier's*.
Oct 1937. "Gun Medicine" (Emley). *Action-Packed Western*, pp. 104–115.
26 Feb 1938. "Pinto York." *Collier's*, p. 12.
9 Jul 1938. "The Little Kid." *Collier's*, pp. 16, 28.
16 Jul 1938. "Sundown Corral." *Collier's*, p. 38; re-printed in *Star Western*, Gramercy, 1995.
20 Aug 1938. "Impersonation." *Collier's*, p. 20.
26 Nov 1938. "Uncertain Wings." *Collier's*, pp. 15–16, 39–40, 42–43.
Jan 1939. "Wild Horse Valley" (Emley). *Complete Cowboy Mag.*, pp. 90–116.
6 May 1939. "Fight at Painted Rock." *Collier's*; reprinted in *Popular Book of Western Stories*, Popular Library, 1948.
29 Jul 1939. "West of Nowhere." *Collier's*.
2 Sep 1939. "Aces in his Hair." *Collier's*, p. 19.
4 Nov 1939. "Interrupted Takeoff." *Collier's*, pp. 14–15, 42, 44, 46.
23 Mar 1940. "Feud Fight." *Collier's*.
22 Oct 1940. *North West Mounted Police* (film). Paramount (U.K. release was renamed *The Scarlet Riders*.).
18 Mar 1942. *Reap the Wild Wind* (film). Paramount (screenplay).
1943. *Useless Cowboy* (book). Farrar and Rinehart.
29 Apr 1944. *The Story of Dr. Wassell* (film). Paramount (screenplay).
22 Jul 1944. *The Adventures of Mark Twain*. Warner Bros. (screenplay).
Aug 1944. "Dead Man Ambush" (Emley). *Texas Rangers*, pp. 58–62.
Sep 1944. "Star on His Heart" (Emley). *Ten Story Western*, pp. 63–69.
Oct 1944. *Trailin' West*. Short for TV (Old Man Coffee).
Jan 1945. "Six-Gun Magic." *Thrilling Western*, pp. 29–33.
Jan 1945. "Smokeless Powder" (Sheriff Horn). *West*.
19 Jul 1945. *Along Came Jones* (film). United Artists ("Useless Cowboy").
28 Dec 1945. *San Antonio* (film). Warner Bros..
1947. "Baldy at the Brink." *Western Stories*, Dell, pp. 133–146. Reprint, see 23 Nov 1926.

6 Jun 1947. *Cheyenne* (film). Warner Bros. (reissue title *The Wyoming Kid*).

1 Jul 1947. *Gunfighters* (film). Warner Bros., (from Zane Grey's *Twin Sombreros*) aka *The Assassin*, UK.

Dec 1947. "Hell for Breakfast." Bantam, reprint of "Useless Cowboy."

1948. "And Him Long Gone." *Bantam Western Triggers*, pp. 128–147. Reprint, see 27 Aug 1932.

1948. "Fight at Painted Rock." *Popular Book of Western Stories*, pp. 91–102. Reprint, see 6 May 1939.

Jun 1948. "Wild Justice." Bantam (*The Smoky Years*).

25 Aug 1948. *Tap Roots* (film). Universal International (screenplay, from James Street novel).

Sep 1948. "Trail Driver's Luck." *Bantam Western Roundup*, pp. 174–189 (reprint, see 5 Jul 1930).

13 Jan 1949. *Trailin' West* (20 minute pilot film, Old Man Coffee). LeMay-Templeton, Warner Bros..

5 Mar 1949. *The Walking Hills* (film). Columbia (Spanish Crossing).

4 May 1950. *The Sundowners* (film). LeMay-Templeton, Eagle Lion (from *Thunder in the Dust*).

3 Nov 1950. *Rocky Mountain* (film). Warner Bros. (*Ghost Mountain*).

7 Dec 1950. *High Lonesome* (film). LeMay-Templeton, Eagle Lion (original screenplay).

15 Mar 1951. *Quebec* (film). LeMay-Templeton, Eagle Lion.(original screenplay).

Apr 1952. *Bug Eye*. Short Stories.

15 Jun 1952. *I Dream of Jeanie* (film). Republic.

25 Dec 1952. *Blackbeard the Pirate* (film). RKO (original screenplay).

15 Nov 1953. *Flight Nurse* (film). Republic (original screenplay).

6 Nov 1954. *The Avenging Texans* (part 1). *Saturday Evening Post*, pp. 17–19, 42, 44, 46–47, 49–50. Serial version of The Searchers.

13 Nov 1954. *The Avenging Texans* (part 2). *Saturday Evening Post*, pp. 36–37, 92, 95–98, 100.

20 Nov 1954. *The Avenging Texans* (part 3). *Saturday Evening Post*, pp. 50–51, 97–98, 100, 102.

27 Nov 1954. *The Avenging Texans* (part 4). *Saturday Evening Post*, pp. 44, 77, 83–84, 86, 89.

4 Dec 1954. *The Avenging Texans* (part 5). *Saturday Evening Post*, pp. 45, 59–62, 64, 66, 68.

1954. *The Searchers* (book). Harper & Bros.

1955. "Mountain Fortress." TV episode in *Cheyenne*.

17 Nov 1955. *The Vanishing American*. Famous Players — Lasky (screenplay, from book by Zane Grey).

8 Dec 1956. "Missing in Action." *Saturday Evening Post*, pp. 34–35, 108, 110–113.

13 Mar 1956. *The Searchers* (film). Warner Bros. (1954 novel).

1957. "Misfire." TV episode in *Sugarfoot* (aka *Tenderfoot* in UK).

16 Mar 1957. *"Kiowa Moon"* (serial, part 1). *Sat. Evening Post* (*The Unforgiven*).

23 Mar 1957. *"Kiowa Moon"* (part 2). *Saturday Evening Post*.

30 Mar 1957. *"Kiowa Moon"* (part 3). *Saturday Evening Post*, pp. 43, 90, 92, 94, 96.

6 Apr 1957. *"Kiowa Moon"* (part 4). *Saturday Evening Post*, pp. 51, 148, 151–152, 154, 156.

13 Apr 1957. *"Kiowa Moon"* (part 5). *Saturday Evening Post*, pp. 51, 99–104.

20 Apr 1957. *"Kiowa Moon"* (part 6). *Saturday Evening Post*, pp. 49, 103–104, 106–109.

27 Apr 1957. *"Kiowa Moon"* (part 7). *Saturday Evening Post*, pp. 59, 110, 114, 116, 120.

Sep 1957. *The Unforgiven* (book). Harper & Bros.

1958. *The Little Black Book*. N. Doubleday.

Oct 1958. "He-Women of the West" (Probably same as "Ten Nights Over a Barroom"; Apr 1946). *True Western Adventures*, pp. 34, 36–37, 72–74.

1959. "Red Water North." TV episode in *Bronco*.

1959. *The Siege at Dancing Bird*. Fontana (U.K. printing of *The Unforgiven*).

1960. *The Unforgiven* (film). United Artists (1957 book).

1962. *By Dim and Flaring Lamps*. Harper & Bros.

1962. "Memory of a Filly." TV episode in *The Wide Country*.

1962. "Straight Jacket for an Indian." TV episode in *The Wide Country*.

_____. "A Gift from Korea." Unpublished.

_____. *Passport* (TV series). Unpublished.

Notes

Chapter 2

1. Reported in Sophie's autobiography, and her son John LeMay's autobiography. Both are brief, handwritten, and unpublished. See the LeMay Family Collection in the annotated bibliography.

2. E.F. Hollibaugh, *Biographical History of Cloud County, Kansas.*

3. Oliver Lamay was Alan LeMay's grandfather. See note on the spelling of Lamay in the annotated bibliography.

4. T.A. McNeill, *The Last Indian Raid in Kansas.*

5. *Biographical Record of Prominent and Representative Men of Indianapolis and Vicinity* (Chicago: J. H. Beers & Co., 1908). Lake High School no longer exists, so further details such as the years he taught there are not available.

6. Maude LeMay to Dr. Lincoln Hulley, President, Stetson University, June 15, 1916. See Archives, DuPont-Ball Library, Stetson University, DeLand, Florida.

7. Doubleday, Doran, & Co., 1928.

Chapter 4

1. *Kingdom Coming,* by Henry Clay Work, 1862, was originally written in Negro slave jargon but is better known without those lyrics because of its catchy tune. Alan apparently was familiar with the original because his first line of the chorus was, "He lost his shirt, ha, ha! In the original it was "De massa run, ha, ha!..."

Chapter 5

1. Reported in the *Aurora Beacon News,* June 18, 1939.

Chapter 6

1. Lasky, 1973, p. 195. See Annotated Bibliography.

2. Ibid.

3. Ibid., p. 202.

4. A roadshow release was an advance set of showings with reserved seats, higher prices, and occasional personal appearances by the stars.

Chapter 7

1. April 27, 1940; May 4, 1940; and May 25, 1940.

Chapter 9

1. The cemetery is in LaPorte County, Indiana. The gravesite is at N 41° 29.585' W 86° 46.659'.

Chapter 16

1. Printed in *Collier's* January 28, 1933. Reprinted in (among others) the anthology *Spanish Crossing*, a Five Star Western first edition, published in conjunction with Golden West Literary Agency, copyright © 1998 by Dan B. LeMay.

Chapter 18

1. See annotated bibliography.

Chapter 19

1. Bill Faralla was an experienced producer and director Alan first met during the filming of *Reap the Wild Wind*.

Chapter 21

1. *Road and Track*, June 1955, p. 23.
2. Ibid. October, 1955, p. 24–25.
3. Alan to Evan Thomas, Harper & Bros., Nov. 21, 1956. Copy in Harper & Row Archives, University of Texas, Austin.

Chapter 22

1. April 7, 1954. Copy in Harper & Row Archives, University of Texas, Austin.
2. Evan Thomas to Alan LeMay, April 22, 1954. Harper & Row Archives.
3. May 3, 1954. Harper & Row Archives.
4. Ibid., June 22, 1954.
5. *New York Times* Best Sellers list for fiction, January 16, 1955.
6. Jon Tuska, *The American West in Film* (University of Nebraska Press, 1988), p. 56.
7. *The Searchers* (New York: Harper & Brothers, 1954), chapter 32.
8. Arthur M. Eckstein, *The Searchers: Essays and Reflections on John Ford's Classic Western* (Detroit: Wayne State University Press), p. 335, essay by Tom Grayson Colonnese, "Native American Reactions to The Searchers."
9. Broome, *Dog Soldier Justice* (Lincoln, Kansas: Lincoln County Historical Society, Lincoln, Kansas, 2nd printing, May 2004), p. 12.
10. Ibid., pp. 10, 18
11. Ibid., p. 28, and Gregory and Suzanne Michno, *A Fate Worse than Death* (Caldwell, Idaho: Caxton Press, 2007), p. 315.
12. Ibid., pp. 326, 459.
13. Broome, p. 89.
14. Unpublished autobiography of Sophia Karen Jensen. Copy in LeMay Family Collection.
15. Ingalls, *Only a Week Away* (Covington, Kentucky: Lavassor Park Publishing Co., 2007), chapters 51 and 52.
16. John LeMay, unpublished autobiographical notes, Wichita, Kansas, December 4, 1964. LeMay Family Collection.

17. T. A. McNeill, "The Last Indian Raid in Kansas," *The Western Star*, Topeka, Kansas, January 23, 1920.

18. Broome, pp. 138, 144. Also Michno, p. 325.

19. Letter to Evan Thomas, April 8, 1954. Harper & Row Archives.

20. See, for example, Scott Zesch, *The Captured* (New York: St. Martin's Press, 2004), p. 42, and Michno, p. 459.

21. UCLA Collection 880, Westwood, California. There are many pages of typed and hand-written research notes on Indians scattered throughout the collection, but primarily in Box 23.

22. Eckstein, p.1.

23. Wikipedia, "Fort Parker Massacre."

24. April 8, 1954. Copy in Harper & Row Archives.

25. Letter, June 9, 1958. See UCLA Collection 880, Box 23

26. Ibid., January 26, 1960.

27. Ibid., December 12, 1960.

28. Ibid., May 8, 1957.

29. Broome, p. 28–29, 68–69, 145. See also Michno, p. 318, 326, 459.

30. According to Ford's daughter Barbara. See John Ford, John Ford Papers, Lilly Library Collection, Indianapolis, Box 11, Folder 34.

31. Original film manuscript page 140, copy in USC-Warner Bros. Archives, Los Angeles, California.

32. The "as shot" film transcript is available at the USC-Warner Bros. Archives.

33. Pauline Center for Media Studies, Culver City, California, *The Searchers: Epic of Hope*. See chapter entitled "The Story: LeMay or Ford/Nugent?" Also end of chapter entitled "Moving with the Spirit and Change."

34. Eckstein, p. 13

35. LeMay, *The Searchers*, chapters 9 and 21.

36. Alan LeMay to Evan Thomas, November 18, 1954. Copy in Harper & Row Archives.

37. *The Unforgiven* (New York: Harper & Brothers, 1957), chapter 46.

38. John LeMay, unpublished autobiographical notes, December 4, 1964. Reproduced in part in The Alan LeMay Collection, p. 5. See annotated bibliography.

39. Alan to Evan Thomas, Harper & Bros., Nov. 21, 1956. Copy in Harper & Row Archives.

40. Dennis Schwartz, *Ozu's World Movie Reviews—The Unforgiven*, January 18, 2005. See also Wikipedia.

41. See, for example, *The Film Daily*, March 30, 1960; *Daily Variety*, March 30, 1960; *The New Yorker*, April 16, 1960; and a contrary opinion by Dwight MacDonald in *Esquire*, June, 1960.

42. Plus royalties at up to $10,000 per year; see Annoted Bibliography.

43. Contract, December 8, 1954.

44. *Variety*, January 29, 1957.

45. Ibid.

46. Alan LeMay to Max Wilkinson, September 28, 1959. See UCLA Collection 880, Box 23.

47. Telegram, Writers Guild of America West, Inc., to Alan, October 10, 1959. See UCLA Collection 880, Box 23.

Annotated Bibliography

Pertaining to Alan LeMay

Arfran Productions, Inc. Named after Alan's wife, Arlene, and George "Dink" Templeton's wife, Fran, Arfran was registered with the California Secretary of State as No. C0240851, filed December 6, 1949. The film credits and most reviews of *The Sundowners*, *High Lonesome*, and *Quebec*, do not mention Arfran, but name "LeMay-Templeton Productions" or "A LeMay-Templeton Picture." The California Secretary of State has no record of any LeMay-Templeton corporation. Apparently, the LeMay-Templeton name was unofficial, but was used in the credits for better name recognition.

Crowell-Collier Publishing Company Records, 1931–1955. New York Public Library, Manuscripts and Archives Division, New York. Various authors and dates. A collection of editorial correspondence among the *Collier's* editors, authors, and authors' agents. It covers the period of the 1930s when *Collier's* was the primary "slick" magazine publishing Alan's short stories and serials. The collection consists of 808 file boxes of chronologically-sorted material containing about 140 pages of LeMay-related correspondence of interest, spanning the years 1934 through 1942. There is no index, but *Collier's* had a system of assigning permanent folder numbers to each author or agent, then reusing those numbers each year. Alan LeMay was assigned folders numbered 493. His agent, Curtis Brown, was filed under "Brown, Curtis," and was assigned folder number 110.

Harper & Bros. book contracts: *The Searchers* contract was signed April 6, 1954, and provided for an advance payment of $5,000 against future royalties of 10 percent of the retail price on the first 5,000 copies, escalating to 12.5 percent on the next 2,500 copies, and 15 percent thereafter. Royalty payments were capped at $10,000 per year, with anything over that carried forward. The contract is a standard printed Harper's form with a number of modifications, such as: exclusive rights limited to the United States and Canada rather than the world; copyright to be in the name of the author, not the publisher; royalties based on retail price rather than average wholesale; and exclusion of motion picture rights and most subsidiary rights. The contract for *The Unforgiven* was signed June 11, 1956, and is identical. Copies of both contracts are in the LeMay Family Collection.

Harper & Row archives, Harry Ransom Humanities Research Center, The University of Texas at Austin, 21st and Guadalupe Streets, Austin, TX 78712, www.hrc. utexas.edu. The collection covers the publishing archives of Harper & Bros. from 1928 through 1969. The company was known as Harper & Row after 1962. Material of interest includes correspondence between Alan and his long-time friend and editor at Harper, Evan Thomas. Most of the letters are from the period 1954–1956, and concern *The Searchers* and *The Unforgiven*. Because of their friendship, the letters also contain personal sidelights.

Lamay, Oliver, (Sr.) Homestead. Situated at N 39° 34.013' W 97° 51.362' in Cloud County, Kansas, the homestead of Oliver Lamay (Sr.) comprised the south east quarter of the south east quarter of Section 34, Township five (Grant) south of Range five west, and the north east quarter of Section three, Township six (Summit) south of range five west. The two parcels are adjacent and total 155 acres. Today they are two miles south of Jamestown on the west side of Thomas St. (CR 765), split by Plum or Rock Road (CR 360). As recounted by John LeMay, Alan's father, in his brief unpublished biography, Oliver Lamay (Jr.), Alan's grandfather, started a homestead in 1873 about 70 miles farther west, on the Solomon River in Phillips County, but stayed less than four years. Both Olivers usually skipped the Jr./Sr. title, and the omission can cause confusion in the old records.

Lamay name change. The spelling of LeMay changed from time to time during the last 300 years. The French newspapers in Trois Riviere, Canada, spelled it Lemay at the tercentennial celebration of the marriage of the first Lemay in America in 1659. This was changed for a brief time to Lamay for supposed better phonetics (to avoid LEEmay,) but Alan's father, John LeMay, changed it back to LeMay because Lamay was too often pronounced Lammy. Alan preferred Le May, with a space in the middle, but the family no longer uses that because it confuses computers.

Lasky, Jesse L, Jr. *Whatever Happened to Hollywood*. New York: Funk & Wagnalls, 1973. Chapter 18. Jesse co-authored Alan's first two screenplays for DeMille (*North West Mounted Police* and *Reap the Wild Wind*) and in this autobiography buttresses Alan's recollections of how it was.

***Alan LeMay Papers*.** UCLA Collection 880, 1919–1964. Department of Special Collections, Charles E. Young Research Library, University of California, Los Angeles. These papers were given to the library by Alan LeMay's widow, Arlene, in 1964. There are 23 file boxes containing original manuscripts, early drafts, unpublished stories, outlines of stories, research materials, and correspondence.

LeMay, Alan. *Painted Ponies*. George H. Doran Company, 1927. Alan's first book-length novel. The story takes place in Kansas and Nebraska in the summer of 1878, the same time and locale as the Last Raid in Kansas by Chief Dull Knife's Northern Cheyenne. Chief Dull Knife is identified by name, as are some of the locales such as the Republican River. The hero of the story has problems with evil white men because of a false rumor that he is a half-breed, and he is befriended by Dull Knife's warriors as they fight their way north to their homeland in the Black Hills. The story is sympathetic to the Indians for wanting to escape the disease and starvation on their Oklahoma reservation, but is biased and historically inaccurate in omitting their gratuitous murdering, raping and scalping. Alan was a rookie writer trying to sell his first novel, and probably thought that this angle would sell better. His grandmother, Sophie Jensen LeMay, who lived on the Kansas frontier during Dull Knife's last campaign, might have disagreed with Alan's portrayal. But she died a year before the book was written.

LeMay Family Collection. Various authors and dates. This collection comprises 10 file boxes of letters, albums, photos, clippings, articles, manuscripts, published and filmed works of Alan LeMay, and genealogy records collected by the current family and by past generations. Most of the genealogy work was done by Mary Ann LeMay. Alan LeMay wrote about 400 letters to his parents between 1937 and 1952 that were saved for this collection by his father and contain a great deal of information used in this book. While this raw material is not publicly available, much of it is edited into *The Alan LeMay Collection* © Dan LeMay, 2006. Copies were donated to the Indiana Historical Society, Printed Collections and Artifacts, Indianapolis, Indiana; the Fairbanks Center for Motion Picture Study, Beverly Hills, California; Stetson University, DuPont-Ball Library, Deland, Florida; and the Cloud County Genealogical Society, Concordia, Kansas.

Padres Writers Group. Founded informally by Eugene Lyle, Jr., in 1925 as a means for getting San Diego writers together to socialize, discuss their work, and hear invited speakers. Writing is a solitary occupation, and San Diego had no literary cafes like Paris or Greenwich Village, so the group was needed and became popular. Meeting every other Thursday, usually at a member's home or at a building in Balboa Park, they were never formalized with bylaws, officers, or dues. Early members, from a list compiled by Ethyl Mintzer, San Diego historian and daughter of Murney Mintzer, included:

Lawrence (Larry) Blochman (1900–1975), fiction author, *Bombay Mail* (1934), *Blow Down* (1939), etc.

Charles G. (Charlie) Booth (1896–1949), *The House on 92nd St.*, Academy Award for Best Story.

Lyman Bryson (1888–1959), lecturer, educator, writer on philosophy, government, faith and education.

Jim Clark

Charles W. Diffin, science fiction writer.

Stuart N. Lake (1889–1964), *Wyatt Earp, Frontier Marshall.*

Alan LeMay (1898–1964)

Eugene P. Lyle, Jr. (1873–1961), journalist, pulp fiction writer.

Syl MacDowell (c.1909–1980), *Gone to Texas.*

Frederick (Fritz) Mertz

Max Miller (1899–1967), *I Cover the Waterfront.*

Murney Mintzer (1896–1961), editorial writer, Copley Press.

Eddie Orcutt, editorial writer for Copley Press.

Col. S. B. Pearson

J. D. Phelps

Leslie (Doc) Quirk

Gil Strick, cowboy advisor to Alan LeMay, listed as co-author on several LeMay short stories.

Frank (Spig) Wead (1895–1947), fiction writer for *Saturday Evening Post*, eight screenplays.

Magner White, journalist, Pulitzer Prize winner, 1964.

Horatio (Hod) Winslow

Pertaining to *The Searchers*

Academy of Motion Picture Arts and Sciences, Fairbanks Center, Margaret Herrick Library, 333 South La Cienega Blvd., Beverly Hills, CA 90211. This is a non-circulating library with a large collection of films and related material. Of particular interest are their clipping files, which contain notes of interest from publications such as *Daily Variety, The Hollywood Reporter,* newspapers, etc. Each file is listed under the name of a film or an actor. Clipping files are available for both *The Searchers* and *The Unforgiven*.

Buscombe, Edward, *The Searchers.* London: BFI Publishing. This is an 80-page review in the British Film Institute Film Classics Series. It gives a scene-by-scene analysis of the film, explaining intent, and comparing the film with the film script and occasionally with the novel and the serial versions. Extensive endnotes document the source material. Chapter XV describes the complex contractual relationships that were being negotiated among C.V. Whitney Pictures, Merian C. Cooper, Columbia, Warner Bros., John Wayne, and others in the era when the major studios had lost their domination of the industry to the so-called independents.

Eckstein, Arthur M., and Peter Lehman, eds. *The Searchers: Essays and Reflections on John Ford's Classic Western.* Detroit: Wayne State University Press, 2004. A collection of 12 essays on *The Searchers* by 12 authors, presented at a 1996 conference at the University of Maryland. The film is analyzed from every angle, down to the background music and the feminist view. Some reviews mostly review other reviews. Of greatest interest is the essay by Indians who saw the film and discussed it from their viewpoint. They thought it went farther than any western before it in fairness to the Indians, but it still didn't go far enough. They were offended by the Navajos being portrayed as Comanche while speaking Navajo.

Etulain, Richard, Introduction © 1978, Pocatello, Idaho, in the 1978 reprint of *The Searchers.* Etulain notes that in his later career, LeMay departed more and more from the formula Western, and became centered on the realism of frontier life. He particularly praises LeMay's realism in dealing with the Comanche. He states, "LeMay knows a great deal about the social and cultural customs of the Comanches, and thus his descriptions of the Indians are not gratuitous portraits of nameless and faceless savages."

Eyman, Scott. *Print the Legend, the Life and Times of John Ford.* Simon & Schuster, 1999. An in-depth biography that shows Ford's domineering character, and paints a vivid behind-the-scenes view of the making of his films. It gives insights into Ford's relationships with screenwriter Frank Nugent and cameraman Winton Hoch. It devotes a chapter to *The Searchers,* which Eyman gives a thoughtful, mostly favorable review.

Ford, John. John Ford Papers. Lilly Library, Indiana University, Bloomington, Indiana. Various authors and dates. The John Ford Collection contains original scripts, production materials, correspondence, and other papers. Material pertaining to *The Searchers* is found in Box 6 folders 19–22, Box 8 folder 22, Box 11 folder 34, and Box 21 folders 6–7. There are also 82 audio tapes of interviews with John Ford by Dan Ford. *The Searchers* is discussed on tape 23, side 2.

Hui, Arlene. *The Racial Frontier in John Ford's The Searchers.* London: University College, 2004. It reviews and compares *The Searchers* novel versus the film. It focuses on parallels with the divisive issues in America during the 1950s, particularly miscegenation.

LeMay, Alan. *The Avenging Texans.* Original serial version of *The Searchers,* published in *The Saturday Evening Post* in five installments: Nov. 6, Nov. 13, Nov. 20, Nov, 27, and Dec. 4, 1954.

_____. *The Searchers.* Harper & Bros., 1954. The novel is longer than the serial due to the inclusion of more material developing the character of Marty and explaining the motivations of the Indians.

Nugent, Frank S. *Films as Writer.* www.filmreference.com. Lists Nugent's 11 screenplays and presents a brief biography.

_____. *The Searchers* shooting script. A comparison of the script taken to Monument Valley with the final edited film shows the extent of Ford's changes. It gives insight into his darkening of the character of Ethan, and how he conveyed it with pictures rather than words. A copy of the Nugent script is available at the Warner Bros. Archives, USC, Los Angeles.

Pauline Center for Media Studies, Boston. Massachusetts, *The Searchers: Epic of Hope.* 2000. www.daughtersofstpaul.com/ mediastudies/reviews/filmsearcher.html. A source paper for the City of Angels Film Festival 2000. This review presents a rather deep and thoughtful analysis of both the novel and the film, but sometimes stretches for symbolism.

Tuska, Jon. *The American West in Film, Critical Approaches to the Western.* Greenwood Press, 1985. This is a scholarly book about how to analyze and categorize western films. It presents countless examples of how Hollywood has idealized the Old West into a state of mythology and symbolism. It condemns *The Searchers* as "Ford's most vicious anti–Indian film yet" and adopts the view that "the Comanches are misrepresented and exploited in this film," a view that fails to recognize the reality of the hundreds of Indian raids of the times.

USC–Warner Bros. Archives, School of Cinematic Arts, University of Southern California, 3716 South Hope St., Room 113, Los Angeles, CA 90007. The collection contains correspondence, photos, scripts, etc. generated in the making of films at Warner Bros. prior to 1968. Of particular interest is Nugent's original as-shot film script.

Pertaining to Indian Raids

Broome, Jeff. *Dog Soldier Justice, the Ordeal of Susanna Alderdice in the Kansas Indian War.* Lincoln, Kansas: Lincoln County Historical Society, 2003, 2nd printing May 2004. This is a well-researched and documented book which focuses on the violent clash of cultures between the Indians and the white settlers in Kansas during the latter part of the 1860s. The perspective is primarily that of the pioneers, and in *The Searchers* that indeed is Alan LeMay's primary perspective because his parents and grandparents were white settlers there.

Hollibaugh, E. F. *Biographical History of Cloud County, Kansas,* 1903, copy held by the State Library of Kansas. It has biographies of the early settlers, including the Rev. Nels Nelson and his family. It also gives many details and firsthand accounts of the Indian raids during the 1860s and 1870s in the vicinity of the Oliver Lamay homestead. See chapter entitled "The Killing of Benjamin White and the Capture of his Daughter, Sarah Catherine White, by the Indians August 13, 1868."

Ingalls, Ethel L. *Only a Week Away.* Historical fiction stories of a Scottish immigrant family coming to the American frontier in the 1870s. Based on extensive family research, the stories give a vivid picture of the living conditions and attitudes of the times. Chapters 51 and 52 are set in the Cloud County, Kansas region where Alan's father was born.

McNeill, T.A. "The Last Indian Raid in Kansas." *The Western Star,* Comanche County, Kansas, January 23, 1920. This article gives a detailed account of the September, 1878 raid. See also The Last Indian Raid Museum, 258 S. Penn Ave., Oberlin, Kansas 67749, which has artifacts and information about conditions on the Kansas frontier in 1878.

Michno, Gregory, and Suzan. *A Fate Worse Than Death: Indian Captivities in the West 1830–1885.* Caldwell, Idaho: Caxton Press, 2007. A 527 page masterpiece of research with many excellent photographs and maps. The experiences of more than 300 captives are recounted in detail; they are described as being just a fraction of the thousands actually captured. The well-documented research is intended by the Michnos to challenge the modern revisionist historians who dismiss the accounts of surviving captives as "largely-fabricated affronts to Native American culture."

Wikipedia. *Fort Parker Massacre.* The online encyclopedia has a comprehensive description of the local conditions on the Texas frontier that made the Fort Parker raid possible. It gives details of the raid, and describes the lives of Cynthia Ann Parker who was captured and lived with the Comanche for 24 years, her Comanche husband Peta Nocona, and their son Quanah Parker who became a famous Comanche war chief. Some reviewers think that *The Searchers* was based on the Cynthia Ann Parker story.

Zesch, Scott. *The Captured: A True Story of Abduction by Indians on the Texas Frontier.* New York: St. Martin's Press, 2004. A well-researched and documented treatment of Indian abductions, showing that conditions on the Texas frontier were very similar to those in Kansas. The author thinks Brit Johnson was the inspiration for *The Searchers*, because of his dogged tenacity in trying to free Indian captives. But Alan LeMay's inspiration for dogged tenacity was his own pioneering family and the other American settlers who "simply keep on, and on, doing the next thing, far beyond all reasonable endurance, seldom thinking of themselves as martyred, and never thinking of themselves as brave." (Epigraph in *The Searchers*.)

Pertaining to *The Unforgiven*

LeMay, Alan. *Kiowa Moon. Saturday Evening Post.* Original serial version of *The Unforgiven,* published in seven weekly installments from March 16, 1957, through April 27, 1957.

_____. *The Unforgiven.* New York: Harper & Bros., 1957.

Index

Numbers in ***bold*** italics indicate pages with photographs.

adoptions 64–66, 120
Adventure Magazine 17
AFL (union) 114
Airevac 150, 152
airplane crashes 38–39
Alderdice, Susanna 171; *see also* captives
Along Came Jones 106, 113; *see also Useless Cowboy*
Amarillo 133
Amarillo Globe-News 132
ancestry chart (LeMay) 8
Antelope Springs 136–137
Arfran Productions, Inc. 130
Army 92
Arnold, Gary 180–181
Audubon 101
Aurora, Illinois 15, 20, 41; Dramatic Club 19; Metal Co. 15
Aurora Beacon News 20
autobiography 17
The Avenging Texans 164, 173, 178

Bacall, Lauren 115
Barber County scouts 169
Barrymore, John, Jr. 130, 132–137, ***138***, 140, 148
Beery, Wallace 98
Bennett, Charles 50–52, 90–91, 97, 99
bestseller list, *New York Times* 166
Beverly Hills house 57
Beverly Hills Tennis Club 57–58, 72
Bischoff, Sam 119
Black Cat Patrol 144–148
Blackbeard the Pirate 152, 163
Blum, Al (business manager) 72, 112
Bogart, Humphrey 112, 115
Booth, Charlie 28
"The Borderman" 96

Box Office (magazine) 126
brain tumor 180
Brandon, Harry 174
Brandt, Erd 152
Breeze, Vance 60
Brentwood house 60
Bridges, Harry 72
British market 128–129
bronchitis 81, 180
Bronco 155
Brown, Daniel Leander "Papa" 6, 10–14, 88
Brown, Harry Joe 118–119, 121
Brown, Maude 11–17, 169
Buckner, Bob 109
buffalo 8
Burnett, W.R. 110
business manager 57, 70, 72, 112, 122; *see also* Heinze, Wally
Butler, Dave 110
Butler, Lois 136, ***138***
By Dim and Flaring Lamps 179

Cadaco-Ellis 77–80
Calamity Jane 108–110, 113
calf pulling 3
California Sports Car Club (Cal Club) 156, 159
Calvet, Corinne 148
Calvin, Frank 53
camping trips 58, 62
Canadian Mounties 141
Canova, Judy 54
"Captain Hornblower" 85
captives 167–174
Carpenter, Elizabeth 8, 10
Carradine, John 88
Carrizo (burro) 25, 26

Carrol, Madeleine 48, 87
Chandlee, Harry 84, 89
Chaplin, Charlie 119
Cheyenne (TV series) 155
"Circles in the Sky" 17, 175
Citadel 142–143
Civil War 168, 179
Clay, Cliff 52
Cloud County, Kansas 6, 10–12, 167–168
Coburn, Walt 27
Collier's 2, 24, 41, 102–106, 152
Colombo, Al 131
Columbia 106, 107, 121
Comanche 169–171, 176
Concordia, Kansas 6, 8, 10–12, 167–169
"The Congo" (poem by Vachel Lindsay) 22–23
Consolidated PBY "Catalinas" 144–145
Consumer Price Index (CPI) 123
Cook, Lucius 59
Cooper, Gary 48, 87, 90, 92, 97–99, *106*, 107, 124
Cordell, Frank 136
Cormack, Bart 46
cost of negative 123, 133
"Cowboys Will Be Cowboys" 24
credits, screen 47–48, 84, 88–89, 107, 110, 114, 121, 123
Crisp, Donald 88
Custer 167

Davey Crockett 129
Day, Doris 110
Deadfall see *High Lonesome*
death toll from Indian raids 169
Demarest, William *106*, 107
DeMille, Cecil B. 44, 46–52, 54, 72, 81, 86, 87, 90–92, 94, 96–97, 99, 101, 103–104, 123–126, 143, 175; ranch 50, 52; yacht 50–52
Department of Defense 152
Detective Story magazine 17
deVoto, Bernard 84
diet and exercise 67, 109–110, 117–118
directing 119, 121, 133, 140–141
distractions 34–36, 41, 63
divorce 5, 40, 73
Dog Soldiers 166–168, 171, 176
Doubleday, Doran, & Company, Inc. 21
Downs, Cathy 130
drowning accident 141–142
Dull Knife, Chief 10, 20, 168–169, 171
Duval, Nikki 148

Eagle-Lion 133–134
Elam, Jack 130, 136
El Capitan theater 54

Emley, Alan M. 4, 35
escape plans 57, 58, 112, 120–121, 125, 163
Everitt, Helen 35

Faralla, Bill 144
Farley, Jim 32
Farrar and Rinehart 105
Fascio, Edouart 124
fatigue 67, 99, 104, 112, 129, 143, 147, 163; temporary blindness 164–165
Faulkner, William 115
Favorite Movies (Jay Cocks) 181
Ferrari Monza 160, *161*
fight song 34, 47
Fleming, Victor 60
Fletcher's Ranch 137
Flight Nurse 148–152, 163
The Flim-Flam Man 125
flood of 1936–37 3, 36
flying lessons, license, stories 43
Flynn, Errol 108–111, 115, 147
Ford, John 1, 166, 170–175, 178, 181
Forman, James Henry 84
Fort Parker Massacre 170–172
Foster, Stephen 150, 152
Foto-Electric games 76–80; Cadaco-Ellis 77; patent 76, 79; royalties 80
Four Minute Man 15
Fox 106
Francis W. Parker school 26
Freeman, Y. Frank
Froelich, Ann 84
The Frontiersman 110–113, 115
Fuller, Clem 136

Gabrilovich, Clara *see* Twain, Mark
Garson, Greer 97
Garvey, Elda 59
gas rationing 60, 72–73
George H. Doran Co. 20
Ghost Mountain see *Rocky Mountain*
"A Gift from Korea" 152, 175
Goddard, Paulette 49
Goldwyn studios 107
Gopher Gulch 22, 23, 29
Gottlieb, Alex 114–115
The Graduate 125
Great Danes 27, 34
Grey, Zane 118–119, 175
The Gunfighters 120, 128
Gus 57, 73, 97, 110; *see also* Roddick, Virginia

Haggard, Edith 36, 41
Haggarty, Don 130, 148
Hampden, Walter 88
Hanford, Harry 158

Hansen Dam 159, *160*
harness business 8
Harper & Brothers 159, 164, 174, 175, 178–179
Hastings, Gretchen 59
Hawks, Howard 60, 101
Haycox, Ernest 38
Hayworth, Rita 97–98
Hecht-Hill-Lancaster 175–176, 178
Height, Rick 178
Heinze, Wally (business manager) 103
Hellinger, Mark 113, 115
Henderson, Jim 145
Hepburn, Audrey 175–178
Hering, Bud, 61–62, 98–99
Hering, Irene 61
Hering, Kip 61
"Hero's Welcome for *The Searchers*" 180
High Lonesome 132–133, 140
Hill, James 176
Hoch, Winton 131, 172, 178
Hoffman, Arlene 43
The Hollywood Reporter 117, 133
Holm, Bill 119, 154
Honeychile 60
Honolulu Advertiser 28
Horton, Edward Everett 59
hospitalization 65
house hunting 63–64, 72
Hurley, Vic 27, 29
Hurricane Harbor 145
Huston, John 175, 178

I Am Villion (play) 18
I Dream of Jeannie 150, 163
independence 130–143
independent studios 128–129
Indianapolis 11, 13
Indians, Alan's treatment of 15, 20, 165–177
Iwerks, David 159, *160*

Jackson, Eileen 27
Jameson, R.D. 18
Jamestown 6–7, 168
Japan 69, 126, 144, 151
Jensen, Sophia Karen *see* LaMay, Karen Sophia Jensen "Sophie"
Johnson, Nunnally 107
Johnston, John Leroy *107*
Jones, Melody 106

Kansas State Militia 168
Kennesaw Mountain, battle of 10
Kimball, Dan 145
"Kingdom Coming" 34
Kiowa Indians 171, 175–178

"Kiowa Moon" 175, 178
Koch, Howard 84
Korea research trips 149–152
Korean war 148

labor unions 72, 74; *see also* strikes
Lake, Stuart 27
Lamay, Harry 9–10
Lamay, Karen Sophia Jensen "Sophie" 6–11, 168–169
Lamay, Oliver [Jr.] 6–10, 169, 171
Lamay, Oliver [Sr.] 7–10
Lamay, Thomas 10
Lancaster, Burt 175–176
Landi, Elissa 59
Landi, Nicki 59
Landi, Toni 59
LaPorte Indiana 10–11
Lasky, Jesse, Jr. 44–46, 48–50, 57, 96
Lasky, Jesse, Sr. 81, 85–86, 101, 104, 111, 175
Last Raid in Kansas 10, 168, 171
Lazy Lightning (brand) *33*, 174–175
Lee, Leonard 110
legal dept. (Warner's) 111
LeMay, Arlene Hoffman 2, 45, 50, 53–54, 56–57, 69, 87, 113, 161
LeMay, Dan Brown 22, 58
LeMay, Esther 4–5, 13–*18*, 19–20, 24–29, 39–40, 69
LeMay, Joan (Jody) 37–39, 45, 161
LeMay, John 6–14, 134, 161, 169; letters 7–8, 134–140, 168
LeMay, Mark Logan 66, 120, 161
LeMay, Mary Karen (Molly) 64, 161
LeMay, Maude Brown 6–14, 16, 71, 169
LeMay Brothers Company 13
LeMay-Templeton Productions 133, 140–141, 144, 148
Leslie, Joan 152
Liberty 105
lightning strike 62–63
Litel, John 130
Littauer, Kenneth (*Collier's* fiction editor) 24, 35–36, 41–42, 103
"The Little Kid" (short-short story) 102
Loftin, Cary 60
Longstreet, Stephen 113, 115
"Look" 164, 174; *see also* Indians, Alan's treatment of
Lookout Mountain house 56
Los Conejos Indians 26, 62
Lovell, Alberto 34
Lula H. 29, 31

MacMurray, Fred 118
MacPherson, Jeannie 46

Maddow, Ben 176
Malibu aquarium 53
March, Frederic 86, 88–89
Marfa, Texas 133–134
Mark Twain (or *The Adventures of Mark Twain* or *The Life of Mark Twain*) 81–90, 94, 102–103; *see also* Gabrilovich, Clara
Marx, Harpo 101
Massey, Raymond 109
MATS (Military Air Transport Service) 150–151
Mazer, Don 77–80
MCA 148
McDowell, Syl 28
MGM 117, 118
Midwest Review 21
Miland, Ray 98
Miles, Johnny 118
Miller, Alan 114
Miller, Christine 136
Miller, Max 27
Miller, Winston 147
Mintzer, Murney 28
miscegenation 172, 174, 177
"Missing in Action" 175
Mission Hills 22
Mojave desert 58
Monaco Drive house 66, 148
Monument Valley 1, 172
Morgan, Dennis 67
Morgan, Anna 167, 171; *see also* captives
Morgan, James 167, 171; *see also* captives
motorcycle riding 60, 73, 92
Mrs. Cafferty 60
Mrs. Miniver 97–99
Murphy, Audi 176

name changes 107
National Guard, Alan's volunteering in 16
Navy 90, 92, 143–149
Nelson, Rev. Nels 6, 167–168
New Orleans 20, 180
Night by a Wagon Road 132; *see also High Lonesome*
Nopal Ranch 137
North West Mounted Police 44–49, 52, 55, 81, 85, 97, 104, 123, 126
Northern Cheyenne 9, 20, 166–169, 171, 176
Nugent, Frank 173–175

O'Brian, Pat 118
O'Conner, Jim 28
Offenhauser engine 158
Office of War Information (OWI) 109

Old Father of Waters 20
Old Man Coffee 20, 130, 154, 183
Orcutt, Eddie 28
Oscar 110, 181
"Out of the Swamp" 17
Overholt, Al 130, 174

Pacific Palisades office *179*, 180
Padres Writer's Club 27
Painted Ponies 20, 169, 171
Palo Duro Canyon 131
Pan American Road Race 159
Panhandle Pioneer Day 133
Paramount 44–46, 52, 54–55, 86, 90, 91, 94–97, 101, 105, 107, 119, 122–123, 141, 144, 148, 150
paraplegic veteran's hospital 75
Parker, Cynthia Ann 170–172
Parker, Quanah (Comanche chief) 170
patent 79–80
Payne Die Casting Co. 13
PBY *see* Consolidated PBY "Catalinas"
Pearl Harbor 126
Pease River, battle of 170
Pelican Coast 21
"peon" games 26
Peta Nocona (Comanche chief) 170, 172
The Philadelphia Story 123
Pi Club 11
Pickford 119
Pine, William 48, 52, 96, 124
Pinhook 58, 121
Pinto Canyon 136–137
plagiarism risk 127
plots 30, 165
polo 2, 4, 24–27, 30–31, 33, 40, 58, 61, 66, 98, 180; *see also* Riviera Polo Club
Powell, Dick 60
Preston, Robert 130, 133
producer, producing 34, 48–49, 109–117, 121–128, 130–133, 140–141, 154
profit 123–124, 128

Quebec 59, 140–143, 147, 148
Quirk, Doc 28

racing 156–162
racism 1, 152, 166, 173–178
Raines, Ella 121
Rancho Una Vaca 2, 5, 31, 41, 61, 117, 175
Rapp, Lt. Gloria, USN, flight nurse *149*, 150
Rapper, Irving 85
rat experiment 117
Rathvon, N. Peter 130–131, 141
rating of screenplays 53
Ray, Harry 137

reading 85–87
Reagan, Ronald 115
Reap the Wild Wind 50–55, 70, 81–82, 96, 97, 104–105
rejections 4, 36, 40, 42, 152
remakes and sequels 127
Republic Studios 148–152, 164, 165
Republican River 12, 20, 168
revisionist history 110
Ripley, Clements 46
Rivermen Die Broke 21
Riviera Polo Club 34, 61, 66, 117; *see also* polo
RKO 152, 163
Roach, Hal, Jr. 117–118
Road & Track 159
roadshow 49, 54, 89
Rocky Mountain (*Ghost Mountain*) 147
Roddick, Virginia 57, 82, 87, 113, 121; *see also* Gus
Rogers, Roy 150
Roosevelt, Franklin Delano 71–74
Rose, Stuart 164
Rosson, Art 92
Rosson, Arthur 53
Rosson, Hal 53
Round Robin 58
Royal Naval players 30; 22nd Regiment of Paratroopers 141
The Rurales 47–48, 50, 81, 86, 90, 94, 96–101
Ruysdale, Basil 136

Sackal, S.Z. 109
salary, royalties, and sale prices 83, 97, 99, 115, 119, 120, 122–123, 127, 129, 133, 178–179
San Antonio 108–113
San Diego 22, 100
San Diego Union 23
San Diego Sun 30
Santee 30, 31
Saturday Evening Post 105, 152, 164, 175, 178–179
Saxon, John 177
Schurch, Jack 77
Scott, Randy 118–119, 121
Scott, Zachary 109, 115
Screenwriter's Guild 89
"scrutineering" 156
The Searchers 127, 164–181
Selznick 119
"Sergent York" 85
serial rights 35
Sheridan, Ann 108–110
Sherman, Harold 83–85, 89
Sherman, Vincent 112

Shippey, Lee 23
Shivers, Texas Governor Allen 133, 134
The Siege at Dancing Bird 175
Skinner, Rev A.C.V. 13, 19–20
Skinner, Esther 13, 17, 19–20
Smith, Alexis 88–89, 109, 115
So You Want to Be a Producer 125
soddys 7–8, 176–177
Spanish Crossing 117; *see also The Walking Hills*
spooking a horse 59
Sports Car Club of America (SCCA) 156, 159
sports cars 156
squid, giant model 53–55
Stagecoach 172
Stagg, Amos Alonzo 11
Stallion Road 113–115
Stetson University 16–17
The Story of Dr. Wassell 90–95, 97, 99, 144
Strabel, Thelma 50, 54
Street, Julian 84
Strick, Gil 3, 24–26, 28
strike 74; Hollywood 65, 114, 115, 127; Writers Guild 179; *see also* labor unions
Sturges, John 121
subjective writing 164
Sugarfoot 155
Sullivan, C. Gardner 44, 46, 48–49
The Sundowners 130–134, 140, 172; *see also Thunder in the Dust*

Tap Roots 119–120, 148
Taras Bulba 179
taxes 71–74, 108, 122, 127–129, 179
Taylor, Robert 118
Technicolor 135, 137, 148, 181
television 153–155
Templeton, George "Dink" 130, 134–136, **138**, 140–143, 148
Texans 131–133, 136, 171
Texas Panhandle 131
Texas Rangers and Militia 170
"There's a Million Cows in the Greasewood" 24
Thomas, Evan 164, 170
Thunder in the Dust 130–131; *see also The Sundowners*
The Time, the Place, and the Girl 110, 113
Toley, George 58, 154
Tracy, Spencer 81
Treasure of the Sierra Madre, or *Treasure of the High Sierra* 112
Truman, Harry S. 74
Tucker, Forest 152

Tulsa 133
Turman, Lawrence 125
Twin Sombreros 118–119

The Unforgiven 8, 175–178
Unions 72–75, 127–130, 134
United Artists 119
United States Regulars 169
University of Chicago 11, 17, 46; football 18
Useless Cowboy 81–82, 85, 92, 102–107, 166

vacations 6–7, 68, 81, 99–101, 113, 129, 143
The Vanishing American 175
V-E Day 114
Verstappen, Henri 55
volunteering for war effort 10, 15–16, 69–70

Wald, Jerry 109
Walker, Lew 34
The Walking Hills 116–121
Walsh, Raoul 108–109

Wanger, Walter 120
war films 70–71
War Labor Board (WLB) 114
Warner, Jack 112, 115
Warner Bros. 65, 67, 82, 84–87, 89, 99, 104, 108–115, 127, 147, 148, 156; Art Dept. 86
wartime travel 60, 73
Wassell, Dr. 86; *see also The Story of Dr. Wassell*
Watson, Starling 4, 31–32
Wayne, John 1, 166, 172–173, 181
Wead, Spig 46
Western College 17–18
Westmore, Perc 86
White, Sarah 167, 171, 172; *see also* captives
Whitney, C.V. 178
The Wide Country 155
Wilkinson, Max 102–105
Wills, Chill 130, 133
World Premier Dinner 133
World War II 69–75; shortages 77, 80

Yates, Herbert 150, 152